Guns & Other Arms

Cover illustration: *Washington at Monmouth* by Emanuel Leutze.
Collections of the Monmouth County Historical Association,
Freehold, New Jersey.

ANTIQUES
Magazine Library

FOLK ART IN AMERICA
Painting and Sculpture
Edited by Jack T. Ericson

EARLY AMERICAN SILVER AND ITS MAKERS
Edited by Jane Bentley Kolter

EUROPEAN POTTERY & PORCELAIN
Edited by Paul J. Atterbury

Guns & Other Arms

Edited by William Guthman

A Main Street Press Book
Published by Mayflower Books, Inc., USA
New York City 10022

Articles included in this volume are printed as they appeared in the following issues of *The Magazine* ANTIQUES:

Part I: Getting the Gunpowder Going, June, 1950; Firearms Combined with Other Weapons, October, 1925; An Eighteenth-Century Scottish Pistol, May 1934; Highland Pistols, September, 1951; Blunderbusses, July, 1925; Pedigreed Antiques: Historic Duelling Pistols, December, 1924; The American's Approach to European Firearms, October, 1955.

Part II: Forefather Firearms, August, 1930; Colonial Firearms—Part I, February, 1927, Part II, The Firearms of the Queen Anne Period, June, 1927, Part III, April, 1928, Part IV, The Identification of Specimens by Technical Analysis, April 1929; Colonial and Revolutionary Firearms, January, 1940; Revolutionary War Muskets, July, 1952; Charleville Muskets and American Arms, January, 1953; French Officers' Shoulder Arms, December, 1931; United States Musket Model 1795, February, 1947; Continental Property versus Commonwealth of Pennsylvania, February, 1931; The 1814 United States Contract Rifle, April, 1945; Our Martial Pistols, October, 1922.

Part III: Charleston Gunsmiths, July, 1942; Medad Hills, Connecticut Gunsmith, July, 1943; Guardians of the Liberty Bell?, February, 1930; On the Trail of a Gunsmith, September, 1928; The Pedigree of the Pennsylvania Rifle, September, 1932; Jacob Dickert, Lancaster Gunsmith, April, 1952; Peter Gonter, Lancaster Gunsmith, August, 1956; Early Ohio Gunsmiths: A Partial Check List, May, 1943; John Hills, Gunsmith of Vermont, August, 1969; A Key to Rifle Locks, May, 1937.

Part IV: American Silver-Hilted Swords—Part I, November, 1944; Part II, December, 1944; Sword Hilts by Early American Silversmiths, February, 1965; American Silver-Hilted Swords, June, 1955; Swords of California and Mexico in the Eighteenth and Nineteenth Centuries, August, 1946; The Fine Art of Stabbing, June, 1924.

Part V: The Why and How of Engraved Powder Horns, October, 1929; Keep Your Powder Dry, January, 1941; American Engraved Powder Horns, January, 1945; Powder Horns of the French and Indian War, 1755-1763, August, 1978; Decorated Military Americana, July, 1966.

First Edition

Library of Congress Catalog Card Number 79-55757
ISBN 8317-4182-1

Produced by The Main Street Press
42 Main Street
Clinton, New Jersey 08809

Published by Mayflower Books, Inc., USA
575 Lexington Avenue
New York City 10022

Contents

III The Work of Regional Gunsmiths   74

Introduction

Collecting weapons probably dates back to the earliest period that man began to dignify his tools of war with ornamentation. A fascination for newly-invented mechanical devices, along with an appreciation for finely chiseled steel and gracefully carved wood, stimulated a keen interest originally confined to royalty. Great European collections were formed with magnificent gifts of swords, pistols, and long arms presented to one royal house from another, and by those splendid specimens that were crafted by the royal gunsmiths for their sovereigns. Most of these superb weapons remained in the imperial collections, seldom used and never abused.

By the beginning of the 19th century some successful entrepreneurs outside the royal households began to accumulate their own arms collections. Interest in the United States, however, was mostly confined to institutions which accepted gifts donated by families that wished to preserve specific weapons handed down by illustrious ancestors. Since the majority of the articles on arms which have appeared in *The Magazine* ANTIQUES are concerned with American weapons, or with those that have an American association, the articles selected for this volume are those that focus upon that same theme. The period of time covered will not extend beyond c. 1840, the end of the flintlock era.

These limitations notwithstanding, a brief synopsis of the entire span of weapons collecting in America is necessary to this introduction. In the United States the hobby of collecting guns, edged weapons, and military accoutrements became available to the masses when surplus war material was offered for sale at modest prices after the Civil War. Not only of interest to hunters or to others who depended upon weapons as necessary tools in their way of life, these surplus martial artifacts were acquired by many who were merely interested in American history and/or the genius of American invention. The beautifully crafted arms that had been the choice of foreign collectors were often by-passed by Americans, who could not afford them, but were happy to purchase, in their place, much lower priced weapons that could be related to events in American history. Although the Europeans and the British also collected weapons from specific battles of historical significance, as well as weapons that possessed ethnological interest, the major collections abroad were based upon artistic merit.

By the end of the Spanish American War, surplus weapons were available to American collectors from two recent periods of armed conflict, as well as an occasional flintlock musket, carved powder horn, or sword and scabbard from the colonial period. Arms collecting was comparatively new in America in contrast with the established foreign collections that had been formed over a period of many generations, and selectivity was seldom applicable.

In the early 20th century just a few wealthy American collectors had acquired the taste and knowledge (or could retain agents who had those capabilities) to establish first-rate collections which followed the Continental pattern of collecting. Most other Americans interested in antique weapons sought those specimens that were available at lower costs and which could be associated with cowboys and Indians, Pilgrims and pioneers, or a Union cavalry charge against a Confederate artillery emplacement. The average collection was fairly general in content, composed of anything that might have been available at a cost the collector could afford. Sometimes an exquisite inlaid wheel-lock rifle or a 17th-century chiseled-steel rapier would be made available at a reasonable price. But, just as easily, a poorly fashioned "tourist trade" Arabic dagger could have been added to the collection. Such New York dealers as Francis Bannerman and H. K. White offered thousands of surplus war items, as well as European and Oriental weapons, at affordable prices.

Souvenirs, taken as spoils of war by returning Union soldiers, were also coming onto the market, disposed of as clutter by the widows or sons and daughters of the soldiers who had brought them home. Many rare Confederate weapons were scattered in thousands of attics throughout the Northern states. But the age of specialization had not really arrived, and would not until after World War II. There were, however, a few major collections that had been formed prior to this period by knowledgeable enthusiasts who had had the sophistication to specialize and the financial means to accomplish their goals. The more prominent collectors included William Henry Riggs, Rutherford Stuyvesant, George F. Harding, John Woodman Higgins, Henry Walters, Claude E. Fuller, William G. Renwick, Bashford Dean, Joe Kindig, Jr., Rudolph J. Nunnemacher, Herman P. Dean, Charles Darwin Cook, J. H. Grenville Gilbert, Rufus Grider, Edwin Pugsley, and Philip Medicus. Of the number of institutions and organizations that formed major collections of considerable quality, a few of the more prominent were the U. S. Cartridge Company, the First Corps of Cadets (Boston), Springfield Armory, Fort Ticonderoga (the Pell Family), United States Military Academy Museum, the Smithsonian Institution, and, comparable to many of the finer collections of arms and armor in Europe, the Metropolitan Museum of Art in New York City.

At the close of World War II, returning G.I.'s brought home thousands of "liberated" antique weapons. Some of these were of the highest museum quality, confiscated from private and public museums in Germany and Japan. Superb specimens eventually turned up in the marketplace. And, as the postwar economy expanded in the United States, Americans traveling abroad could find reasonably priced specimens in the antiques shops of the still-ailing European and British markets. With the improvement of the American economy, more funds to spend on leisure became available, and arms collecting, along with all of the other areas of collecting, began to grow rapidly. Soon numerous periodicals and books about American weapons and accoutrements appeared on the market, and collecting organizations were established throughout the country, many with their own journals or bulletins.

Collecting interests soon turned to specialized categories: Colts, Winchesters, Smith and Wessons, U. S. martial long arms, Confederate long arms, colonial long arms; pistols in those same categories; colonial swords, Civil War swords, U. S. swords, bayonets, hunting knives, pocket knives; military buttons, prints, paintings, published military manuals, uniforms, headgear, and camp equipment. Eventually there was a separate collecting category for every type of American weapon and equipment that had ever been manufactured. There were, of course, those who still sought the fine foreign arms—and many of these were at bargain prices, compared with the rising cost of American arms. As the economies abroad improved, however, this disparity was eventually corrected. Americans, who found buying trips abroad fruitful in the 1950s and 1960s, now find the Europeans, the British, and the Japanese scouring American markets in the 1980s.

In the years immediately preceding the American Bicentennial, a great deal of American interest turned toward colonial arms, a field that had never been as popular as those involving weapons of the later periods simply because arms and accoutrements of the 18th and early 19th centuries were far more scarce and usually of inferior condition than those that were mass-produced. Although most collectors gravitate towards fields of abundance and familiarity and shy away from scarcity and the unknown, an amazingly large number of articles have appeared over the years in ANTIQUES about weapons and accoutrements of the earlier period. Throughout its entire period of publication, in fact, the editorial staff of ANTIQUES has expressed a strong interest in the early arms that played such an important role in the history of this country. And for an excellent reason: Military weapons and accoutrements, as well as the accessories of the hunter, trapper, fur trader, and explorer, were as much in evidence in the everyday life of the colonist as the bannister-back chair, pewter porringer, or printed almanac.

Armed conflict was no stranger to the inhabitants of the New World throughout the 17th, 18th, and early 19th centuries. Warfare was synonymous with the settlement of the thirteen original colonies, all of which had been exposed to bloodshed since the establishment of the first permanent settlement in 1607. The colonists' struggles ranged in dimension from small local skirmishes to major intercolonial expeditions. Enemies varied from aborigines to neighbors involved in rebel-

lion or religious disagreement as well as soldiers of foreign nations. The wars that strained the purse strings of European governments during the 17th and 18th centuries had their counterparts in the colonies over control of the North American continent. A militia system had been established early in the 17th century and had remained in existence until the Civil War. For almost two centuries, almost every American male between the ages of sixteen and sixty, except those engaged in essential work, were required to report to militia drill four times a year.

Each militiaman was required to supply his own musket, cartridge box or powder horn, knapsack, canteen, bayonet, sword, or tomahawk. The trapper and explorer carried his own firearm, knife, tomahawk, hunting pouch, and powder horn. The settler living on the frontier needed his firearm and powder horn close at hand for survival, and the trader carried his own weapons as well as a supply of cheaper arms to trade with the Indians. The defenses required in clearing the forest in order to plant crops and establish settlements, or in trapping the beaver for its precious pelt, and fighting off Indian attacks or enemy soldiers provided a rich area of artifacts for the antiques enthusiast to collect many years later.

The collection of weaponry is not without concern for artistic quality. American silver swords first began to attract attention in an article in ANTIQUES by Philip Medicus in 1944. A catalogue was published in 1955, illustrating eighty-one examples of American silver-hilted swords that had been displayed at the Corcoran Gallery of Art as part of an exhibition entitled "The Sword in America, 1000-1954." A chapter of Harold L. Peterson's *The American Sword* (1954) is devoted to silver swords, and subsequent articles and books have acknowledged the importance of these handsome weapons in the study and collecting of American silver.

In 1924 Captain John G. W. Dillin's *The Kentucky Rifle* first called attention to the talented craftsmen from Pennsylvania, Maryland, Virginia, and North Carolina who created the magnificent long rifles. In 1960, in *The Pennsylvania Kentucky Rifle,* Henry J. Kauffman enlarged upon the "county characteristics," or regional features, of the long rifles made in Pennsylvania and Maryland. The definitive book on the subject was written by Joe Kindig, Jr., in 1960—*Thoughts on the Kentucky Rifle in Its Golden Age.* One of the earliest students of the long rifle, Mr. Kindig began writing articles about them for ANTIQUES as early as 1932 and, by the time his book was published, had assembled the finest extant collection of these magnificent weapons. Large detailed photographs and scholarly descriptions point out the qualities of these rifles that place some of them in a class with the finest carved Philadelphia furniture and the most sophisticated engraved American silver and brass. In recent years an exhibition was held at the York County (Pennsylvania) Historical Society in which 350 of the finest examples of the Kentucky rifle were placed on view for the public to study, and a book picturing most of them was published in 1976 through the sponsorship of the Kentucky Rifle Association. That organization had sponsored the publication of a similar volume in 1967 and has printed a great deal of valuable information in its bulletins.

Other books about regional firearms have been published,

indicating a growing awareness of the special characteristics applicable to the handcrafted firearms produced in different parts of the country. *Long Rifles Of North Carolina* by John Bivens, Jr., was published in 1968 and is an excellent illustrated scholarly book in which the author describes the long rifle as a form of folk art. *Maine Made Guns and Their Makers* by Dwight B. Demerritt, Jr., published in 1973, is an authoritative and detailed illustrated history of gunsmithing in Maine. Equally important is *The New England Gun,* published in 1975 and written by Merrill Lindsay, with superb photographs by Bruce Pendleton. This fine book illustrates many examples of a long-neglected area of gunsmithing and portrays in great detail the artistic qualities of the New England rifle and fowling piece.

The powder horn, always associated with colonial guns, has been gradually accepted by collectors as an art form as well as an historical artifact. ANTIQUES has periodically included articles about powder horns, the first appearing in 1925 and the latest in the August, 1978, issue. Stephen V. Grancsay's book, *American Powder Horns,* was published in 1946, and, in 1978, two new books on carved horns appeared: *Engraved Powder Horns* by Nathan L. Swayze, and *American Engraved Powder Horns* by John S. duMont. A wide variety of different decorated horns are illustrated in all three books, with little duplication, and all three include many of the watercolor drawings and pencil sketches drawn by Rufus Grider during the last decade of the 19th century.

Militia and regulation U.S. military uniforms, insignia, and decorated accoutrements fall into another collecting category that has recently become recognized by military enthusiasts. ANTIQUES published an article in 1966 which deals with decorated military Americana, including weapons, canteens, drums, swords, knapsacks and headgear. Much of the militia equipment was hand-decorated by itinerent artists, carriage painters, and sign painters. Like powder horns, this category of military Americana is slowly becoming recognized as a form of folk art.

The articles selected for this volume actually parallel the growth of attitudes in this country concerning the importance to collectors of American weapons and accoutrements, and have been divided into five chapters. An overall assessment of the subject is contained in the first section. Chapter II concerns itself with firearms used in America from the colonial period through the end of the flintlock era. The regional characteristics of American firearms and the contributions of particular regional gunsmiths form the content of Chapter III. Chapter IV includes material on edged weapons—on daggers and swords. Finally, Chapter V combines the subjects of powder horns and military uniforms and accoutrements, both aspects of decorative martial art.

I In Pursuit of History

The art of self defense and the most productive and efficient methods of obtaining food have always been accorded man's highest priorities. Today's newspaper headlines reflect the large percentage of the national budget that is allocated for weapons. Vast amounts of taxpayers' money are expended on newer and more sophisticated designs for the sole purpose of killing other men. But those instruments of war used in the 20th century are no longer the same tools used by the 20th-century hunter to obtain his food. Modern techniques of ranching and farming have reduced hunting to a sport. Less than 100 years ago, however, the buffalo hunter was decimating the bison herds with his rifle and defending himself, if necessary, with the same tool.

Two centuries ago provincial soldiers aimed their muskets at British redcoats and, after winning their independence, took many of those same weapons west of the Allegheny Mountains and utilized them for both the defense of their new homes and to obtain meat to feed their families. More than 500 years prior to the American Revolution man was beginning to experiment with gunpowder in the Western world while the crossbow reigned supreme. Man's progress seems to parallel the development of his weapons, and, as they became more sophisticated, so did he.

In the beginning a rock or a stick would have been the most suitable tool for defense as well as for attack; both were surely more effective than man's clenched fist. Eventually, the stick became a club, shaped for better balance, easier handling, and more efficient striking capability. And the idea of securing a rock to a handle was discovered and soon evolved into the hatchet or ax, which was capable of being used for either a work tool or fighting tool. Along with the advancement of ideas for improving the functional ability of his weapons, man conceived different designs with which to decorate them.

Many people dislike thinking of weapons as collectable works of art. Yet it is impossible to open a history book and find any span of time in which man was not fabricating or utilizing weapons. And equally impossible is the task of attempting to isolate designs and styles of any given period from those that adorned the weapons of that same interval. Therefore, a collection of weapons, covering a broad range of time and categories, will reflect, as effectively as any other area of collectable materials, the advancement of mankind in the decorative arts as well as in mechanical invention and ingenuity. Collecting should not be limited to the material objects sought by the collector. The events and other objects that influenced the field being collected should also be studied in order to more easily understand that field. A reference library that is readily available for consultation is a prime requisite for every collector. It should thoroughly cover the subject collected as well as related categories.

One of the most efficient mediums of reference, and a building block for every adequate collector's library over the years, has been *The Magazine* ANTIQUES. Chapter I of this anthology contains a general selection of articles that appeared in that magazine and which offer a simple and effective introduction to the subject of collecting firearms. Lewis Winant's article, "The Development of Ignition in Gun Locks," presents the various methods of firing guns, from the matchlock to the introduction of the metallic cartridge at the end of the Civil War. Excellent illustrations accompany the text, enabling the reader to reach a clear understanding of the evolution of firearms. Lewis Appleton Barker's "Firearms Combined with Other Weapons" offers a view of a fascinating aspect of the world of gun collecting. The lethal combination devised by the inventors of the weapons described and illustrated in this article possibly indicates the mood of the times in which they were conceived.

The anthology continues with two articles about Scottish pistols, weapons that have always delighted American collectors for both their beauty and historic association. An interesting historical footnote, not mentioned in either of these articles, concerns Major John Pitcairn of the British Royal Marines. Major Pitcairn lost his pistols when his horse threw him at the Battle of Concord and the frightened animal carried the Scotch all-metal weapons, still in their saddle holsters, into the American lines. They are now on display at the Lexington Historical Museum, and legend relates that General Israel Putnam acquired them and carried them throughout the Revolution. Subsequently, Pitcairn was killed at the Battle of Bunker Hill, leading a final assault against the American forces.

Another weapon that has held the attention of American collectors is the blunderbuss, the subject of an interesting article by Charles Winthrop Sawyer. Associated by folk lore with the Pilgrims, this impressive looking weapon was in fact used in America during the 18th and 19th centuries. Revolutionary War inventories from West Point and other storage arsenals show numbers of blunderbusses on their lists. Of equal interest is Elizabeth Urquhart's article about duelling pistols, one of which ended the life of Commodore Stephen Decatur. Stephen V. Grancsay's article, "The American's Approach to European Firearms," although it reflects the collecting views of almost twenty-five years ago, is nonetheless a reasoned argument leading to an ineluctable conclusion: "The wide spread of knowledge about firearms, stimulated by gun collectors' clubs in almost every state and by many recent authoritative publications, insures a permanent interest in fine firearms, European as well as American."

GETTING THE GUNPOWDER GOING

The Development of Ignition in Gun Locks

By LEWIS WINANT

Mr. Winant's boyhood fascination with the mechanism of old guns grew into a collecting interest in fine early firearms, of which he now has what he modestly calls "a reasonably good collection." He is a member of the Armor & Arms Club, the Eastern Arms Collectors, and the New Jersey Arms Collectors.

FOR THE LAST FIVE HUNDRED YEARS men have fired guns by pressing a finger against a trigger. But it was not until a Scottish clergyman patented a detonating gunlock in 1807 that the way was clear for modern guns. Before the Reverend Forsyth's invention the powder in the barrel was ignited either by sparks caused by friction or by the direct application of fire.

Except in the matter of ignition there have been no decided changes in the construction of guns since Columbus arrived. By the time the first settlers reached Jamestown guns not only had conventionally shaped stocks, and barrels equipped with sights, but some European guns were repeaters with rifled barrels. Gunsmiths were experimenting with breechloaders even then, but only muzzle-loaders were practicable until Forsyth's idea started them on the road leading to our present self-primed center-fire metallic cartridges.

The first type of lock used was a matchlock, in which a burning piece of chemically impregnated rope, or slow match, was touched to the priming powder.

The German matchlock arquebus shown in Figure 1 (as well as all others pictured here) is loaded by ramming a charge into the chamber from the front end. In this and in all the guns with friction locks, the fire is carried to the charge by a train of powder which runs from a flashpan through a touchhole in the barrel. Priming powder is placed in the pan when the gun is loaded. Pressing the trigger of this match-

lock pulls the curved holder, in whose cleft end a burning slow match is held, in leisurely fashion down to the flashpan. The cover of the flashpan having been first moved aside, the match ignites the powder, and the discharge takes place.

The matchlock mechanism did not produce fire or ignite the powder; it simply moved an already lighted wick to contact with the powder. The next achievement was the invention of the wheel lock, which produced a shower of sparks to ignite the powder *(Fig. 2)*. The wheel lock, which appeared in 1515 or soon thereafter, had the most complicated apparatus ever used to set off powder in a gun barrel. When the trigger is pressed on a loaded and primed wheel lock, a catch moves aside and releases a heavy spring which gives a jerk to a chain wound around the axle of a wheel, causing the wheel to revolve. The serrated edge of the wheel rubs against the flint, or iron pyrites, which is held in the jaws of a doghead. The friction brings a brief shower of sparks in the powder-laden flashpan. To fire each shot from a wheel lock

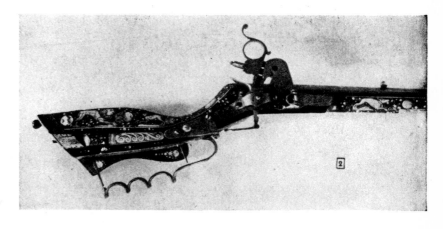

FIG. 2—GERMAN Rifled Wheel-Lock Tschinke *(early seventeenth century)*. This gun is held to the cheek, not to the shoulder, in firing.

it was necessary not only to charge the barrel and prime the pan but also to wind the lock with a spanner that fitted over the axle on the wheel. However, the wheel lock, once charged and spanned, was ready for instant use without further attention. It was clearly a great improvement over a method that required continual watchfulness while a smoldering rope was slowly consumed.

In the wheel lock the objective of touching off the priming powder was attained by suddenly moving the edge of a whirling steel against a stationary stone. In the next development this objective was effected by the reverse method, suddenly moving a stone, or flint, against a steel.

An Italian snaphaunce pistol shows this development *(Fig. 3)*. The squeeze of the trigger on this gun permits the flint, held in the jaws of the spring-driven doghead, to strike the steel. The steel is pushed back by the blow and the sparks

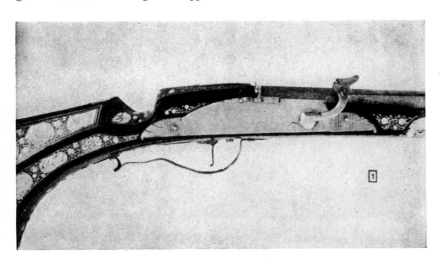

FIG. 1—GERMAN Matchlock Arquebus *(late sixteenth century)*.

fall in the pan whose cover was automatically opened when the doghead, now called the hammer, was released. This sliding pan cover had its counterpart in the wheel lock, and the influence of the wheel lock is apparent in the hammer. Only two major changes in the snaphaunce were needed to give us the flintlock of this country's pioneer days. One of these changes, the com-

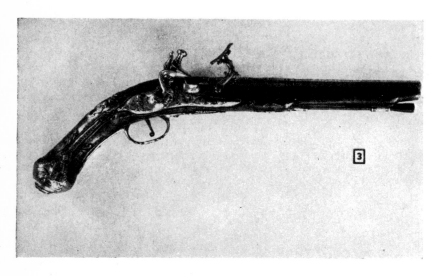

FIG. 3—ITALIAN Snaphaunce Pistol *(early seventeenth century)*.

bining of the steel against which the flint struck, and the pan cover, into one solid piece, came very quickly. The other change, which was the production of a tumbler with a second notch filed in it to provide a half cock, was not realized for at least forty years. The true snaphaunce, as we use the word today, always has the pan cover separate from the steel, and it has no half cock.

The writers of a century ago often defined as a snaphaunce lock what we now call a miquelet lock. In a still earlier day the word snaphaunce probably covered all types of friction locks other than the wheel locks. We now use "frizzen" as the name of the steel against which the flint was struck, though the word was unknown before the percussion era and is not yet to be found in any of the three leading English dictionaries.

The miquelet lock was devised soon after the snaphaunce and was perhaps an independent development. It is possible that both locks were made before 1600. Figure 4 shows a Persian rifle with a typical Spanish miquelet lock. Notice that the steel against which the flint is struck is made in one piece with the pan cover. When the hammer is cocked against the pressure of the heavy mainspring which is mounted on the outside of the lock plate, the toe of the hammer as it moves back uncovers two small holes in the lock plate and permits studs to slip through them. The hammer, if drawn part-way back and rested on the lower

of these studs, cannot be fired by pressure on the trigger. When the hammer is fully cocked and resting on the stud which protrudes through the second opening, trigger pressure will then draw both supporting studs inside the lock plate and let the hammer fall, driven by its heavy spring. This type of lock continued to be popular on guns in Spain well after 1800.

In any gun having a flashpan it is necessary to have a pan cover which will fit the pan tightly, so that priming powder will not fall or be blown out, or become damp in wet weather. Further, in a gun that employs a hammer designed to snap down on a frizzen it is necessary as a safety measure to provide that the hammer need not be held at full cock in order to keep the pan closed.

On the snaphaunce, as the frizzen was separate from the pan cover and could be set well forward, it was possible to have the pan primed and securely covered when the hammer was not cocked. Consequently, the lack of a half cock on the snaphaunce was not of particular importance. However, when the steel and pan cover were made in one piece, designed to be thrown back and open by the blow of the falling hammer, the need of some form of half cock was evident. In the miquelet locks this difficulty was overcome by use of the studs passing through the holes in the lock plates; in the flintlocks a second notch filed in the tumbler permitted setting the hammer in the safe half cock, out of the way of the closed frizzen.

The true flintlock is distinguished by having its steel and pan cover in one piece, by having its mainspring inside the lock plate, and by having both half-cock and full-cock notches cut in its tumbler. Its final development is shown in a pair of English dueling pistols *(Fig. 5)*. The locks have rainproof pans and are fitted with rollers on the frizzens. Their touchholes are bushed with platinum and their set triggers will fire at the gentlest touch. Their refinements increase their efficiency, but basically they do not differ from the first locks of this type made perhaps two hundred years earlier.

In America the flintlock was the only kind of lock made before the percussion era. In Europe, by 1680 the matchlock had run its course, and the brief and limited vogue of the snaphaunce was ended; by 1700 even the men who could afford the expensive wheel locks preferred flintlocks, and the flintlocks reigned supreme until the advent of percussion locks. In Asia, matchlock guns were made in recent years and were used in some engagements in the last war. In Africa, guns of

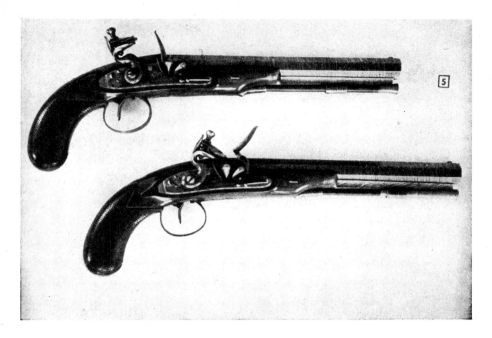

FIG. 5—PAIR of English Flintlock Dueling Pistols *(1826). Above,* lock ready to fire; *below,* in fired position.

believe that detonating locks were made before 1800, perhaps because two guns in particular have been observed dated earlier, though equipped with detonating locks. One of these guns, however, is a converted flintlock; the other is dated just one hundred years before its actual manufacture.

Forsyth's work had not been unnoticed, and by the time he was granted a patent many gunsmiths were working on other forms of detonating locks. The first evolutional change was the use of pills or pellets of detonating material instead of the loose powder. Two American-patented pill-lock pistols made by Mr. Hart of Chautauqua County, New York, with locks described in 1827 as being "ingenious and simple" are pictured in Figure 7. The lock is very simple, yet apparently more efficient than the later pill locks which were used by some American gun makers for many years. In firing one of these pocket pistols, a pellet of fulminating material is placed in the small pan, the hammer is drawn back and the trigger pressed. There is a sliding cover that may be pushed over the pan and held there firmly by the hammer when that is eased down. The gun may then safely be carried loaded and primed. Cocking the hammer automatically pulls the cover back and exposes the primed pan to receive the hammer blow.

The next step was the placing of the detonating mixture in a roll of copper. To prime the English tube-lock duck gun of Figure 8, the hammer is raised and a copper tube, about the size of a half inch of pencil lead and open at both ends, filled with a powerful fulminate of mercury preparation, is partially inserted in the vent leading to the powder chamber. The part of the tube not in the vent rests on an anvil which is integral with the lock plate. A pivoted cover is snapped down to hold the tube in position. When the trigger is squeezed the released hammer drives through an opening in the cover to crush and explode the tube primer.

This tube detonator provided an excellent, strong ignition,

the flint and snaphaunce types continue to be used.

The explosive power of the fulminates of various metals was known before 1700 and many experiments were conducted in attempts to use one or another of the fulminates as a propellant in a gun barrel. A fulminating powder explodes suddenly and violently when struck a quick blow; it does not burn like gunpowder, which must be lighted in a confined space to explode. Experiments with the fulminates were costly in life and property but of no avail until Forsyth turned to the idea of using a fulminate, not as a propellant, but as an igniter only. After some unsuccessful approaches to his problem, he invented and patented in 1807 a method of using loose detonating powder in a magazine that could be moved to drop a few grains in the opening to the gunpowder charge, where they could be crushed and exploded by the blow of the hammer.

An English gun with a lock by General Shrapnel uses this method of detonation *(Fig. 6).* The magazine, which has a screw top to permit refilling, may be pushed back and forth manually on a rail. When the magazine is fully back with the hammer raised, it pushes away the pan cover and drops a few grains of detonating powder into the vent-like pan. The magazine is pushed forward and the pan cover returns to its protective position, where it is lightly held by spring pressure. When the gun is cocked and the trigger pressed, the falling hammer causes the pivoted pan cover to get out of the way before the hammer nose hits the fulminate.

Speaking of the Forsyth patent, Major Pollard said in 1926, "It is undoubtedly the most important invention in firearms since the discovery of gunpowder, for it is in itself the main principle which has permitted us to proceed to the evolution of the metallic cartridge, the effective breech-loading small arm, and all the varied artillery inventions of today." Some antiquarians

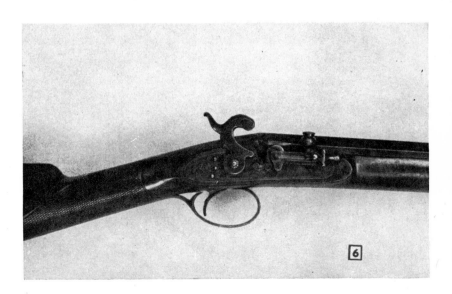

FIG. 6—ENGLISH GUN *(early nineteenth century),* with lock by General Shrapnel using Forsyth method of detonation. Shown ready for firing, with hammer cocked, pan covered, and magazine forward. This and figure 7 are the rarest items shown here.

but the invention of the percussion cap soon stopped any demand for tube locks except in occasional pieces made for heavy charges.

The detonating principle culminated in the percussion cap. This is the primer that has been produced in many thousands of millions to be inserted in the heads of modern cartridges, but which was first used quite apart from a cartridge. The cap is simply a small cylinder of copper with one end closed, and with a coating of a detonating mixture on the inside of that closed end. It is easily possible that percussion caps were invented in the United States before the tube lock was invented in England. However, the tube-lock ignition was used in England before the cap lock was known there and as it is not certain just when, where, and by whom the percussion cap was invented, we rank the cap primer as the ultimate development of the detonators.

The carefully designed pistol of Figure 9 is fitted with a typical percussion cap lock. The cap is pressed on a nipple screwed into the powder chamber. When the hammer strikes the cap, the fire from the crushed fulminate passes down the vent running through the nipple to the powder.

From the time Forsyth challenged the supremacy of flint ignition to the development of the copper cap was barely a dozen years, but it took a half-century more to get that cap fixed in the base of a metallic cartridge. The history of the development of the cartridge, through paper cartridge, metallic cartridge-with-outside-primer, pin-fire, rim-fire, and finally center-fire stages is fascinating—but quite another story.

It has been said that though the Declaration of Independence declared men equal, it was Colonel Colt who made them so. The revolver known to collectors as a Thuer Colt is the first type of revolver made in the United States to use an all-metal, center-primed, reloadable cartridge *(Fig. 10)*. It is also, incidentally, the first type of revolver made by Colt to use a metallic cartridge of any sort. It employs a patented cylinder ring which controls both the firing of the cartridges and the ejecting of the shells. The cartridges are slightly tapered, being of less diameter at the primer end than at the bullet end, and are loaded into the cylinder chambers from the front. Both the Thuer cylinders and the Thuer cartridges used in Colt revolvers were first issued in 1868. Though there have been many improvements in the components of cartridges, in shape, weight, and ingredients, eighty years have gone by with no basic changes in the ignition of gunpowder.

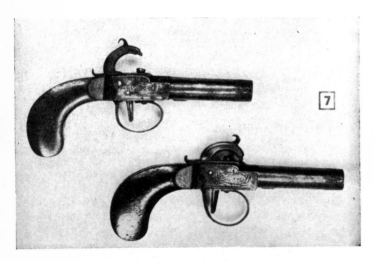

FIG. 7—AMERICAN-PATENTED Pill-Lock Pocket Pistols *(c. 1827)*. *Above,* shown in firing position; *below,* in fired position, with hammer resting on pan cover.

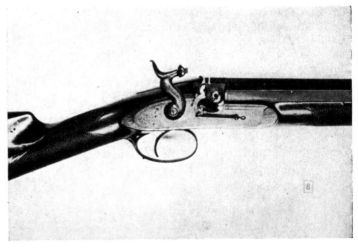

FIG. 8—ENGLISH Tube-Lock Gun *(early nineteenth century)*. Shown with both hammer and cover raised.

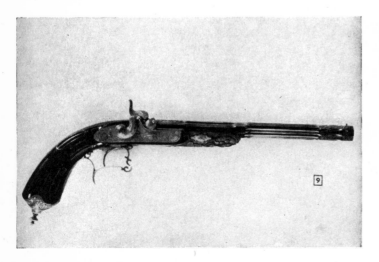

FIG. 9—PISTOL with Typical Percussion-Cap Lock. One of a pair made in Liège in 1867 by Julian and engraved by Potgisser.

FIG. 10—THUER Colt Revolver *(c. 1868)*.

Fig. 1 — CROSSBOW AND PISTOL (*c. 1625*)
A richly decorated compromise between the mediaeval and the modern in weapons. The upper part constitutes a crossbow. Underneath is the wood encased barrel of a pistol. *Owned by Sumner Healey.*

Firearms Combined with Other Weapons

By LEWIS APPLETON BARKER

WHY is it that we are so chary of accepting any-thing new or strange, no matter how great an improvement over what we have been accustomed to? Inventors have learned this to their cost; for, whatever the reason, innovations are regarded with suspicion; and this was just as true in the fourteenth century, when gunpowder first came into European use, as it was in the early nineteenth, when steam vessels were still equipped with sails because of doubt concerning their new power; and later, when we refused to remove our gas fixtures upon installing electric light; and clung to the old fashioned cistern with its accompanying pump at the kitchen sink, long after an enlightened municipality had taxed us generously for a modern water supply. Somehow, confidence is always placed in what is known to be tried and true, and reliance upon the clumsy but oft proved tools of our fathers is likely to be greater than upon those of a more modern type.

This has been particularly true in the use of firearms, where protection of life and limb has been involved. The chivalry, and, indeed, those of all classes of the period trained to war (and this included most of the male inhabitants not connected with the clergy), were very suspicious of the new death-dealing power of bullet and barrel. They were dubious,—and with abundant reason,—as to whether the weapon would go off when, and as, desired,—a consideration of some importance when the life of the owner might hang in the balance. In addition, there was considerable hatred and scorn on the part of our warlike ancestors toward weapons which, fired by one man, could mow down dozens; or which, in the hands of the veriest tyro in arms, could overcome in a flash the flower of knighthood. The feeling of the day is well expressed by the statement that Conan Doyle puts into the mouth of a grizzled English bowman, speaking of a cannon:

There is what hath done scath to good English bowmanship, with its filthy soot and foolish, roaring mouth. I wonder that a true knight, like our prince, should carry such a scurvy thing in his train.

With such feelings prevailing, while it would have been the height of folly utterly to ignore and refuse the aid of a new device with which an opponent might inconveniently be equipped, the soldier felt far safer if, connected with whatever form of firelock he carried, he might also have a sword, an axe, or a crossbow,—some one, indeed, of the weapons with which he was familiar, and which had stood the test of centuries. So it came about that, while hitherto armourers had been content to turn out single weapons of a kind, not uniting in one piece both sword and axe, or spear and crossbow, they now taxed their ingenuity to make combinations of one or all of these weapons with some form of firelock. Other combinations could be devised so that such an innocent appendage as a walking-stick might contain deadly properties in different forms.

Such things were cunningly made, and were, therefore, expensive. Being so, they were not as a rule fabricated in types or in quantities, but rather in odd and single pieces; and, since the price might be of no object to the purchaser, master gunsmiths of the day spared neither pains nor time in perfecting both mechanism and ornamentation. Hence, the examples of such workmanship as have come down to us are naturally scarcer than those of the ordinary weapons of daily use.

Thus, we find, in the fourteenth century, the simplest of both axe and hand cannon in one piece, part of the handle of the axe being a steel tube with a pan at the side, but with absolutely no mechanism, or even a serpentine or slow-match holder. Equally crude was a piece belonging to the reformer Zwingli, who died at the battle of Cappel, in 1531. This was a plain axe of half moon shape, the entire handle being a steel tube, thirty-four inches in length, with a touch hole on the top.

As the serpentine for holding the match came into use, we meet with more elaborate axes, both in Europe and in the Orient, the handles of which form match-lock pistols, to which are attached knives that unscrew from the barrel before the piece can be discharged. By the end of the

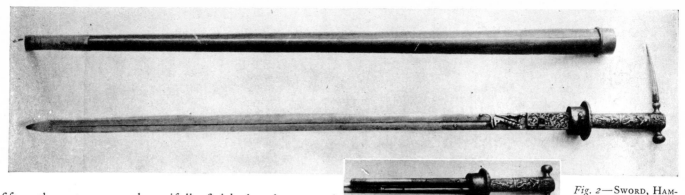

Fig. 2 —Sword, Ham-
mer and Pistol
An elaborate and in-
genious combination.
*Owned by Sumner
Healey.*

fifteenth century very beautifully finished and engraved battle-axes were combined with wheel-lock pistols, inlaid with ivory and silver. Even in the late seventeenth century, when the flint-lock had very generally superseded the wheel-lock, we find that the axe had not been entirely relegated to the scrap heap; as there are extant some rare examples of axe and firearms in conjunction.

Perhaps the most curious combination of this nature that can be imagined is a very heavy English mace or war club of the reign of Henry VII (1500), which unscrews in the centre and is furnished with a *gonne*, as it was then termed. It is needless to add that this was simply a steel tube equipped with a touch hole.

For additional defense at close quarters, the forked rests, which were thrust into the earth to help bear the weight of the heavy early muskets, were sometimes provided with a wheel-lock pistol. In the Historical Museum of the Monbijou Palace at Berlin is such a one, five feet, two inches in length. It is a three sided dart of steel, damascened with gold: fastened to it is a wheel-lock pistol. This weapon belongs to the sixteenth century.

Even the *martel de fer*, or war hammer, was not exempt from shooting aid. There is one of the reign of Queen Elizabeth (1580), furnished with a pistol, beautifully engraved, and having a hook to hold it at the saddle bow. One of the time of James I (1603) has within it a *tuck* or sword; while a magnificent piece of the period of William III (1690) contains a sword and firelock pistol.

The form of crossbow known as a *prodd* was a favorite type with which to combine a pistol. Perhaps the most beautiful specimen of this in America is that owned by Sumner Healey of New York City. It is reproduced herewith. It is of the period of Charles I (1625), and is very elaborately ornamented. Both lock and barrel bear

armourer's marks. The bullet leaves the barrel of the pistol directly below the spring. A peculiar feature is the ramrod (half of which is shown), which is telescopic; that is, in two parts which screw together. It is made of iron. The two triggers (which form the hair trigger combination known as the *stecher*) discharge the pistol, while what appears like a trigger guard for the latter is also a trigger for the bow.

The ornamentation of stock and pistol panel, consisting of engraving and inlay of ivory, is exceptional. With a magnifying glass, if not with the naked eye, one may readily discern the running hare on the ivory plate at the butt, and the face just over the wheel, as well as the dragon on the forestock of the pistol. The engraving on the cock or hammer forms a dragon's head, below which is half a face and a grotesque animal. They were master workmen who turned out weapons like this, and could command any price.

But probably the most unique bow combination in the world is one in the Meyrick collection in England. It is a German longbow of steel, of the fifteenth century. It hinges in the middle and may be folded together, and held so by a cross-bar, so that it then resembles a sword with two blades side by side and pressed together, the handle of which forms two small *gonnes*, each to be fired by an unattached match. In the same collection is something equally unusual. This is one of the weapons termed by different authorities, respectively, a *holy water sprinkler* and a *morning star*, and in this case is described

Fig. 3 — Pocket Ingenuities
Top, right to left: double barreled French flint lock (*1700*); double barreled English flint lock (*1790*). *Below:* double barreled English flint lock with bayonet; double barreled English percussion cap. *Period of Crimean War.*

in the language of the time as, "with gonnes at the end." This is nothing more nor less than a long wooden mallet or club, bound with iron, and furnished with iron spikes at the end, in its ordinary form. This awkward weapon, prior in point of date to the invention of the match-lock, and therefore not later than the reign of Edward IV (fifteenth century), was made to hang at the saddle bow instead of a mace. An iron cap at the end was furnished with a slender, spear-like blade, and opened on a hinge to reveal the muzzles of four short barrels; each of which could be fired by a match.

A most extraordinary piece of this class is another item owned by Mr. Healey. It is a walking staff containing a long, double-edged sword, a wheel-lock pistol, and—in the handle—a war hammer. The cane is made of various colored strips of wood with bone inlay; mouth and ferule are of gilt bronze. As may be seen in the accompanying photograph, the handle of the sword—of chiseled bronze, heavily gilt—is exquisitely decorated with figures in bas-relief. There is no other such piece in America, the only similar one known belonged to a former Doge of Venice, and is now in the Meyrick collection in England (*Fig. 2*).

From the reign of Elizabeth—if not before—down to the Crimean War, swords have been combined with pistols of the match, wheel, flint, percussion, and even cartridge locks. Canes, with swords and daggers enclosed, as well as canes with pistols, are not uncommon. A peculiar piece is an alpenstock with a flint-lock pistol in the handle.

Once begun, the custom of combining weapons was not easily given up. During the eighteenth century, flint pistols, and during the nineteenth, percussion and even cartridge pistols and revolvers, had frequently a dagger or bayonet which sprung forth, either from the top, bottom, or side of the barrel.

A peculiar and interesting dagger of Belgian manufacture is one of sixteen inches in length, with a short barrel each side of the blade, fitting into the sheath. The hammers are made to represent quillons, and are fired by one concealed trigger, the right barrel going off with the first pull, and the left with a second pressure.

Another combination, a favorite with thugs, combines the butt or handle of a pistol or pepperbox with a sort of brass knuckle with which to strike. These were made in variations from 1860 to 1880. The most pretentious of the lot is one that possesses an entire set of four brass knuckles, which, unfolded, form the handle of a six-shooting pepperbox revolver. A small, wavy bladed dagger that unfolds to the front, adds further attractiveness to this cheery little pocket companion.

Fig. 4 — POCKET CARTRIDGE PISTOLS
A variety of types developed from 1860 on. The central item of the group, with its knife blade and "knuckle dusters" in addition to its cartridge cylinder and barrel, is not an alluring object.

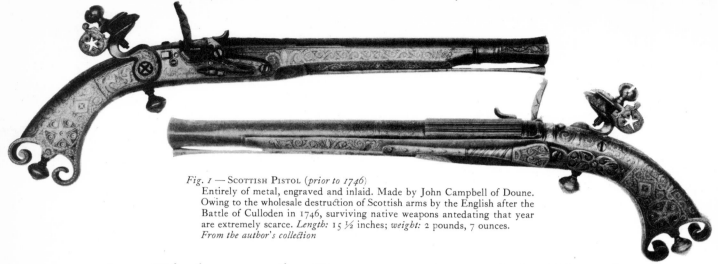

Fig. 1 — Scottish Pistol (*prior to 1746*)
Entirely of metal, engraved and inlaid. Made by John Campbell of Doune.
Owing to the wholesale destruction of Scottish arms by the English after the
Battle of Culloden in 1746, surviving native weapons antedating that year
are extremely scarce. *Length:* 15 ½ inches; *weight:* 2 pounds, 7 ounces.
From the author's collection

An Eighteenth-Century Scottish Pistol

By Doctor J. R. Mayer

Drawings by the author

Scene: *Edinburgh. Holyrood Castle. The first levee of George IV, 1822.
As the old Celtic chiefs, in plaid and philabeg, and flowing tartan passed
in review — each with the badge of his clan — the dress that had distinguished his name for centuries — colours that had been so oft paraded in
those very apartments — the picture was full of martial show and anima-
tion. The basket-hilted sword — the Ferrara of other times, the hereditary
palladium from father to son — recalled the party feuds and patriotic
struggles in which it had been so oft displayed as the sole arbiter from which
there was no appeal. The richly inlaid pistols, generally of the famous
Doune manufactury, and the dagger of Damascus metal — all arranged in
the girdle, gave the wearer more the aspect of a corsair prepared for a cruise
than of a courtier in the presence of his sovereign. . . .*

— David Beattie's *Scotland*

PRIOR to the beginning of the second half of the seventeenth
century the gun trade of Scotland was almost entirely under foreign influence. Ideas were imported from Spain and Italy, material
from Sweden and England, finished arms from Germany and the
Netherlands. In the few Scottish arms of the time this alien quality was
universally in evidence. All metal construction was German; long,
graceful stocks were Italian; tulip-shaped butts, Dutch; dog locks, ball
triggers, circular fences on snaphaunce pans, and the upturned stocks of
the long guns were Hispano-Moresque. The leading
smiths of the time were Alex Pryde, Gordon, and
Smith, with shops at Dundee and St.
Andrews. With the advent of the
eighteenth century, however, this
situation underwent a complete
change. Craftsmen in the gun-
smitheries freed themselves from
Continental influences. Reaching
back into the antiquity of their own
land, they revived the decorative
motives of their Celtic forbears,
cultivating a style and form essentially Scottish, unique because in-
digenous, having roots in the soil.

The incentive to the manufacture
of firearms in Scotland occurred as
follows: After the English Civil War
and the Continental wars of the first
half of the seventeenth century
(Thirty Years War and the War of
the Fronde), Scotch mercenaries returning to their native land brought

Fig. 2 (above) — Silver Inlay Panel from Butt
Fig. 3 (right) — Bronze
Brooch: Celtic (*seventh
century*). A saucer fibula
crisply embossed

with them a great variety of weapons. Clock- and locksmiths at Leith,
Dundee, Doune, Stirling, and other towns along the eastern seaboard
undertook to repair these imported arms. From such beginnings guilds
of hammermen or tackemakers (pistolmakers) grew up. Early in the
eighteenth century these craftsmen had begun to fabricate a characteristic type of all-metal pistol — rugged, graceful, and remarkably decorated. Bright steel surfaces were engraved, and on blued surfaces, where
incised ornamentation proved ineffective, designs were executed in gold
and silver inlay. Since these pistols were admirably adapted to their
picturesque costumes, Highland chieftains eagerly purchased them.
After the abortive revolt under Prince Charlie Stuart the Pretender had
culminated in the English victory at Culloden in 1746, most of the existing Scottish arms were captured and destroyed. Hence surviving examples of the early period are today excessively rare.

A pioneer in the firearms trade was Thomas Caddell, who came to
Doune in 1640 and in 1646 there established a shop. Caddell was a remarkable man. With little or no education or training, he distinguished
himself as a leading gunsmith, the founder of a notable line of artisans
who manufactured many of the finest Scottish arms. Two more Thomas
Caddells followed the first. About 1700
John Campbell, an apprentice, took over
the business and was eventually succeeded
by two others of the same name. Toward
the end of the century John Murdoch was
the leading smith at Doune.
Thereafter the influx of cheap arms from England
destroyed the domestic manufacturers.

An early eighteenth-century Highlander pistol from the shops of these
smiths is here illustrated to demonstrate
the distinctly national character of
Scottish arms. The piece is all
metal, fifteen and a half inches
long, and weighs two pounds,
seven ounces. The .56 calibre barrel
retains all of the original bluing.
It is ten and a half inches long,
delicately fluted at the breech,
octagonal and flared at the muzzle.
The surface ornamentation is
engraved. The steel stock retains
much of the original bluing and is
enriched from end to end with silver inlay. The butt is of the ram's

Fig. 4 — Details of Engravings on Barrel

*Fig. 5—*Illumination *(enlarged)* from the Lindisfarne Gospel *(early eighth century)*

horn, or spiral, type, fitted with a silver knob picker. It is slightly cast off to the right to overcome the tendency to fire to the left as the scear is released by the trigger pull. The belt hook is pierced, engraved, and inlaid. The lock is seen to be of the early flint type, the hammer and the frizzen shafts having no bridles. The scear action is horizontal, embracing a stud which pierces the lock plate holding the hammer at the half-cock position. The swan-neck hammer is decorated with the very effective star-pierced lobe. The trigger knob, like that of the picker, is of engraved silver. The ram-rod is an inaccurate restoration. The lock plate is signed *John Campbell*.

The application of surface decorations embracing ancient Celtic motives enhanced the uniqueness of Scottish arms already highly distinctive in design and material. On the pistol here described, the barrel, as illustrated in Figure 4, is engraved with variations of the spiral or trumpet form, a Celtic device of the seventh century. The pattern on the breech is a familiar form; the one above it, a connected system of spirals, though foliate in appearance is nevertheless aphyllomorphic. Noteworthy are the geometric designs within the central spindle. The four-petal floral form is a common decorative adjunct to the spiral. The venerable antiquity of these ornaments will remain unquestioned after Celtic paleography is consulted. Particular reference is made to the illuminations of the Lindisfarne Gospel and the Book of Kells, the former Anglian, the latter Hibernian, both probably of the early eighth century. To demonstrate the point, an illumination from the Lindisfarne Codex is reproduced in Figure 5.

On the silver inlaid butt (*Fig. 2*), we see how effectively the spiral complements the geometrical stars, squares, and crosses. The Celtic star is, perhaps, the remotest contrivance, for it dates back to pagan times. A fine example of this motive is shown in Figure 3, from a bronze saucer brooch of the seventh century at Fairford, Gloucestershire, England. It is embossed with a central star and peripheral runes.

On the under side of the stock (*Fig. 6*) occurs a woven pattern, consisting of a single twisted strand or guilloche intertwined with running loops terminating in spirals. The ancient artists multiplied these strands, creating a braid or plait, and then, by diverse cutting and joining of loops, formed an interlace of which there are about eight hundred varieties. The interlace design evolved during the eighth century was Christian Celtic in origin. Other peoples used a similar ornament, especially the Christians of Byzantium and the Moors of Spain. In Celtic England and Ireland, however, the motive was most highly developed.

The side of the stock reveals the running scroll or vine reproduced in Figure 7. Its archetype is discoverable in many of the ancient sculptured Celtic crosses erected during the seventh century. A panel from the famous Bewcastle cross in Cumberland, England, is depicted in Figure 8. This vine pattern, not to be identified botanically, symbolizes in a purely conventional manner the Church as a compact unit supporting and sustaining.

Celtic art as portrayed in the ancient codices, stone monuments, and bronze objects was practiced in Great Britain and Ireland from the fourth and fifth to the eighth and ninth centuries. Although other contemporary peoples used similar devices, it may be averred that the system was native to these islands. Whether the art was primarily Anglo-Saxon or Hiberno-Saxon is beside the point, as these races learned the technique from their Celtic predecessors. Its revival for ornamentation by the Scottish gunsmiths of the eighteenth century contributed in no small measure to the excellence of their products. These firearms were sought by magnates of the time as unique and reliable weapons. They are coveted by connoisseurs of today as rare objects of art.

Bibliography

Jones, Owen: *The Grammar of Ornament*; London, 1856.
Brown, Baldwin: *The Arts in Early England*; London, 1921.
Hamlin, A. D. F.: *A History of Ornament*; New York, 1916.
Saunders, O. Elfrida: *English Illuminations*; Florence, 1928.
Champneys, Arthur C., M. A.: *Irish Ecclesiastical Architecture*; London, 1910.
Pollard, Major H. B. C.: *History of Firearms*; London, 1930.
Farquharson, Major V. A.: *Firearms and Gunlocks*; London, 1898.
Whitelaw, C. E.: *A Treatise on Scottish Hand Firearms of the XVIth, XVIIth, XVIIIth centuries*; London, 1923.

(The author wishes to express his appreciation to Miss Mary E. McConnell, Art Librarian of the Memorial Art Gallery of Rochester, New York, for her generous assistance in the compilation of the bibliography.)

Note. Major H. B. C. Pollard, in his *History of Firearms*, sounds a warning to would-be owners of such pistols. "The high prices paid for these Scottish weapons," he writes, "have resulted in a good deal of ingenious reproduction by careful, if non-ethical, craftsmen. Some excellent forgeries have sold for high prices under the hammer, and in no department of antique firearms is greater care needed."

Fig. 6 (below) — Interlace Panel from the Stock (Silver Inlay)

Fig. 7 (below) — Silver Inlaid Panel from the Stock

Fig. 8 (right) — Bewcastle Cross: Celtic *(late seventh century)* Panel on column of stone 14 feet 6 inches high

HIGHLAND PISTOLS

By IAN FINLAY

As Assistant Keeper in the Department of Art, Archaeology, and Ethnology at the Royal Scottish Museum, Mr. Finlay is well versed in all branches of Scottish arts and crafts.

FIG. 1—PAIR OF STEEL PISTOLS mounted in silver *(second half, eighteenth century)*. Maker: John Murdoch of Doune. "Scroll-butt" type. Length, 11½ inches. *Royal Scottish Museum.*

THE WEAPONS of the Scottish Highlander are making an ever-growing appeal to American collectors. My correspondents on this subject have ranged from a New York connoisseur who has made valuable contributions to our knowledge of the field, to people for whom the weapons have a mere passing, romantic appeal. Since the war a number of American students in Edinburgh have gratified me by calling to discuss prospective purchases in the antique shops of the Old Town.

Choicest among the old Highlander's weapons was his pistol, or dag. Good Highland pistols by celebrated makers now fetch high prices in the salesrooms, but often enough in old Scottish country houses I have come on lovely pieces hanging high and neglected on a staircase wall. Few know the real thing from the imitation. Early in the nineteenth century, Highland regiments of the British Army were equipped with mass-produced imitations of the ancient form of pistol, and those clumsy and almost worthless pieces are to be found in hundreds up and down Scotland, and beyond, even in public collections. Many have the name *Bissell* stamped on the lock plate. My first advice to a collector would be: beware of Bissell. His pistols are not Scottish. They are genuine "Brummagem"–made in Birmingham, England.

There are several distinct types of Highland pistol. The earliest type is now excessively rare. It has what has been termed a fishtail butt. A very few, probably the prototypes, have wooden stock and butt with silver or brass mounts. One is in the Royal Scottish Museum, Edinburgh *(Fig. 4)*. There is a pair—are they there still?--in the Dresden Museum, probably relics of Highland adventurers of the wars of Gustavus Adolphus of Sweden. They have snaphaunce locks of primitive but graceful form, and belong to the early seventeenth century. A variety of the same type is carried out entirely in brass. Illustrated in Figure 3 is one which I believe to be now in a Continental collection, with characteristic engraved

rosettes. Scots soldiers of fortune have left those pieces behind them in considerable numbers on their travels, and fine examples are in the Berlin Zeughaus and the Royal Armory, Stockholm.

Although Scottish, the fishtail-butt pistol may not be strictly a Highland pistol at all. The same may be said of the very long pistols with heart-shaped butts *(Fig. 2)*. These last are probably an east-coast type, but no doubt found their way to the clans. They are all-steel, like the true Highland pistols, and are inlaid with silver. They appear about the time of the Covenanters, toward the end of the seventeenth century.

But the pistol most widely associated with the Highlands has what is sometimes called a ram's horn, and at others a scroll butt. Whether the horns developed from the fishtail or not we shall never know. Features of the scroll-butt pistol are its all-steel construction, its beautifully flared, octagonal muzzle, its flowing butt with spirited scroll terminals flanking the engraved silver knob of a screw-in pricker, and the graceful S-shaped dog-head operating the flint. In good examples, not only the pricker-knob but the trigger, butt plates, and all inlay are of silver. The silver inlay on butt and stock loops and swirls with great intricacy and with the delicacy of damascening, and alternates with areas of equally fine and skilled engraving *(Fig. 1)*.

Now it is this very artistry and craft skill which exalt these little weapons in the eyes of connoisseurs. They set a problem which no one has yet solved satisfactorily. A big proportion of the finest pistols was produced by a few families in the small village of Doune, in Perthshire, a village on the border of what in the eighteenth century was the "Highland Line"—a line dividing Scotland roughly from Angus to Loch Lomond. Doune was probably tiny even then. How is it this remote hamlet should have given us pistols so lovely that they are today prized second only to the work of such artists as Cominazzi of Brescia? The medium, steel, is far more intractable

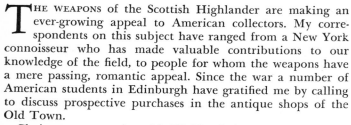

FIG. 2—STEEL PISTOL inlaid with silver, of "heart-butt" type *(late seventeenth century)*. Length, 20⅜ inches. *Royal Scottish Museum.*

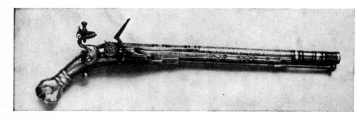

FIG. 3—HIGHLAND PISTOL of brass, engraved *(early seventeenth century)*. "Fishtail-butt" type. *Private collection in Europe.*

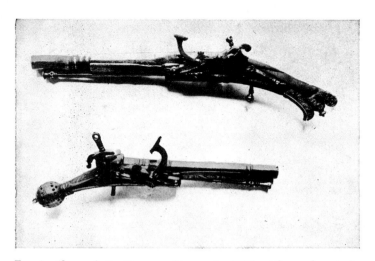

FIG. 4—*Above:* SILVER-MOUNTED PISTOL *(c. 1650),* with wooden stock. "Fishtail-butt" type; snaphaunce lock. Probably a prototype of the Highland pistol. Length, 15⅞ inches. *Below:* BRASS-MOUNTED PISTOL with snaphaunce lock *(probably late seventeenth century).* Crude type. Length, 12½ inches. *Both from The Royal Scottish Museum, Edinburgh.*

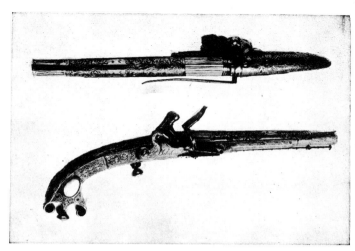

FIG. 5—PAIR OF "SCROLL-BUTT" PISTOLS of steel, inlaid and mounted in gold *(mid-eighteenth century).* By John Campbell of Doune. Length, 11½ inches. *Colville Collection, National Museum of Antiquities of Scotland, Edinburgh.*

at least than the walnut butts and stocks of Brescia, and yet the technical excellence never falters.

In an article in ANTIQUES for May 1934 Doctor Mayer of Rochester, New York, discussed the decoration of a pair of Highland pistols, comparing details of their ornament with an illumination of the famous Lindisfarne Gospels of the early eighth century and with a panel of the Bewcastle Cross. He saw in the pistol ornament a revival of Celtic art by Scottish gunsmiths of the eighteenth century. I have myself subscribed to this view and attempted to follow it up. After long pondering it, however, I feel one has to be cautious in these comparisons of similar motifs, and point rather to the traditional mastery of metalworking in general which can be traced back from those village gunsmiths to the ancient Celts, whose talent made them supreme in central Europe several centuries B. C. But there are many stone carvings, done by the Picts, much nearer to Doune than the mainly Anglo-Saxon Bewcastle Cross, and those Pictish carvings may have inspired the smiths of the village.

Most of those master-craftsmen signed their works. Their names appear on the lock plates of the pistols. The most recent and most authoritative list, including all known Scottish makers of pistols, appears at the end of the late Charles E. Whitelaw's treatise printed with Jackson's *European Hand Firearms* (London, 1923). The great names among Doune makers include Thomas and Robert Caddell (late seventeenth to mid-eighteenth centuries), three generations of Campbells, John Christie (mid-eighteenth century), and John Murdoch who was still at work in 1798, the year of the *First Statistical Account* of Scotland. John Campbell was the author of the magnificent pair of pistols with gold mounts instead of silver and inlay, now in the National Museum of Antiquities of Scotland *(Fig. 5).* I have had the privilege of examining another gold-mounted pair preserved in the Royal Armory at Windsor Castle. But Doune had no monopoly: the clansmen seem to have been supplied by craftsmen in many of the large and small towns bordering the Highlands—Inverness, Elgin, Aberdeen, Brechin, Dundee, Stirling.

It should be said that, in their original state, most of the scroll-butt pistols had their steel parts blued. Only a few have survived with traces of the bluing. The effect is to enhance the silver mounts and inlay to a pitch which must have delighted the Highlander, whose garb, music, poetry, and whole

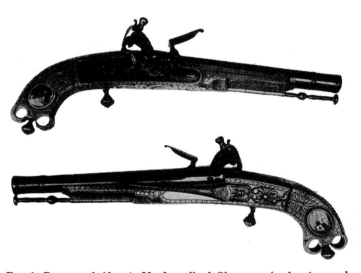

FIG. 6—PISTOLS of Alastair Macdonnell of Glengarry *(early nineteenth century).* Blued steel with gilt mounts inset with enamel plaques. Signed *Murdoch,* but barrels bear Birmingham proof marks. *Private collection in Scotland.*

attitude toward life are all animated by the old Celtic love of color and contrast.

Rather strangely, the craft of pistol-making survived the pacification of the Highlands which followed the Rising of 1745 under Prince Charles Edward—strangely, because the Disarming Act forbade the Highlander to carry weapons or wear his traditional dress. Clansmen hid their arms away, when they could. Many a targe (shield) was found doing service as the lid of a butter churn! But if weapons were still made, there is a noticeable difference between those made before and after the middle of the century. They became smaller, less workmanlike, more delicate, and decoration grows more elaborate and pretentious. It is obvious they have turned into show pieces, adjuncts of the dress, permitted again after the repeal of the Act.

In the end the pistols become stereotyped. Their manufacture is taken over by gunsmiths in the south, although a famous Doune name may still appear on the lock plate as it does on the pistols of Macdonell of Glengarry *(Fig. 6).*

Blunderbusses

By CHARLES WINTHROP SAWYER

BLUNDERBUSSES differed radically from other smooth bore guns in two main particulars; first, they were made solely for defense, and that at close quarters; second, they were not made to be arms of precision, but instead, merely special agents of destruction incapable of selecting foe from friend. To accomplish these ends the barrel of a blunderbuss was made a funnel, not a cylinder.

The eruption of a mine beneath the feet of a multitude could hardly be more disastrous than the cyclonic blast from a large blunderbuss. The latter's hail of missiles forms no regular pattern, comprises both empty and congested areas within its danger zone, is liable to leave unscathed the actual intended victim, and, at the same time, cut to shreds every animate thing within its path. A blunderbuss affords—or afforded—its user no certainty of hitting any desired place or thing: it is, of all weapons, a blunderer.

In the English speech of a few centuries ago, the term "blunder" meant just what it means today. The word "buss" meant *kiss*, in the sense of a loud smack. The name "blunderbuss" seems much more probably compounded of blunder and buss than derived, as philologists claim, from the German words *donner-busche* (thunder box or barrel). The assumed German derivation seems far fetched and fantastical.

Blunderbusses were of European, not American, origin. They were not extensively in use, either abroad or in the colonies, much earlier than 1750, although they may have been originated a bit before 1600, and were in use scantily for military purposes as early as 1650. Although usually equipped with flint locks, some of the early ones had match, and some wheel locks.

Blunderbusses in great numbers came to America in due time, but not in Pilgrim time. One of the commonest anachronisms committed by illustrators is that of portraying a Pilgrim Father, on his way to church, overtaken by a shower of arrows and vainly threatening the source of the shower with a huge bell-mouthed blunderbuss. Probably not one blunderbuss was in America at that period, and probably not one Pilgrim, unless perhaps Standish, had ever seen one. Artists appear to visualize the Pilgrims themselves as blundering, adult children; but they were not, and they were not blunderbuss users.

In America, except for sea service, the blunderbuss never had the vogue that it enjoyed in its home countries. Thousands of the weapons came here with the constant in-pouring stream of Europeans; and thousands more came as trade goods. Some, out of all that came, served as guardians of homes and of vehicles; but the majority became dormant weapons, stored away against a time of possible need.

In their home countries, blunderbusses were made for three specific services—military, home-defense, and stagecoach protection—and, to adapt them precisely, each to its kind of service, they were made in three types, one for each sort of service. In the heyday of their fashion, of course, each type was subject to infinite variation and even to crossing with other types: but, in early days, distinct types outranked the mongrels, and, furthermore, they hold first place in the esteem of arms collectors of these present times.

Many foreign countries issued blunderbusses to their soldiery as regulation military arms. America did not; and our government made none until after 1800, and then

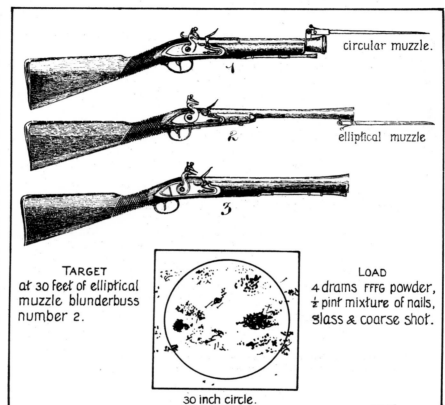

TARGET at 30 feet of elliptical muzzle blunderbuss number 2.

30 inch circle.

LOAD 4 drams FFFG powder, ½ pint mixture of nails, glass & coarse shot.

C.W.Sawyer

Fig. A — STAGECOACH BLUNDERBUSSES

1.—English. Length 29 inches; with bayonet 40½ inches. Brass barrel. Muzzle caliber 1⅝ inches. Weight 6½ pounds. The bayonet, when folded, is held and released by the catch shown in the rear of the cock. *Period, about 1770.*

2.—English. Length 33 inches; with bayonet 40½ inches. Brass barrel, with elliptical muzzle calibering 1⅞ by 2¾ inches. Weight 6¼ pounds. Bayonet catch under fore end operated by moving the trigger guard. *Period, about 1800.*

3.—English. Length 31½ inches. Brass barrel; muzzle caliber 2 inches. Weight 6 pounds. *Period, about 1780.*

only a few to enable our navy to cope with Mediterranean and West Indian freebooters. But our privateers in Revolutionary times and our merchant marine of the next two decades bought and carried and used quantities of foreign-made blunderbusses, and found them admirable arms of defense against boarders. Still later, in the days of clipper ships and the China trade, blunderbusses on American ships bloomed in profusion—but that is for subsequent telling.

Figure B shows the principal varieties of military blunderbusses. All are sizable weapons, as are the home-defense ones, as well; but military blunderbusses are distinguishable from the others by definite characteristics. Thus Number 3, by its great weight and its swivel for mounting, must have been made particularly for use over a ship's rail or in a land fortification. Numbers 1 and 2 are recognizable as military arms and not home-defense ones, not only by the government ownership marks on them but, likewise, by their military pattern stocks and furniture. Numbers 4 and 5, little ones for use by horsemen, are distinct from the stagecoach weapons for the same reasons and causes. The characteristics of each type are apparent in the three pictures portraying them.

Figure C shows the principal varieties of the home-defense type of blunderbuss. Blunderbusses of this type were patterned after shotguns as to butt shape and kind of furniture. They were sizable arms usually about a foot longer than their little brothers that rode on coaches. As a rule they were much more carefully and accurately made than the military pieces—stocked with a good quality of figured walnut and often provided with neatly engraved furniture.

Home-defense blunderbusses however among gun-wise men did not rank with shotguns. Their name even—blunderbuss—was a somewhat contemptuous term. Nevertheless they usually served the double purpose of guarding the home against robbers and of providing the young male hopeful of the family with a gun of a sort which supplied him an occasional tame rabbit or starling and returned but a weak kick, provided its load was coarse powder and real lead shot. Speaking generally, the use of shot in a home-defense blunderbuss was sacred to occasional hunting jaunts. When the arm was returned to its pegs by the fireplace, it was given its accustomed load of scraps of iron, chopped sheet lead, and broken glass and crockery: it was most potent then.

Some individuals in that far off time —wise or cautious men, or shooting men who used double barreled shotguns — preferred to guard their homes with double barreled blunderbusses. These arms, whether with round or elliptical muzzles, whether with or without spring bayonets, all belonged to one or other of the two varieties illustrated in Figure C, by pictures numbered 3 and 4. Both of these are shown with their bayonets folded. On pulling the catch which held the bayonet's tip, the bayonet would fly, with incredible speed, into the rigid position shown in Figure A by pictures numbered 1 and 2.

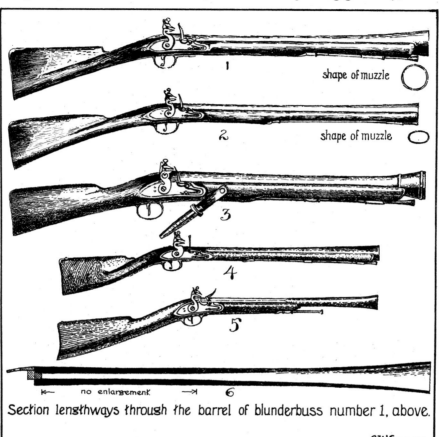

shape of muzzle

shape of muzzle

no enlargement

6

Section lengthways through the barrel of blunderbuss number 1, above.

C.W.Sawyer

Fig. B — Military Blunderbusses

Land and sea service, regulation (governmental, army and navy); and secondary (militia and privateer).

1.—English; navy. Length 42 inches; 26 inch iron barrel. Muzzle caliber 3¼ inches. Weight 8 pounds. Marked with *Tower, Crown, GR*, and old Birmingham proof stamps. Revolutionary War service possible on both British and American ships. *Period, probably about 1765.*
In this variety of the military type, barrel lengths ran between 20 and 30 inches.

2.—English; navy and internal revenue. Length 40 inches; 24 inch light brass barrel with elliptical muzzle calibering 1⅜ by 2½ inches. Weight 6¾ pounds. Marked as Number 1 with the added stamp of *IR* (Internal Revenue). Revolutionary War service on either side, or both sides, possible. *Period, probably about 1770.*

3.—British; land and sea service. Length 42 inches. Weight 37 pounds. Muzzle caliber 4 inches. Old London proof stamps legible; other marks not legible. *Period, about 1790.*

4.—English; army (?). Length 31 inches; 16½ inch iron barrel. Muzzle caliber 1¾ inches. Weight 6¼ pounds. Marked with *Claude, London* crossed sabres under a crown, and the interlaced *GR* of George the First. Probably not issued to cavalry but to a mounted branch of the excise service. Colonial Wars and Revolutionary War service possible. *Period, about 1735.*

5.—French; army. A governmental regulation issue to the Mameluckes of the Guard. Length about 31 inches. Muzzle caliber about 1½ inches. Iron barrel. Provided with the same style of lock and ramrod thimble as the Model 1793 rifle. *Period, about 1800.*

In both of these Figures—A and C—are also shown average targets, which average blunderbusses made at thirty feet, which is the practical limit of effectiveness for this class of weapon. Neither target caught all the missiles fired at it, perhaps not over two-thirds; but what did strike were far more deadly in massing and in cutting and tearing than a charge of shot from a shotgun, besides covering several times the area.

Figure A shows the remaining type, the coach or stagecoach blunderbuss. The coach blunderbuss never had in America the extensive use on vehicles that it had in Great Britain and France. That was because America was a land of poor roads and few stagecoach lines; and very few private coaches used for long journeys. In Great Britain, however, roads were well kept after the year 1700; and, as the years passed, they were constantly improved and extended. Stagecoach communication between hundreds of cities and towns was constant: private traveling coaches were fashionable and abundant; and, after 1784, when government mail carrying by coaches was established, the byways as well as the highways were rolling with wealth that needed blunderbuss guardianship from predatory highwaymen.

Much the same was true of France and of lesser portions of continental Europe. Great Britain, in particular, and Europe, in general, therefore, produced stagecoach blunderbusses in enormous numbers, and quantities of them came to America. But in this country they were used—when used at all—principally in city homes.

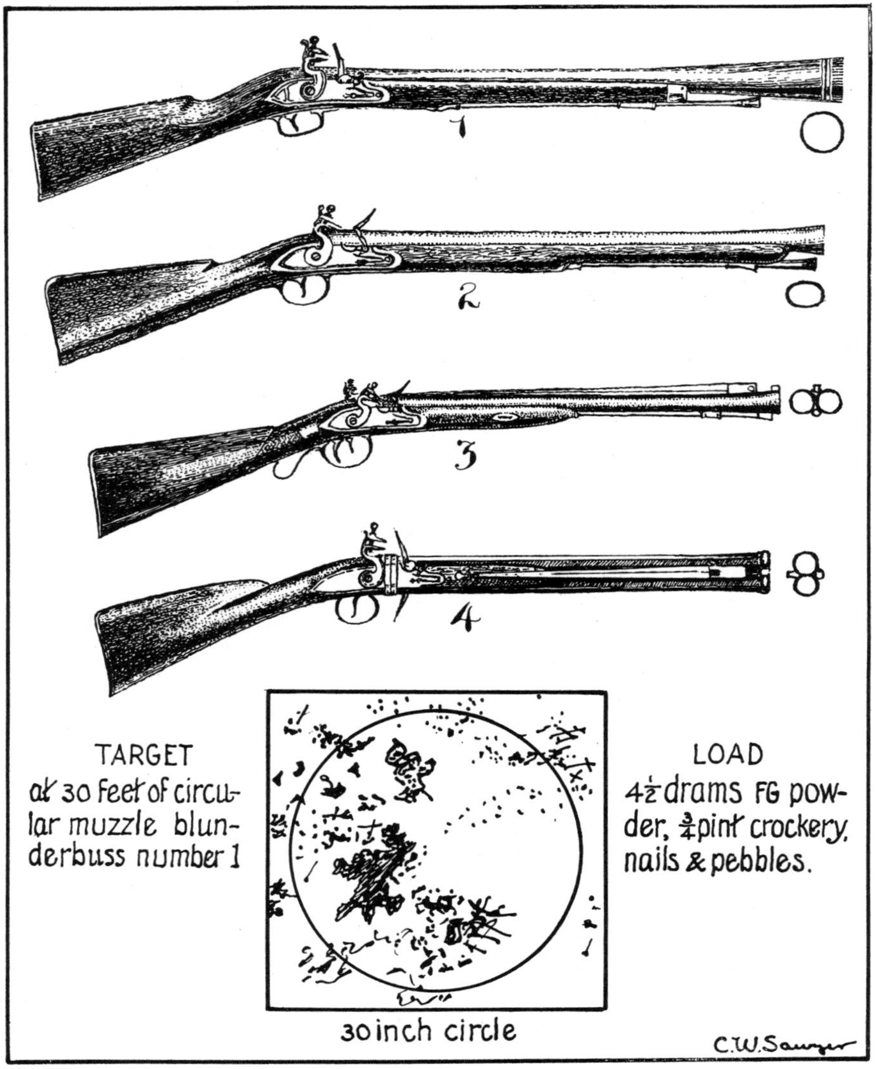

Of all the coach—stagecoach and other coach—blunderbusses now in existence, both abroad and here, it is safe to say that ninety per cent were made between 1750 and 1850; and, of that number, at least three-quarters were made after the Revolutionary War. The period of manufacture can be approximated closely by means of the proof marks on the barrels, the names on the locks, and the style of the furniture; for fashions changed in firearm furniture at certain periods.

The variety of the stagecoach blunderbuss that was, in its time, considered the highest grade, and that today is liked best by arms collectors was the carefully made specimen with the brass barrel, octagonal at the rear and ringed and belled at the front, equipped with a spring bayonet on the top of the barrel. This sort was carried, not only by government mail coaches, but also by the coaches of persons of wealth or title.

The elliptical shape of the muzzle of some stagecoach and other blunderbusses was formed for the purpose of causing the charge to proceed in the form of an ellipse, with the long axis horizontal, so as to avoid wastage into sky and ground, and to afford the utmost percentage of destructiveness. The theory seems sound but practice disproved it: a blunderbuss gave a blundering buss, whatever the shape of its mouth.

TARGET at 30 feet of circular muzzle blunderbuss number 1

LOAD 4½ drams FG powder, ¼ pint crockery, nails & pebbles.

30 inch circle

C.W.Sawyer

Fig. C — HOME-DEFENSE BLUNDERBUSSES

1.—Belgian. Length 3 feet 4 inches; 24½ inch iron barrel. Muzzle caliber 2¼ inches. Weight 8 pounds 14 ounces. Marked with the Liège proof master's stamp of the period, *1780-1790.*

2.—English. Length 38½ inches; 22½ inch brass barrel with elliptical muzzle calibering 1¼ by 2¼ inches. Weight 8¼ pounds. Marked, *Bailey, Newark, 1760.*

3.—English. Double barrel. Length 34 inches with bayonet folded. Iron barrels and furniture, the former of plain twist, the latter engraved. Sixteen gauge, with muzzle caliber of ⅞ inch. Weight 8 pounds. Marked *Egg*, old London proof stamps, and on the silver name plate an heraldic device, the initials *JP*, and date, *1781.*

4.—German. Double barrel over-and-under. Length 33½ inches, with bayonet folded. Barrels of iron, octagonal, of different gauges, and with bayonet on one side and ramrod on the other. Muzzle calibers 15/16 and ¾ inches. One lock for both barrels. They turn on a pivot and are held and released by a catch operated by the forward and rearward movement of the trigger guard. The bayonet, therefore, is alternately on the right and on the left. *Period, about 1775.*

Pedigreed Antiques

Historic Duelling Pistols

By Elizabeth Urquhart

DUELLING is no part of our life today. But a century ago it was recognized as an honorable and reasonably satisfactory method of settling personal differences. Perhaps the likelihood of being called to account on the field of honor for idle slander and groundless vilification kept some tongues in leash that might otherwise have done dangerous wagging. Perhaps the occasional sinful query as to whether life today might not really be more peaceful with the restoration of duelling as a silencer for blatherskites accounts for our interest in relics of the time when that drastic procedure was in good repute.

The pair of duelling pistols here pictured, however, did their share to destroy that good repute in the United States; for one of them put an untimely end to a gallant sailor, whose life was far too valuable to be sacrificed in the settlement of a petty dispute, — Commodore Stephen Decatur. That was back in 1820; — March twenty-second of that year, to be exact. And the place was Bladenburg, Maryland.

Commodore Decatur will be remembered as the American naval commander, who, in the Tripolitan war of 1801–1805, led a daring expedition into the harbor of Tripoli, boarded and burned the captured *Philadelphia* and then made his escape. Nelson pronounced this performance the "most daring act of the age."

Promoted to the rank of Commodore, in 1808, Decatur still further distinguished himself by skill and bravery in the War of 1812. In 1815 he fought against the Algerine pirates of the Barbary Coast, and forced the abolition of tribute. The following year he was appointed Navy Commissioner; and it was in the course of fulfilling the duties of this office that he became involved in the controversy which culminated in a fatal duel.

Commodore Barron, commander of the *Chesapeake*, in 1807 had been surprised by the *Leopard* and obliged to surrender his vessel.* For this he had been duly court-

---

*This event, which occurred at the port of Norfolk, was an expression of the British policy of impressment out of which grew the War of 1812.

martialled and suspended for five years. His sentence expired with the opening of the War of 1812; but the sulky Barron made no move to apply for a reinstatement and, with it, for an opportunity to wipe out his earlier disgrace.

At the close of the war, however, he sought reinstatement. This was opposed by Naval Commissioner Decatur. His reasons were, and are, obvious. Nevertheless, a bitter controversy arose between the two men. It was maintained by angry correspondence. At length Barron challenged Decatur to a duel; and the encounter was arranged at Bladenburg, Maryland.

The challenger was near-sighted: the distance between the duellists was but eight paces. They fired simultaneously, and both fell wounded —Decatur so seriously that he died on the field.

* * *

The pistol which ended Commodore Decatur's career is the upper one of the two pictured. Shortly after the duel, the pair were sold to the Honorable John Scott of Virginia, whence they descended to a great grandson, Mountford S. Wilson, of Burlingame, California, the present owner. Mr. Wilson is, however, about to deposit the pistols, as a personal gift, with the Leland Stanford University Museum.

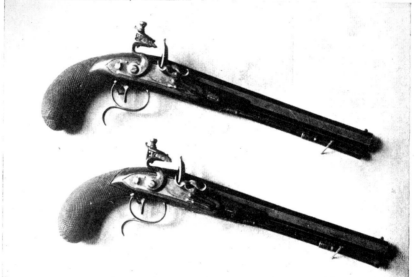

DUELLING PISTOLS

A pair so finely made and so reliable in action that they are said to have been frequently borrowed for settling affairs of honor. They were used in the famous encounter between Commodore Decatur and Commodore Barron in 1820, in which the former was killed. *Owned by Mountford S. Wilson.*

The connoisseur of firearms may be able to perceive from the picture wherein lay the popularity of these pistols for duelling purposes. It is said that they were constantly being borrowed to aid in settling disagreements.

They balance well and the sights are excellent. The barrels, octagonal in shape, are ten inches long from muzzle to rear sight. Weapon length is fifteen inches over all. The ramrods terminate each in a worm, or corkscrew, for extracting anything which may lodge in the barrels. Metal parts are engraved, and the walnut butts are chased to afford a sure grip. The name of the makers, Wogden and Barton, is inlaid in brass on each barrel as well as on the lock plate.

At eight paces, what deadly weapons these pistols must have been!

BY STEPHEN V. GRANCSAY

The American's approach

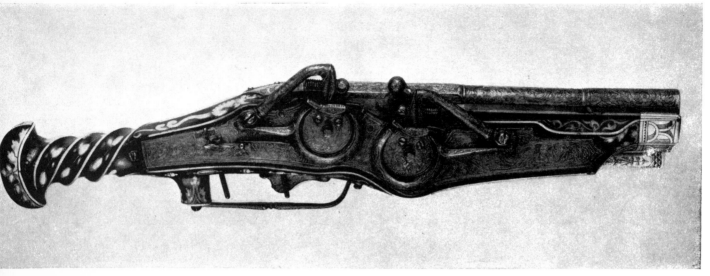

Double-barreled wheel-lock pistol made for the Emperor Charles V by Peter Pech of Munich about 1540.
The most important European firearm in America. *William Henry Riggs collection, Metropolitan Museum of Art.*

THE CLOSE RELATIONSHIP BETWEEN American and European firearms gives the American collector a logical interest in the art of the European gunsmith. European arms have been used here since the days of exploration, and European techniques and design are at the basis of all early American firearms. In 1609 the French explorer Samuel de Champlain supplied the first firearms used in Indian warfare. German and other European rifles, brought by immigrants from their homelands influenced the development of American rifles. A brace of pistols that belonged to George Washington, now in the museum at West Point, bears London proof marks and the name of the London gunsmith Hawkins. A pair of pistols of Alexander Hamilton, in the Metropolitan Museum of Art, was made at St. Etienne by Jalabert Lamotte. It has been recorded that the first shot of the American Revolution was fired at Lexington by Major Pitcairn from a Scottish all-steel pistol.

Still, the average American collector of firearms naturally has an overwhelming interest in those made in America. He is familiar with their historical background; he knows about the individual gunsmiths and firms that manufactured them. Furthermore, the study of American firearms is complicated, and the collector has a long road to travel before he can have even a nodding acquaintance with the subject as a whole, without extending his studies to Europe.

Many Americans want to show a sequence of principal mechanisms in their collections and therefore seek to include the earliest type, the matchlock musket that was used extensively in the Colonies. Captain John Smith in his *Generall Historie of Virginia* (1624) advised that colonists be provided with a "long peece five foot and a halfe, neere musket bore." Such muskets were common in the Colonies but, because they were plain pieces in daily use, they had little pecuniary value and fair wear and tear ultimately rendered them useless. A matchlock musket that is definitely known to have been made or used in the Colonies is a great rarity—so great that almost any collector of American firearms will gladly settle for a European matchlock just to have the type in his series.

The American is interested in the Kentucky rifle, which from the standpoint of achievement was the premier weapon of the world for over a century. He is interested too in the Colts and Deringers of the old West, especially the rare Colt Paterson and Colt Walker revolvers. The sequence of Colt revolvers commands more attention than that of any other firearm in America. They are vital souvenirs of stormy periods of this country's history, such as the conflicts with the Seminole Indians, the hazards of the pony-express riders, the Border trouble involving the Texas Rangers, and the Mexican and Civil Wars. Many collectors start with obsolete Colt models, Deringers, and the martial arms of the United States, guns as well as pistols.

The serious collector to whom the use and knowledge of firearms is an all-absorbing hobby will go further. Besides a matchlock musket of the type used by the colonists in the 1620's, he will try to get a flintlock used by Washington's Virginia riflemen, and a rifle carried by

to European firearms

Jackson's backwoodsmen at New Orleans. He will seek such famous old military muskets as the British Brown Bess and the French Charleville, brought to America during the French and Indian wars. The more ambitious collector will look for the Ferguson breech-loading flintlock rifle, which has the combined interest of unusual construction and great historical associations: this was the first breech-loading arm carried by organized troops of any country. Other rarities are a flintlock revolver invented in 1810 by Elisha Collier, who was born in Boston but made and sold most of his arms in England, and the Forsyth firearms using the first form of percussion ignition. Cased pistols by English and Continental gunsmiths are also in considerable demand. When the American collector's interest has extended to these pieces it is an easy step to the earlier European historical types, many of which are of superb workmanship and signed by such distinguished craftsmen as Lazarino Cominazzo, Nicolas Noël Boutet, Caspar Spät, or Nicolas Bis. They belong to a period when artistry was stressed as much as utility.

European firearms have been collected and appreciated in America for about a hundred years. The first to be exhibited in the Metropolitan Museum of Art (then in the Douglas Mansion, on West 14th Street) were lent by H. Cogniat in 1875, and included some richly inlaid wheel locks and a pair of pocket pistols by Napoleon's gunsmith, Boutet, engraved with scenes illustrating fables of La Fontaine. At about this time, William Henry Riggs, an American living in Paris, was adding to his collection of arms and armor, which was donated to the Metropolitan Museum in 1913. Among its many extraordinary items, one is the most important European firearm in this country: a wheel-lock pistol of the type brought to America by the conquistadores fifty years after Columbus first appeared in armor before the startled American Indian. This pistol belonged to the Emperor Charles V and bears his motto, *Plus Ultra* (More Beyond), referring to the New World.

An extensive collection of fine European firearms was displayed in the Columbian World Exposition at Chicago in 1893. This was the Richard Zschille collection of Grossenhain in Saxony, an illustrated catalogue of which was published. Many of the Zschille firearms were purchased by Tiffany and Company, whose agents collected fine arms and armor whenever they could get them. Some of the Zschille firearms have found their way back to Chicago and are in the George F. Harding Museum.

By the beginning of the present century American interest in European firearms was already considerable. Rutherfurd Stuyvesant, a trustee of the Metropolitan Museum from its founding in 1870 until his death in 1909, was a keen collector of arms and armor. The published catalogue of his collection, written by Bashford Dean, includes such magnificent examples as the finest Brescian firearm in America, a seventeenth-century snaphaunce fowling piece with lock and mountings by Carlo Botarelli and barrel by Gio. Lazarino Cominazzo. In their own time Cominazzo barrels were renowned, and today it is the ambition of practically every collector of firearms to have a pair of pistols with barrels bearing the Cominazzo name. Henry Walters also had some remarkable firearms in his collection, now in the Walters Art Gallery in Baltimore, including a fine pair of Brescian flintlock pistols with locks, stocks, and barrels signed by the masters who made them—the barrels by G. B. Francino, locks by Piero Alsa, and stocks by Gio. Marno. Bashford Dean, who inspired and encouraged other collectors of arms and armor, himself owned many important items, notably those from the collection of Prince Liechtenstein of Castle Vaduz. A number of superb examples from

Rare three-barreled wheel-lock pistol (German, sixteenth century). *Edward Hubbard Litchfield collection, Metropolitan Museum of Art.*

the Dean collection, which has been dispersed, are in the Metropolitan Museum: a wheel-lock hunting gun with stock overlaid with plaques of ivory carved with scenes from the story of Perseus; a self-winding, breech-loading wheel-lock gun dated 1638; and a wheel-lock hunting rifle, dated 1668, with stock by the Augsburg stock maker Elias Becker and metalwork by Caspar Spät, who worked for the Bavarian court.

Edward Hubbard Litchfield, who collected until 1930, had been a big-game hunter so that he was familiar at first hand with good firearms, and he had traveled widely. His collection, which was sold at the Parke-Bernet Galleries in December 1951, included a pair of English flintlock pistols of George Washington, a remarkable pair of Brescian wheel-lock pistols, double- and triple-barrel wheel-lock pistols, and a hundred other European firearms and accessories of high quality. The Litchfield collection was a good example of what an ample pocket-book, knowledge, and a passion for collecting firearms can accomplish. It would be easy to name a hundred American collectors, some of them world-famous art collectors, who assembled at least a good series of European firearms.

After both World Wars, there was a quickened interest in collecting. When the arms and armor collection of Henry Griffith Keasbey, an American who lived abroad, was sold at the American Art Galleries in 1924 and 1925, the introduction to the sale catalogue justly asked, "Where else today would one find so fine a pair of ivory mounted Dutch pistols, a pair of beautiful High-landers by Christie, elaborate Brescians or Saxon dags? And guns of the finest quality, decorated with delicate intarsia and with sculptured barrels?" The sale also offered numerous richly inlaid and sculptured wheel-lock pistols and guns which would be noticed in great museums, and a series of powder flasks of high quality. Other great sales of arms and armor offering important firearms, those of the Archduke Eugen (1927) and of Prince Liechtenstein of Castle Vaduz (1926 and 1928), played a great part in developing interest here in fine early European firearms. During World War II many museums and private collections in Europe were plundered, and ancient firearms which fell into the hands of American soldiers and dealers have now been widely scattered among American collectors.

A number of American museums have given European firearms a prominent position among their exhibits. The Metropolitan was fortunate in acquiring the peerless collections of the Duc de Dino and William Henry Riggs as well as selected pieces from the Daly, Dean, Morosini, Schott, and Stuyvesant collections, an advantage which gives it first rank. The collection, incidentally, is extremely popular not only among specialists but also among casual visitors, who stand hour-long before the cases and examine with great attention the beautifully designed and elaborately decorated firearms, the intricately ornamented powder flasks and accessories.

The City Art Museum in St. Louis has some fine pieces, especially those from the Hearst and Mackay collections, and in 1940 held a special exhibition of selected pieces of artistic merit and historical associations from the William Goodwin Renwick collection. Comprising several thousand items, both European and American, the Renwick is the most comprehensive collection in America of firearms of the pre-quantity-production era. One of its great pieces is the early seventeenth-century fowling piece made for Louis XIII of France. The Cleveland Museum of Art has ninety firearms and accessories from the Frank Gair Macomber collection of Boston. The extensive Rudolph J. Nunnemacher collection was bequeathed to the Milwaukee Public Museum in 1900, much of it acquired abroad in the last years of the 1800's. This is predominantly American but also includes several hundred European pieces, with the aim of showing the evolution of firearms.

In the forty years that I have been in this field, I have seen little change in the American's approach to European firearms. There has always been a brisk demand for fine pieces. Today firearms are being collected in America as never before, and those that are works of art are sought not by a few collectors merely, but by many. The wide spread of knowledge about firearms, stimulated by gun collectors' clubs in almost every state and by many recent authoritative publications, insures a permanent interest in fine firearms, European as well as American.

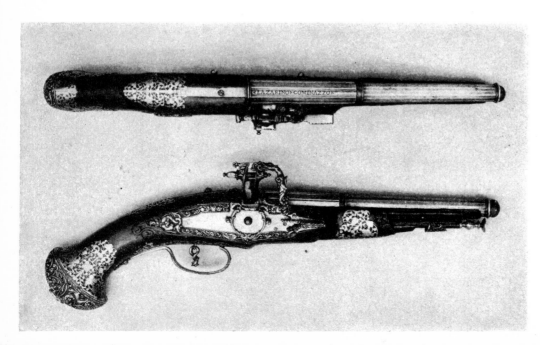

Pair of wheel-lock pistols
with barrels
by Lazarino Cominazzo
(Brescian, 1650).
*Duc de Dino collection,
Metropolitan Museum of Art.*

II Firearms—From Colonial Times to the End of the Flintlock Era

During the 17th and 18th centuries, America's economic status was no different from that of any other colonies under the rule of Great Britain or of the European powers. Always under rigid trade regulations, America exported produce to England in return for most of the manufactured goods required by the colonists. Firearms were no exception, and, as a result, a majority of the guns that have colonial association were manufactured abroad. Extremely few firearms were produced in North America prior to the Revolution. A majority of those that were domestically manufactured usually consisted of several imported parts, such as the barrel, lock, trigger guard, side plate, butt plate, trigger, screws, pins and the flint. It was much cheaper to import these parts than to manufacture them at home, and usually the imports were of better quality.

Utilizing one or all of the above-mentioned imported parts, firearms that were stocked in this country in American wood may today legitimately assume the label of an American-made weapon. It is now difficult, in fact, to differentiate between those weapons that were originally made from new imported parts and others that were re-stocked from an older weapon that had been broken or worn out. Such American stocked guns of the 17th and 18th centuries are quite scarce and eagerly sought by collectors. Even rarer, and more highly sought after, are those few weapons that were completely made in North America. Early Pennsylvania rifles, long Hudson Valley (New York) fowling pieces, and graceful, slender, or club butt New England fowling pieces of the 18th century have always commanded premium attention from collectors. Because of this fact many forgeries have appeared on the market, as have reconstructed and assembled pieces. Greater detail will be given to specialized regional firearms in Chapter III.

Next in collector demand are those 17th- and early 18th-century English and European weapons that were brought over to America and today have documented backgrounds. These are just as rare as those early weapons manufactured in America, and many times, because they have had broken parts replaced, are difficult to properly identify. In addition, a large proportion were re-stocked, utilizing the same parts and same style as the original, thus complicating the difficult task of identification.

Those English and European firearms of the second and third quarter of the 18th century that are typical of the weapons used in this country during that period qualify for the next category of collector demand. Here, however, the condition of the individual pieces becomes more critical than in the first two categories. Weapons with authentic historic provenance in this class are, and always have been, extremely rare and, when available, are offered at a premium over similar examples with unknown backgrounds. Here, too, the forger has profited over the years.

Collecting 18th-century British and European military firearms in proper chronological order, and in the best obtainable condition, has become popular with students of the French and Indian and Revolutionary Wars. Those weapons that have legitimate markings indicating American military usage command the highest degree of recognition from collectors. Included in this group are cheaply made Indian trade guns. Unscrupulous dealers have often substituted African trade muskets to unsuspecting and naive collectors.

During the American Revolution, thousands of firearms were imported from Europe and stamped (surcharged) with "U.S." markings. Similarly stamped were those muskets that were captured from the British and Hessian troops and the exceedingly rare muskets that were manufactured according to each colony's specifications by local gunsmiths. The latter guns are the most highly sought-after Revolutionary War arms, and the wary collector should note that authentication, unconditionally guaranteed, should accompany every purchase.

Recent research has brought forward an entirely new point

of view regarding surcharged or stamped muskets with Revolutionary War attribution. When the Revolution ended, the United States had many thousands of surplus muskets in storage. These were eventually surcharged ("U.S.", or "U. States", or "United States") and issued to the new Federal troops, as well as to the militia, between June 3, 1784—when the Federal army was first established—through 1794—when General Anthony Wayne defeated the Confederation of Indians at Fallen Timbers.

Because foreign weapons were also surcharged during the Revolution, the question of how to distinguish between those stamped during the period 1775-1781, and those stamped between 1784-1794, presents an interesting dilemma. Many collectors wish to acquire only those weapons used during the Revolution, although they were no different from the surplus arms issued after the war. And, although there should be no difference in collector value between the two periods, there most definitely *is*.

By the end of 1794, after Wayne's stunning victory over the Indians, the supply of surplus Revolutionary War weapons was depleted, and the United States began to import military arms from England. In 1794 a contract for rifles was placed with a handful of Pennsylvania gunsmiths. All of these weapons are great rarities today.

Congress authorized funds in 1794 for the establishment of national armories for the manufacture of small arms at Springfield, Massachusetts, and at Harpers Ferry, Virginia. Springfield, the site of a Revolutionary War repository, began to manufacture muskets in 1795, but Harpers Ferry did not begin production until 1800. In order to supplement the slow production of the national armories, the government also issued contracts to private manufacturers. The muskets were patterned after the 1763 French model, and the pistols were copied from the 1777 French pattern.

Fig. 1 — AN EARLY BLUNDERBUSS
A flintlock weapon with barrel expanded at the mouth so as to spread the charge of slugs, bullets, or other missiles with which it was loaded. This specimen dates from the early eighteenth century.

Forefather Firearms

By CHARLES D. COOK

ONE result of the Boston tercentenary is likely to be a reawakened interest in the furniture of the Pilgrim period as well as in all kinds of other relics from May-flower days. There will be a great scurrying about for old-time pine and maple furniture and for all the lesser habiliments of the early Colonial house. For months to come, it will be almost impossible to enter a New England home or walk a New England thoroughfare without stumbling over articles solemnly averred to have come to these shores in the *Mayflower* — albeit they bear the imprint of the Bennington pottery or the pattern number of Reed and Barton britannia.

The Mayflower joke is, to be sure, a musty one, yet so long as the Mayflower complex holds New Englanders in its thrall, it will continue to evoke agnostic smiles. But whatever the Pilgrim fathers did or did not carry with them on their crowded over-sea adventure, we may be certain that they took good care to supply themselves with firearms and ammunition. They could exist almost without houses, completely without furniture; but they cherished no misconception of the dangers surrounding them in the American wilderness or of the close relationship between future food supplies and accurate marksmanship.

If any artist has ever depicted a Pilgrim father unaccompanied by a gun, we fail to know of it. Always a gun, usually a Bible as well; but, in case of trouble, the weapon served as court of first resort. It was the *sine qua non* of primitive equipment. And, just as a portrayal of a Pilgrim father is incomplete without its protective firearm, so is a Pilgrim style dwelling to be considered incomplete unless above its fireplace stretches the menacing length of steel barrel and walnut stock.

We have now reached the text of these brief notes. We are not particularly concerned with the license which artists may exercise in portraying the Pilgrim countenance and clothing. Neither do we care very much whether those who live in the semblance of seventeenth-century dwellings outfit their abodes with Carver chairs or Victorian ottomans. The latter are the more comfortable of the two; and we can see no good reason for accepting discomfort and inconvenience in articles of utility for the sake of playing that we are our ancestors. When, however, we attempt to create an atmosphere quite apart from considerations of utility, there is no excuse for perpetuating anachronisms. If we are bent on hanging an ancestral firearm athwart a seemingly ancestral chimney breast, we should see to it that the weapon is truly of the type that it purports to represent.

But how is the peace loving twentieth-century householder to know what is what in Pilgrim weapons? He will find plenty of magazines with the gay covers of their Thanksgiving numbers adorned with Pilgrim fathers hunting in high hats and buckled shoes, regardless of the weather, and offering a desirable and conspicuous target for lurking Indians, and an equally disconcerting warning to even the most confiding and unsuspicious of wild turkeys. Usually the stern-faced hunter is armed with a strange-looking weapon, in shape closely resembling a modern automobile horn, though in action probably somewhat less deadly. This contrivance, commonly known as a blunderbuss, was not widely employed until long after the Pilgrim fathers had yielded place to their Pilgrim sons unto the third and fourth generation. It was a stagecoach and shipboard weapon intended to wreak wide damage at close quarters. It is first mentioned in a Rhode Island inventory of 1712. But there is no convincing artists of this fact, or of firearm facts in general. Even a recent statue of Daniel Boone by a renowned sculptor shows that doughty woodsman carrying a rifle of the vintage of 1840, instead of the long-barreled Kentucky arm that was the companion of the great marksman of old.

Let us, however, abandon our digression into the realm of art and return to our muskets, where we can, perhaps, indicate some of the points by which firearms of the Pilgrim century — that is, of the period between 1620 and 1720 — may be identified.

The distinguishing features that enter into any consideration of a firearm are: first, the firing mechanism; second, the barrel; third, the stock. Every effort to increase the effectiveness of such arms, since the invention of gunpowder, has been directed toward speeding the process of loading and firing, toward extending carrying power — that is, range — and toward improving accuracy. Evidently such changes as are to be observed in the aspect of firearms as they have evolved through centuries will begin with the firing mechanism. As that improves, other parts of the arm will be altered to take full advantage of the increased speed of fire.

When the Pilgrims first landed in America, their muskets were equipped with either one of two kinds of firing mechanism. One of these was the so-called matchlock — already verging on the old-fashioned — which exploded the powder in the barrel by means of a fuse or slow match. The other was the wheel lock, in which a serrated steel wheel, released by a spring, came into sufficiently sharp collision with a piece of iron pyrites to strike a stream of sparks and thus ignite the powder in the barrel. Somewhere about 1630, an improvement was made, and remained in use until long after the Revolution; that was the substitution of a hammer holding a flint in its jaws and so arranged as to strike a spark against a piece of steel known as

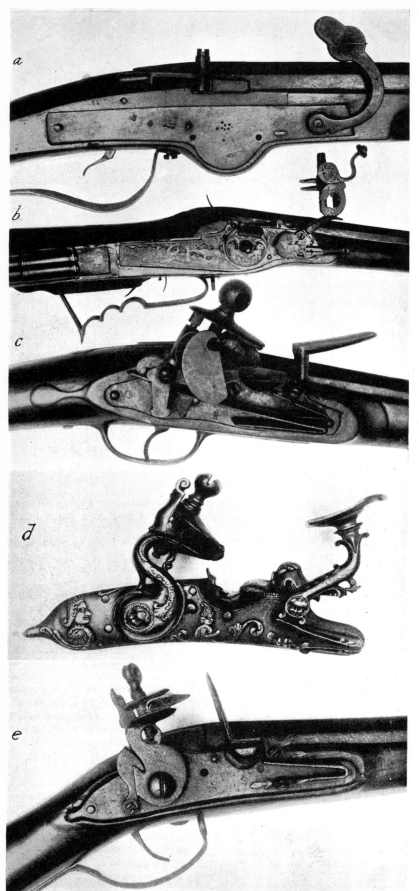

the battery, or frizzen. The different types of locks in use between 1620 and 1720 are pictured in Figure 2.

Now for barrels. Instead of being short and stocky, as artists love to depict them, Pilgrim muskets were long. They had to be. Their barrels were smooth bore. It was necessary to confine the expansive force behind the bullet as long as possible and to get the bullet started as straight as possible on its way to the mark. Only a long barrel accomplished these results. Pilgrim-century musket barrels will measure about thirty-six to sixty or more inches in length. Apply a tape measure to the barrel before you are caught by a seemingly ancient lock.

Again, it is well to remember that the barrels of weapons of the Pilgrim century are usually held to the wooden forestock by pins, and seldom by surrounding metal bands. There are, of course, exceptions. Bands were occasionally used on the Continent in the seventeenth century. France used one band and pins on 1717 models. In general, however, the banding method of securing barrels did not become common before 1728. Figure 3 illustrates several Colonial muskets ranging in date from the seventeenth to the eighteenth century. All are fairly typical and the group as a whole sufficiently exemplifies the variety from which the neophyte may hope to choose.

As for stocks, there is no telling. All sorts of accidents may happen to the woodwork of a hard used firearm, and hence necessitate its replacement. So it is just as well not to place too much emphasis on the aspect of that part of an ancient weapon. Between 1620 and 1720, nevertheless, the material ordinarily used for gunstocks was walnut in England and walnut, maple, and fruit wood in the Colonies.

Now a word about the source of our early Colonial weapons. Those first brought over were doubtless for the most part of English or Dutch make. When the French and English came into collision over territorial rights, the French armed their Indian allies with French military muskets. The American Colonial troops were equipped with the military muskets of England, in type somewhat different from the personal hunting weapons belonging to gentlemen of quality.

But all was grist that came into the hands of the early settlers. Captured French muskets, English

Fig. 2 — EARLY FIREARM LOCKS

a, MATCHLOCK. The slow match, or coal, was placed in the end of the serpentine, which, when released by the trigger, swung back to bring the coal in touch with the powder.

b, WHEEL LOCK. The jaw of the lock carried a piece of flint, or iron pyrites. This, when brought backward in contact with the wheel, which revolved by action of a spring, sent off a shower of sparks to ignite the powder.

c, MIQUELET. An early form of flintlock, a French type used in the Colonies. The powder was ignited by a spark when a flint was struck against the frizzen, or upright piece of steel above the pan. The miquelet has its spring mechanism outside the lock.

d, SNAPHAUNCE. Similar in operation to the miquelet except that the operating spring is inside the lock. This specimen is an unusually ornate one.

e, FLINTLOCK. A late seventeenth-century type, known as a doglock, because of the dog, or catch, at the rear of the cock. In this illustration, the frizzen, against which the flint strikes, is shown in place over the pan. Later flintlocks omit the dog catch.

Fig. 3 — EARLY FIREARMS

   a, Matchlock musket of the type used by early settlers in New England.
   b, Typical matchlock musket of the seventeenth century.
   c, A transitional type combining matchlock and wheel lock features.
   d, A typical wheel lock musket.
   e, An early miquelet used in America in the eighteenth century.
   f, Flintlock with dog catch at the back of the cock.
   g, Typical flintlock musket (*dated 1748*). Made in England, and representative of a form extensively used in the Colonies.

fowling pieces, English military arms — all found their way into the Colonial home and were made to serve every requirement of war and the chase. So we shall be perfectly safe to hang above the family hearth any one of quite a variety of arms. But to make assurance doubly sure, I recommend a careful study, both of the specimens pictured and of the details shown in previous numbers of ANTIQUES.

Once in a while, it would be a good idea to take down the weapon above your fireplace, oil its stock with boiled linseed oil, and give its barrel, inside and out, a liberal coating of Winchester gun grease to prevent rust. During the process, study all parts of the weapon until you find yourself beginning truly to sense their individual meaning and their relationship one to another. That accomplished, you will be ready to dig really deep into the lore of firearms. Here we have not even scratched the surface of it. A couple of collectors of arms might spend seven successive evenings wrangling over the position of a single screw, the shape of a trigger guard, the curvature of a trigger, and the interpreta-

tion of the cryptic marks often found on ancient musket barrels. In the end, they would probably remain in utter, but amicable, disagreement.

Perhaps we have offered suggestions sufficient to prevent the reader from falling into the most obvious trap spread for the unwary — that of completely misdating old-time muskets. Of the other snares — the more or less modern pieces made up to imitate the old, the assembled pieces constructed of shreds and patches of souvenir junk, the repaired pieces, which represent successive generations of tinkering with the same old trusty — it were better to say nothing. Avoidance of them is sometimes difficult even for the canniest collector.

Colonial Firearms

Part I

By HOWARD M. CHAPIN AND CHARLES D. COOK

Illustrations from the Cook collection, except as noted otherwise

IT is hard for us in the security of our modern complex and well-policed civilization to realize the importance of firearms in the humdrum routine of the daily life of the early settlers of America. To the pioneer, indeed, the long-barreled rifle was literally the staff of life. For years many of our New England villages were in constant danger of Indian attack, and it was absolutely essential that dependable means of self-protection should constantly be at hand, in every household.

Early Colonial legislation in regard to firearms gives proof of the urgency of this need. Then too, the meat supply of the early settlers and, for many years, the supply for a large proportion of New England's population consisted chiefly of game bagged by the hunter. Fur, too, was one of the chief exports of the infant colonies, and the extensive, lucrative, and important trade in peltry rested to a considerable degree upon the use of firearms.

Traders, explorers, and hunters, all alike, lived primarily by the use of their muskets or rifles; and the folk of all frontier settlements, whether those along the coast in 1630 or those inland in later years, depended upon similar weapons for their security. The oceans of those uncertain days, too, were as unsafe as the land, and no vessel put to sea without a supply of small arms and ammunition. All the larger vessels mounted cannon. In a word, the settlement of New England would have been impossible without firearms. Upon the use of such arms, security, livelihood, and commerce depended; guns, powder, and shot were as much a part of daily life — as much a household necessity — as most of the so-called necessities are to us today.

In delving into the history of America's past, antiquaries, collectors, and philanthropists have built up large public collections of books, of furniture, of Indian objects, and of household utensils in pewter, glass, and pottery. But where is there a great public collection of the types of arms illustrative of the periods of our Colonial and Revolutionary history? Nowhere. Firearms, indeed, constituted one of the rarest categories of the utensils that were extensively employed in the early days of our history.

Few, very, very few, of the arms used in America during the seventeenth century have come down to the present. The first half of the eighteenth century, likewise, makes but a scant

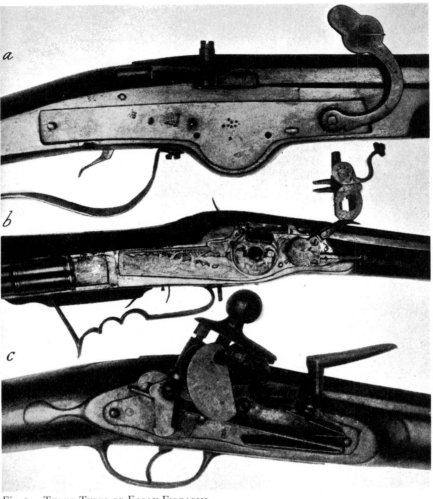

Fig. 1 — THREE TYPES OF EARLY FIREARMS

a. MATCHLOCK
The slow match, or coal, was placed in the end of the serpentine, which, swinging backwards, would bring the coal in touch with the powder.

b. WHEEL LOCK
The jaws of the cock carried a piece of flint, or iron pyrites, which, when brought backwards in contact with the wheel, would send off sparks when the wheel was set in motion. The lock is ornamented with hunting scenes.

c. MIQUELET
An early French flintlock of the miquelet type, showing the outside mainspring, the L-shaped frizzen, and the early form of cock. This piece was made in France but used in the American colonies.

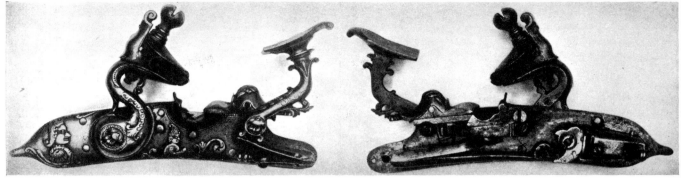

Fig. 2 — Snaphaunces

(*Left*) — Snaphaunce
An early flintlock, showing the snaphaunce type of frizzen, having the mainspring inside, and an early form of gooseneck cock. The lock is rather ornate
(*Right*) — Snaphaunce
Internal mechanism of snaphaunce shown at the left.

showing, and it is not until we reach the Revolutionary period that we find enough arms extant to warrant many definite conclusions as to the details of the types used. The reason for this is that obsolete arms are cumbersome and awkward to handle; hence, a weapon outworn is usually made over or thrown away. Remarkably few have been preserved for sentimental or decorative reasons; yet it is this few, together with some others, saved by carelessness rather than design, that makes up the remnant of early specimens still extant.

First Arms and Armor

The early colonists of New England brought the civilization of old England to the new world. As part of this civilization they carried military accoutrements; *armor, halberds, pikes, half-pikes, swords,* and the various sorts of cannon then in use; *saker, culverin, demi-culverin,* as well as flintlock muskets, often called *snaphaunces* — then something of a novelty — the reliable old matchlock muskets, and a few of the more expensive wheel locks.

The armor that our ancestors bore from England is illustrated in many portraits of the worthies of early New England. Some of these portraits, notably those of William Penn, Sir Nathaniel Johnson, and Fitz-John Winthrop have been reproduced in Mrs. Earle's *Two Centuries of Costume in America.* Samuel Gorton, the eccentric founder of Warwick, Rhode Island, imported a suit of armor which he presented to his friend, the Indian sachem Miantonomi. The donation proved most unfortunate for its recipient, for, when the Narragansetts were routed by the Mohegans,

Miantonomi, overwhelmed by the weight of his armor and unable to keep up with his fleeing braves, was overtaken and captured by his enemy Uncas, by whom he was soon afterward put to death.

Halberds, though powerful weapons in mediaeval Europe, were not serviceable in the guerrilla warfare of our primeval forests. The portrait of Thomas Venner, of Salem, shows his halberd over his shoulder, but in some thousand inventories in Essex County made between 1635 and 1682 only ten mentions of halberds have been found.

Attributing Firearms

How often are we regaled with the story of the unearthing in a dingy attic of an ancient musket that doubtless saw service in the days of Miles Standish! Occasionally such a yarn proves true, but more often the weapon is of a much later time. Our friends, the collectors and connoisseurs of furniture, or pewter, or pottery, who report the stories of rare old firearms, are seldom able to test the validity of these extraordinary tales. Often a long personal trip has to be made, or the gun has to be packed and shipped a considerable distance before a competent expert can determine its age and shed some light upon its history. Yet, while the collector of antiques infrequently has the knowledge to classify firearms — even approximately — with regard to age, it is really not difficult to determine, within relatively few years, the date of manufacture of almost any old musket or rifle.

The most puzzling phase of the problem of date assignment is attributable to two very common circumstances.

Fig. 3 — Jireh Bull Lock
A transition form of early flintlock, used in King Philip's War
Owned by the Rhode Island Historical Society Museum.

Fig. 4 — Jireh Bull Lock
Internal mechanism of lock shown in Figure 3.
Owned by the Rhode Island Historical Society Museum.

In the first place, a great many old guns, *as found*, are what might be called *assembled pieces;* that is, they were not made at one time, but are constituted of parts produced sometimes in widely different periods, by various manufacturers. Again, confusion arises from the circumstance that the locks of many ancient muskets have been transformed from *flintlocks* into *percussion locks*.

ANALYZING A FIREARM

To fix the date of any firearm we must first learn to analyze the weapon, to judge its major parts separately and then in their assemblage. It must be borne in mind, therefore, that the musket, or rifle, for purposes of historical study, is usually divided into three parts; the *lock*, the *stock*, and the *barrel*.

FAMILIAR LOCKS

The lock, of course, is the first part to demand our attention. The guns found in old farmhouses in America are usually of three types: (1) *flintlocks*, (2) *flintlocks that have been made over into percussion locks*, and (3) *percussion locks*. Percussion lock pieces belong in the nineteenth century, and date certainly since 1820, probably later even than 1840. Indeed, even so recently as the Mexican War (*1845*) the United States government had not given up the use of flintlocks.

The flintlock that has been transformed into a percussion lock is easily recognizable by the *nipple* or *cone* that has been screwed into the barrel at the touchhole, and by the *shape* of the lock plate. As a general rule, the flintlocks that have been transformed into percussion locks represent a rather late period of their type—say, from 1763 on. The reason for this is, that when transformation occurred, sometime between 1820 and 1850, most arms surviving from a period earlier than 1763 would have been too obsolete to be worth remodeling.*

An untransformed flintlock may be found that dates from the seventeenth century; or it may be as late as the early part of the nineteenth century; but it will probably be a survivor from the time of the later Colonial Wars or from the Revolution. In some rare instance a collector may stumble upon a wheel lock or a matchlock piece of the seventeenth century, but such finds are too uncommon to be hoped for. Matchlocks and wheel locks were, however, occasionally made over into flintlocks.

MATCHLOCKS†

The earliest mechanical form of ignition was supplied by the *matchlock*. A piece of slow match was held at the end of a curved metal arm, called a *serpentine*, which, by means of a lever or trigger, was, as a rule, brought backward and downward so that the lighted end of the slow match would ignite the charge of powder. This charge of powder, called a priming charge, had been placed in a small metal pan on the side of the barrel, from which a hole led through the side and into the breach of the barrel

itself. When the slow match ignited the *priming charge* of powder in the pan, the fire passed through the hole in the barrel and ignited the heavy charge of powder within. The consequent explosion expelled the bullet.

Better results were obtained by using a fine powder in the pan and a coarse powder in the barrel.

The disadvantages of the matchlock were that the slow match had to be kept lighted to be of use, and *that at night this light could be seen by an enemy. Furthermore, the lighted coal of the slow match is said to have interfered with correct aiming of gun.*

WHEEL LOCKS

The wheel lock consisted of a steel wheel which was revolved rapidly by a spring mechanism released by a push-button or trigger. This wheel revolved against a piece of flint or iron pyrites, and, by throwing sparks into the powder, ignited it. The wheel lock was superior to the matchlock in that it displayed no light, and that it called for no constantly ignited match. On the other hand, its mechanism was complicated; for the spring of the wheel lock had to be wound up, it was expensive, and liable to get out of order, particularly in unskilled hands.

FLINTLOCKS

In the flintlock, a piece of flint is held in the jaws of a hammer operated by a spring which is released by a trigger. When released, the hammer drives the flint against the steel *frizzen*, or upright part of the pan, thus sending off sparks that ignite the priming powder.

PERCUSSION LOCKS

The percussion lock does away with the pan. In the early period of this type, the priming charge was placed in a cap that was put on the nipple. A blow from the hammer on the nipple ignited the fulminate in the cap and the spark passed through the nipple to explode the powder in the barrel. In a still more modern development, the hammer falls directly on the end of a cartridge which encloses powder and bullet together in a single package.

ASSEMBLED PIECES

In studying an old firearm, after the age of the lock has been approximated, the *barrel* and the *stock* must be examined before judgment as to the age of the piece as a whole is determined. For if, as is so often the case, the arm has been assembled, the lock, stock, and barrel may all be of different periods.

STOCKS

The stock of a rifle or musket is likely to be most modern of the three parts. Since it is made of wood, it is particularly subject to breakage. If this wood has been derived from some of our native fruit trees, such as apple, pear, or cherry, it is probably of American manufacture. Nevertheless, it may have been made to replace an earlier English-made stock on an English-made gun.*

---

*The Kentucky rifle would be an exception.

†It is to be remembered that the desiderata of firearms are: (1) rapidity of fire; (2) accuracy of fire; (3) range of fire. The effort to achieve these ends, either singly or as a whole, accounts for the evolutionary changes which human ingenuity has wrought in projectile-throwing arms.

---

*While it has generally been assumed by collectors that gun stocks made of native American wood were produced in the Colonies, this judgment may not be entirely justifiable, for, from a letter written August 10, 1657, by Evert Pietersen, a school teacher at New Amsterdam, it appears that it was at least planned to export such wood to Europe. Pietersen wrote: "Your Honors are also informed that there is considerable black walnut timber here to make gun-stocks with; you

Fig. 5 — A TYPICAL FLINTLOCK (*middle of the eighteenth century*)
Of English manufacture, dated 1748, and used in the colonies. Note the gooseneck cock.

on the inside, perhaps so that Colonial dealers could sell them as their own make.

MARKS

The marks on the stock, butt plate, and trimmings of a gun, and some of the marks on the barrel — particularly numerals such as *58* for *58th Regiment* — are usually marks of ownership.

EARLY MIXTURES OF ARMS

The guns used in the English Colonies in America might well be called *Anglo-American*, for they were generally made in England and imported into the Colonies; and the few produced in America followed the patterns in vogue in England, except, of course, the rifles, which were a development of the middle Colonies during the eighteenth century.

BARRELS

The barrel, in many cases, will prove to be much older than the stock, and often older than the lock. If the barrel bears no marks, it is probably American-made, and not later than the Revolution, although many of the American-made Revolutionary barrels bear proof marks — as do almost all the English and French barrels. Any proof marks on both barrel and lock should be carefully copied or rubbed and shown to an expert. The length of a barrel offers but a poor clue to age or provenance, for a great many of the old gun barrels have been shortened.

The Pequot War occurred in 1637, at a time that might be considered a period of transition for firearms. Many of the old matchlock guns were still in use side by side with the more expensive and elaborate wheel locks. The newer snaphaunces, or *miquelets*, as the early flintlocks were called, though not really perfected, were rapidly coming into use. It is entirely possible that muskets of all three types were used in the Pequot War, although, on account of the meagerness of existing records, it is not possible for us to determine the matter at this late date.

The common-property arms of the Puritans of Boston —

LOCKS

Most French and English locks are marked with the makers' marks, and, if government property, with the Royal cipher as well. A few American-made Revolutionary locks are marked, but not many. The fact that a lock is not marked on the outside does not prove that it was made in the Colonies, for some English makers, especially Ketland, made locks for export and put their mark

can have enquiries made of the gunsmiths what it is worth, and whether they purchase by the stick or foot, and how long the pieces must be, and then calculate the profit to be made on it. It costs only the labor, and makes good ballast, for a great deal of it is worked up at home."

As to the importation of walnut into England, whether for furniture or for other articles, there is abundant testimony in contemporary English advertisements.

Fig. 6 — KING TOM NINIGRET'S GUN
Showing a flintlock transformed into a percussion lock. This musket was made in France and is what is known as a *Charleville 1763*. It belonged to King Tom Ninigret, Chief of the Narragansett Indians, who died in 1769. In the early nineteenth century it was made over into a percussion lock. The pan has been removed and a nipple screwed into the touchhole. A piece of iron has replaced the flint in the jaws, and has been rudely beaten so as to serve as a hammer.

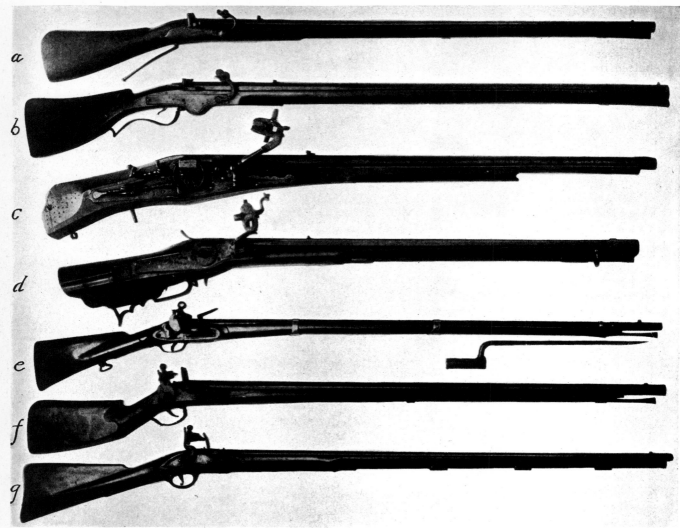

Fig. 7 — Early Firearms

    a. Matchlock musket of type used by early settlers in New England. See Figure 1*a* for enlarged view of the lock.
    b. Matchlock musket typical of the seventeenth century.
    c. Combination matchlock and wheel lock musket. An unusual example of the transition type.
    d. Typical wheel lock rifle. See Figure 1*b* for illustration of lock.
    e. An early miquelet used in America in the eighteenth century. See Figure 1*c* for illustration of lock. The bayonet is a later addition.
    f. Samuel Gorton's flintlock musket, showing the peculiar form of lock, known as a dog lock, on account of the dog catch at the back of the cock. The lock bears the royal initials J. R. For detail of lock see Figure 8.
    g. Typical flintlock musket. For detail of lock see Figure 5.

even before the Pequot War—numbered a large proportion of snaphaunce, miquelet, or flintlock muskets. Miles Standish at Plymouth carried and used a snaphaunce* in December 1620, and some of the more wealthy of the Boston settlers doubtless owned elaborate and expensive wheel locks.

Indeed, Sawyer believes that most of the guns used in the Pequot War were flintlocks or snaphaunces, as he considers that the old matchlocks were not superior to the Indians' bows and arrows. However, the colonists loaded their muskets with small shot, which, by multiplying the effectiveness of the matchlocks, caused considerable havoc.

The advent of King Philip's War found the colonial soldiers well equipped with flintlock muskets, although not many of these early weapons have come down to our day.

    *Mourt's *Relation*, 1622, p. 19.

AN HISTORIC WEAPON

An interesting gunlock, probably dating from King Philip's War, was discovered in the ruins of the Jireh Bull garrison house at Narragansett when that site was excavated in 1917. The gunlock and part of a gun barrel, both the worse for wear and very badly corroded, were found in the ruins of the house that Mr. Norman M. Isham, the authority on colonial architecture and one of the excavators, identified as the dwelling described in Waite Winthrop's letter of July 9, 1675. The place was attacked December 15 of that same year, and was burned to the ground, with the loss of fifteen lives. The gun to which the ancient lock and barrel belonged was used in the vain defence. In connection with this theory it is interesting to note that a grooveless stone axe-head, or *celt*, was found in the same ruins. Such stone celts were in common use among the Narragansett Indians of the time.

The lock under discussion is particularly interesting because it has the main spring on the inside, as in a snaphaunce, and yet shows a rather early form of frizzen arm with bridged frizzen spring, which harks back in design to the serpentine of the wheel lock.

There is, unfortunately, more or less confusion, or at least variance of opinion, as to what differentiation constitutes a snaphaunce, a miquelet, and a flintlock. Even those living in the sixteenth and seventeenth centuries used the names vaguely and to some extent indiscriminately, so it is not surprising that modern writers are not always in agreement as to terminology.

The wheel lock, of course, as a rule had the main spring on the inside, and, since the various early forms of flintlocks developed from the wheel lock, it would seem probable that the earliest types would have the main spring on the inside. On the other hand, whoever was experimenting with a new type of ignition would be likely to follow the easy procedure of placing the mainspring outside. Indeed, wheel locks are found occasionally with the mainspring on the outside; but such wheel locks are very scarce and probably belong to the early period of the type.

In the case of snaphaunce and miquelet, it is not possible to say which of these two similar types antedates the other. In fact, the two were, for a considerable space, manufactured contemporaneously in different parts of Europe; those made in or near Spain being called *miquelets*, after Spanish marauders (miquelitos), and those made in or near Holland being called snaphaunces, after the hen thieves (snaap-hans). Indeed, the differences between the miquelet and the snaphaunce may be in reality too unimportant to justify classing these weapons as different types.

Fig. 8 — A DOG LOCK
Detail of Samuel Gorton's musket shown in Figure 7f. The weapon may have been used in America before the beginning of King William's War (*1690–1697*).

Perhaps the most salient characteristic of each of the three types of flint ignition locks are: the outside mainspring, and the *L*-shaped frizzen and pancover of the miquelet; the inside spring, and the frizzen arm which is attached to the middle of the frizzen of the snaphaunce; and the inside spring, the *L*-shaped frizzen and pancover, and the gooseneck-cock of the true flintlock.

THE BULL LOCK

The *bull lock* is a flintlock, in contradistinction to a miquelet or snaphaunce (both of which are indeed, in a broader sense, themselves variant flintlocks) and is certainly an early form of the third or latest of the three types, the type usually distinguished by the term *flintlock*. It dates unquestionably from the seventeenth century and perhaps from its early years. In this, the cock, although a gooseneck, is of an early and primitive design, and the complicated frizzen spring mechanism also points to an early period. Three unusual dogs, or pauls, are placed between the cock and the frizzen spring, which give proof that the piece belongs to an early, and, one might even say, experimental period in the development of the flintlock.

The Tower of London contains flintlocks marked with the Royal initials *J.R.* and *W.R.*, and it seems probable that similar firearms were used in the American Colonies during the reigns of James II and William III.

Our illustration (*Fig. 7f*) shows the so-called Samuel Gorton gun, which bears the initials J.R. This gun, which has been handed down in the Gorton family, was probably owned by Capt. Samuel Gorton, who died in 1724, leaving, according to his inventory, "three guns." This musket may have been in America before the beginning of King William's War.

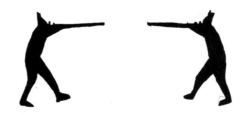

Colonial Firearms

Part II

The Firearms of the Queen Anne Period

By HOWARD M. CHAPIN *and* CHARLES D. COOK

Illustrations from the Cook collection

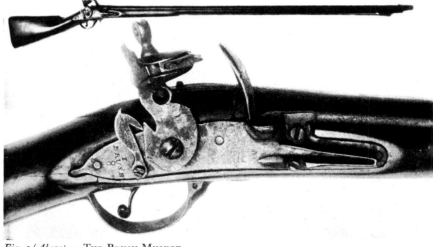

Fig. 1 (Above) — THE BRUSH MUSKET
Restocked in the Colonies. Detail shown below.

(Below) — QUEEN ANNE DOG LOCK
Marked with the maker's name *Brush* and with the royal initials.

SHERLOCK HOLMES' oft repeated criticism of the professional detective's "generalization from too few data" might apply likewise to discussions of firearms. Even the most extensive collections of weapons are remarkable for their paucity of examples of seventeenth-century muskets, and, indeed, a survey of all the principal collections together fails to discover a sufficient number of specimens to justify many conclusions that may be considered quite scientifically sound.

Queen Anne's War (*1702–1713*) witnessed a period of military activity in the American Colonies, and probably resulted in the importation of many muskets from England.

In general appearance, the English muskets of this period did not differ noticeably from those of the two reigns preceding that of Anne. Only those locks and barrels that bear the royal initials *A.R.*, or are dated, may at present be certainly identified as of Queen Anne's reign; although it is probable that further research will disclose some makers who worked only in that period. In such case, the maker's name on a musket would of course serve to date the piece.

THE DOG LOCK CHARACTERISTIC

While it is unsafe to generalize from meagre information, it seems highly *probable* that most of the military muskets made for use in Queen Anne's War were equipped with dog locks; that is, locks supplied with a dog, or pawl, that caught on the back of the cock and held the hammer safe at half cock. Such a dog must have been one of the earliest safety devices used on muskets. A dog lock, marked with the royal initials *A.R.* between broad arrows, beneath the royal crown and above a broad arrow, is shown in the illustration (*Fig. 1 Below.*) The initials are in Roman and not in script as was the case in the *J.R.* lock illustrated in the previous article.

This lock, which may be taken as a typical Queen Anne military lock, bears the maker's name *Brush*, and it is interesting to note that, in the Tower of London Collection, there occurs a musket lock (No. 77) carrying the royal initials *A. R.* and the maker's name *Brush*. The barrel of this Tower musket, however, dates from the time of James the Second, and bears the mark *J.R.* The Tower of London Collection likewise includes one other musket lock (No. 78) marked *A.R.*, and this lock, which is a dog lock, also bears the maker's name, *R. Wolldridge.* Another lock (No. 79) of the same collection, marked *Wolldridge*, doubtless dates from this general period, if not actually from the reign of Anne.

In the vast majority of instances, indeed in all which have come under our observation, the dog locks of military muskets have been fitted with reinforced gooseneck cocks, except, of course, when the contemporary cock has been replaced by a more modern mechanism. Another characteristic of the locks of Queen Anne's War and of contiguous periods, is the fact that *three* screws instead of *two* were used to hold the lock.

LATE LOCKS AND EARLY BARRELS

Many of the Queen Anne locks were assembled with earlier barrels, dating from the times of James and of William. Throughout the later Stuart period, barrels that were round their entire length, as well as barrels that had a half-octagonal surface on the upper side of the breech, were in use. In fact, the musket barrels made during these several reigns display no marked differences in form and

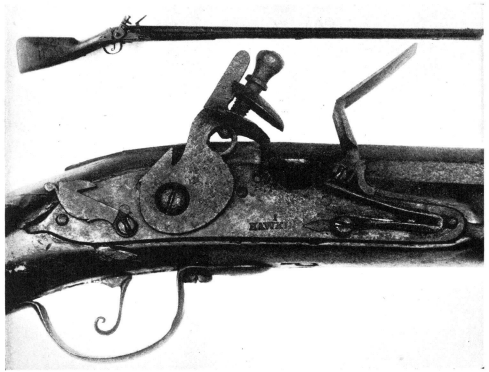

illustrated (*Fig. 1*) was, undoubtedly, restocked in the Colonies — not at all an unusual occurrence. Stocks were often broken by rough usage, for the muskets commonly served as clubs at close quarters, and in the hands of a strong man would do great execution. Even pistols were thus used, as, for instance, during the Bahama revolution in 1701, when the old privateer captain John Warren, one of the ringleaders of the uprising, struck Governor Haskett over the head with his pistol, cracking that high official's crown in several places, and forcing acquiescence in the disturbingly sudden change of government.

The lock marked *I. Hawkin* (or *Hawkins*) is characteristic of Queen Anne's period, although the Hawkins' lock, shown in the previous article, dates from the reign of James, and bears the script initials *J. R.* Hawkins most probably was a locksmith who worked during the three short reigns of James, William, and Anne, and perhaps even for a longer period (*Fig. 2*).

Fig. 2 (Above) — THE HAWKIN MUSKET
(*Below*) — THE HAWKIN LOCK
    Typical of the Queen Anne period. The dog and hammer differ slightly from those of the *Brush* musket. *The stock is original.*

construction. It is virtually impossible to determine the exact age of any barrel of the time, except as it bears the royal initials.

Another musket bearing the earmarks of this period has

CLASSIFICATION BY REIGNS FALLACIOUS

In studying and classifying English firearms, there is a great temptation — and we must confess that we have yielded to it — to arrange the arms by reigns, when, perhaps, the differentiating changes have occurred without relation to sovereignty. So little research has been applied to the history of early English gunsmiths, and so little reliable material on this fascinating subject is available in print, that it is almost impossible, at present, to determine upon a suitable system of classification for type and period. That is why the student has, as a rule, grouped the arms roughly by reigns; and he has been encouraged in the habit by the custom of marking government-owned muskets with the sovereign's initials.

MARKS AND EXAMPLES

The *Brush* lock musket, here

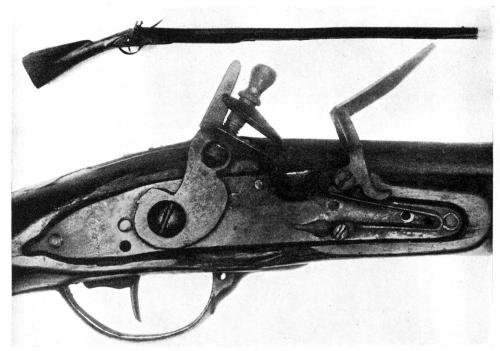

Fig. 3 (Above) — THE NUTT MUSKET
(*Below*) — THE NUTT LOCK
    Originally a dog lock, but the dog has been removed and the cock trimmed.

a plain round barrel with proof marks apparently earlier than the reign of Anne, and a lock bearing the maker's name *W. Nutt* (*Fig. 3*). The stock is so evidently of Colonial manufacture that it seems safe to conclude that the gun was restocked in America. The lock itself, however, bears, in addition to the maker's name, the broad arrows, the well-known mark of government ownership, which is almost conclusive proof in a case of a lock of this type and period of English manufacture. The lock was originally a dog lock with a reinforced gooseneck cock, but the dog has been removed and the cock trimmed down so that the lock presents a most unusual and, at first glance, puzzling appearance. It is unquestionably as early as Queen Anne's War, and may well date from an even earlier period.

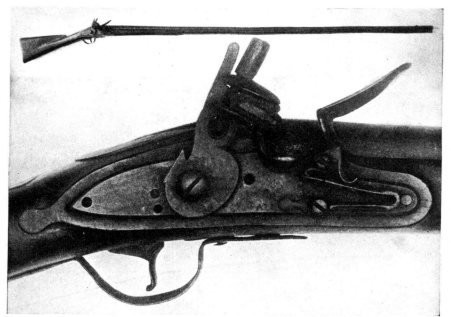

Fig. 4 (Above) — THE ALLEN MUSKET
Seven feet and seven inches long, this huge weapon was doubtless designed for garrison house use.
(Below) — THE ALLEN LOCK
Like the *Nutt* lock, this was originally a dog lock. In this specimen, the cock has not been trimmed and still shows the catch for the dog. Note the lower screw hole where the dog was originally attached.

The Allen musket is a remarkable piece, seven feet, seven inches long, and, of necessity, very heavy, weighing twenty pounds. From its great length and weight, and from the fact that it is 80 calibre,

Fig. 5 — AN EARLY BLUNDERBUSS
This specimen dates from the early eighteenth century, and possibly from as early as Queen Anne's War. The flare of the barrel is elliptical.

this musket would seem almost without question to have been intended for garrison use. It certainly dates from the days of Queen Anne's War. The barrel, round for its entire length, bears English proof marks, and the maker's name *E. Allen*, while the lock, which is a dog lock with the dog missing, is marked *R. Allen*, but bears no proof marks. The musket was restocked in the Colonies, and only two of the three lock screws were used.

Occasionally a barrel marked *A. R.* will be found assembled with a later lock and stock; for instance, musket No. 80 in the Tower of London.

SPORTING ARMS FOR WAR

There is reason to believe that during all the Colonial wars, many of the officers carried non-military weapons; that is, rather elaborate sporting arms, generally orna-mented to some extent, which had been acquired before the call to service, or were occasionally purchased because of their decorative aspect.

DOG LOCKS CHARACTERISTIC OF THE AGE OF ANNE

Dog locks, although occasionally used earlier, are particularly characteristic of Queen Anne's reign, and in general their manufacture was not continued to any extent in the time of the Georges.

BLUNDERBUSSES

The blunderbuss is said to have come into its own during Queen Anne's War, though, of course, this wide-mouthed weapon was made and used before that time. Indeed, a blunderbuss now in the London Museum was used in the attempted assassination of William III in 1696.

The blunderbuss is usually a short-barreled gun with a pronounced flare at the barrel mouth. In a few cases this flare is elliptical, but generally it is circular. Blunderbusses, although often shown in fanciful pictures of the Pilgrims, were not in general use in America in the early seventeenth century, and their appearance in such pictures must be attributed to the ignorance or the carelessness of the artist.

The blunderbuss, or "bell-mossell gun," as it is named in the inventory of William Whipple's estate taken in Providence, Rhode Island, in 1712, was designed to scatter small shot, and was used most effectively at short range, as on shipboard to repel boarders. It might, indeed, be considered primarily a naval weapon. At a later period, particularly during King George's War (*1739–1748*) blunderbusses were mounted on shipboard as part of the vessel's equipment.

It was required by law in those days that, before a privateer could sail, the captain must make a return to the Vice Admiralty office, reporting the name, tonnage, and owners of the privateer and also her armament. As an instance of the use of blunderbusses on American privateers, the return made for the brigantine *Prince Frederick* of Newport, Rhode Island, November 26, 1745, states that she is a vessel of 170 tons, armed with 18 carriage guns, 30 swivel guns and *18 blunderbusses*. As the small arms used by the crew were never included in these returns, it follows that these eighteen blunderbusses were part of the ship's equipment, and were probably mounted on swivels. In 1744 the ship *Hercules* of London, 400 tons, is described in a contemporary newspaper as mounting 24 carriage guns (both nine and six pounders) 40 swivel guns and *30 swivel blunderbusses*.

When enlistments for the Canadian expedition of 1711 were lagging, a proclamation was issued offering inducements to volunteers. One of these inducements was the promise that each soldier "might keep as his own forever the Queen's musket that would be furnished." Through some exigency, or mismanagement, the Rhode Island soldiers failed to obtain their promised muskets at the end of the war. But in 1721, ten years later, the soldiers were given twenty-five shillings each by the Colony "in lieu of their guns, which by proclamation

they were to have." The lock plates of these muskets were doubtless marked with the royal initials *A. R.*, and are still occasionally found in old farmhouses. One such musket, doubtless distributed by one of the other colonies, is described as "one gun, one of the Queen's arms," in the inventory of the estate of Obadiah Brown of Providence in 1716.

QUEEN ANNE PISTOLS

The cannon-shaped, brass-barreled pistol made by George Ogilvie, a Scotch gunsmith, and dated 1716, is a good example of the type of Scotch Highlander pistol of the Queen Anne period, although made a few years after the monarch's death, in the early part of the reign of George I.

A typical example of the English-made pistols of this period is the brace of pistols handed down for years in the Holden family. They unquestionably belonged to the second Randall Holden of Warwick, who was chosen "Major of the Main" in 1706. This curious Colonial title signified that its bearer was commander of the militia on the mainland of the Colony of Rhode Island, as distinct from the militia on the islands in Narragansett Bay.

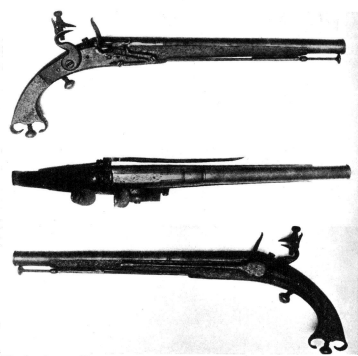

Fig. 6 — SCOTCH HIGHLANDER PISTOL (*1716*)
Made by George Ogilvie and dated. Typical of its place and period.

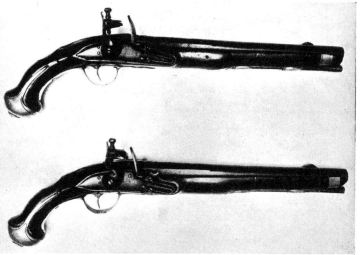

Fig. 7 — ENGLISH PISTOL (*early eighteenth century*)
Belonging originally to the second Randall Holden, of Warwick, Rhode Island.

Colonial Firearms

Part III

By Howard M. Chapin and Charles D. Cook

Illustrations from the Cook collection

FIREARMS, like all other complicated human tools, are constantly undergoing slight changes and improvements, which, though often scarcely discernable to the contemporary layman, are readily detected by the expert technician, who, on the basis of various small details, is usually able to judge approximately the date of manufacture of any recent specimen which comes to his attention.

What is true today undoubtedly held good in the eighteenth century; but the knowledge which the eighteenth-century gunsmiths possessed, the result of their personal experience, died with them. Meagreness of written records and paucity of specimens — the oft heard complaint of the latter-day antiquary — retard the study of early firearms; yet much can be learned from examination of the few specimens extant. While the conclusions thus derived may not be tied up with the precision of year dates, yet they are likely to hold good for general periods.

The lines of division between such periods will, however, remain rather vague and undefined, partly because of the overlapping of the periods during which certain types of arms were used, and partly because of the occurrence of transitional forms. For example, the dog lock, which was characteristic of the Queen Anne period, was used even before that time, and, in all probability, continued to be used extensively during the reign of George I. One such dog lock musket, marked *G R*, appears as Number 80 in the Tower of London Collection.

As a general rule, war stimulates improvements in firearms. Hence the peaceful period of George I, during which England fought no important war, probably saw few important changes in the English military musket, which, unquestionably, until the

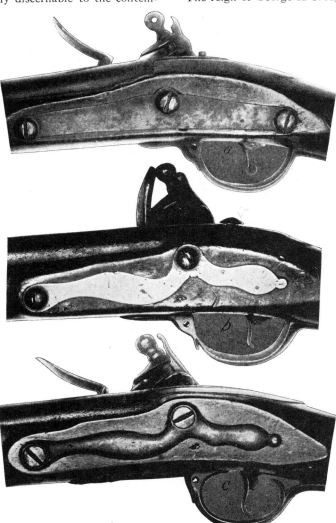

Fig. 1 — Showing the Change in Screw Plates
a. Plain, flat screw plate of the reign of Queen Anne. *b.* Decorative flat screw plate of the reign of George I. *c.* Convex screw plate of the reign of George II, *1743.*

outbreak of the American Revolution, served as the principal military weapon in the American colonies.

The reign of George II brought the War of the Austrian Succession, often called King George's War by American writers. This struggle immediately stimulated improvements and changes in the English military musket, or at least consolidated and utilized any experimental changes that may have developed subsequent to Queen Anne's War.

The most salient changes that appear in the muskets used in King George's War, as contrasted with those of Queen Anne's War, are: (1) the shift from the dog lock with reinforced hammer to the goose neck hammer without any safety dog device; (2) the abandonment of the method of fastening the barrel by a screw that came *up* from the under part of the lock in front of the trigger in favor of the use of a screw that went *down* from the tang of the breech plug to a screw plate in front of the trigger; (3) the addition of an arm running from the pan to the head of the screw of the frizzen; (4) the addition of a fence back of the pan to protect the eye from the flash; and (5) the reduction from three to two in the number of screws holding the lock plate.

These changes probably did not occur all at once, but were doubtless gradually accepted improvements, introduced between 1715 and 1740. And it is quite likely that some of them were made on sporting arms long before they appeared on military weapons; for the development of the military arm, often, if not usually, entrusted to a tape bound bureaucracy, generally lags behind that of the sporting arm, the improvements in which are obvious to the user and thus enhance sales value.

English military muskets dated during the last years of King George's War (*1739 to 1748*) show further differentiation from their predecessors. The trigger guard becomes lighter, and the knob at the end becomes more ornamental, taking on the form of a double knob, or embryo acorn which, in later years, was to develop into the true acorn finial. The lock plate becomes convex, and begins to show a downward curve behind the hammer; and, on the reverse of the musket, the screw plate becomes convex and is occasionally engraved. The butt plate runs up the comb of the stock to a distance of some six inches, instead of only about three, as on the earlier muskets; and the plate itself becomes much more ornamental, and shows a kind of graduated tapering form along the comb. The comb of the stock itself becomes thinner, and is scooped out in a concave curve where it joins the wrist or grip of the musket. The forward curl at the top of the hammer likewise makes its appearance.

The Seven Years War, otherwise known as the Old French and Indian War (*1756–1763*) might be expected to mark at least a few slight changes in the military musket. The English muskets of the latter part of this war seem to have reverted to the straighter form of lock plate, without the noticeable drop-back of the hammer that was characteristic of the muskets of King George's War (*1739–1748*). A small brass plate is likely to be found on top of the wrist or grip of the butt on these later muskets, and this plate usually bears the letter and number of the company and regiment to which the weapon was assigned.

Changes in the English military musket during the middle of the eighteenth century occur chiefly in somewhat unimportant accessories rather than in essential mechanism; yet these changes serve to assist the student in the dating of unmarked firearms.

Probably most of the military muskets used in the later Colonial period in America were English military muskets; but of course a good many Colonial-made muskets were also used — doubtless in ever increasing quantity as time went on.

As the colonies aped English fashions but lagged behind them, so the Colonial gunsmiths aped English models but, quite naturally lagged behind them, and often copied models that had become more or less obsolete. The chief earmarks of Colonial-made muskets are, of course, the absence of proof marks on the lock and on the barrel; the use of native American wood for the stock, (which, except in the case of unusual wood, such as fruit tree wood and curly maple, is not conclusive), and the archaic form of the stock. Most of the Colonial stocks made in the early half of the eighteenth century follow the heavy, crude form of the English seventeenth-century stocks. Of course, occasionally, the latest English model might be copied by a particularly progressive artisan, and, especially during and after King George's War,

Fig. 2 — SHOWING THE DEVELOPMENT OF THE BUTT PLATE
a. Queen Anne musket. *b*. George I musket. *c*. Musket of 1748. *d*. Musket of 1762, showing the number plate on the wrist of the stock.

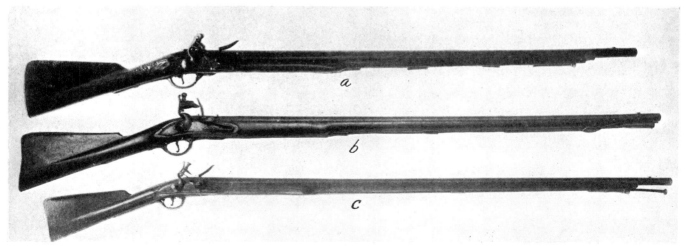

Fig. 3 — EIGHTEENTH-CENTURY MUSKETS
a. Musket of reign of George I. *b*. Musket of 1748. *c*. Musket of 1762.

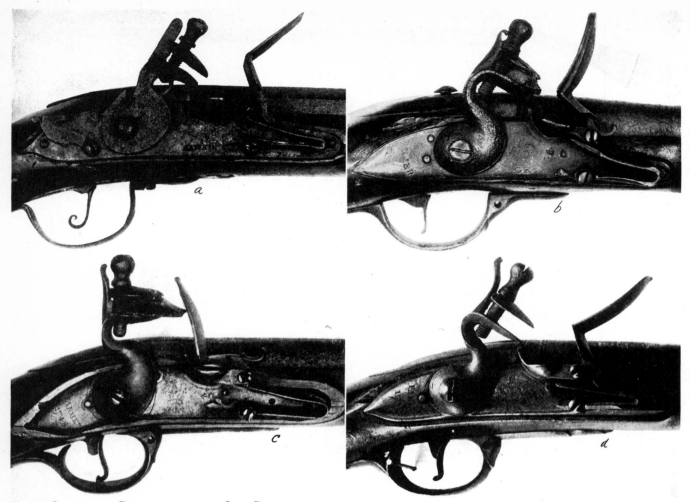

Fig. 4 — SHOWING THE DEVELOPMENT OF THE LOCK PLATE
a. Queen Anne musket showing flat lock plate with dog lock. b. Musket of reign of George I. c. Musket of 1748. d. Musket of 1762.

the lighter French stock seems to have been imitated. Of course French influence in America, both on account of the immigration of French artisans and on account of the capture of French arms, increased as the century grew older, and this serves to add new complications to an already complicated problem.

The determination of the date of manufacture of the extant specimens of Colonial-made firearms is certainly a very intricate problem. Each case must be judged on its own merits, taking

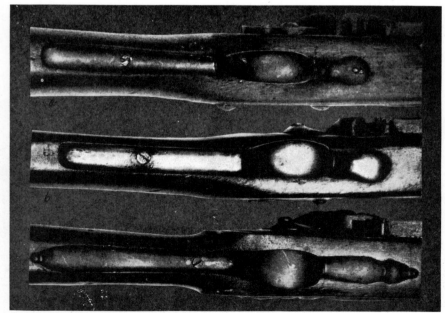

Fig. 5 — SHOWING THE DEVELOPMENT OF THE TRIGGER GUARD FINIAL
a. Queen Anne musket. b. Musket of reign of George I. c. Musket of 1748.

into consideration the possibility of restored parts, the tendency of the Colonial gunsmith to follow obsolete or archaic models, and the contemporary development of English and foreign military and sporting arms Indeed, the sporting arm, which usually showed changes in advance of the military arm, might be copied in the Colonies in the ambiguous arms which were made partly for hunting purposes and partly for military service should necessity for the latter arise.

Fig. 1 — THREE VIEWS OF THE COOKSON GUN

Colonial Firearms

Part IV
The Identification of Specimens by Technical Analysis

By HOWARD M. CHAPIN *and* CHARLES D. COOK *

Illustrations from the Cook collection

DETERMINING the date of manufacture of a Colonial firearm offers a very intricate problem whose solution depends on the examination of various salient details, which in any two instances are almost never precisely alike. The analysis of a few specific specimens will throw more light upon the problem and the method of its solution than many pages of glittering generalization.

I. THE COOKSON GUN

Let us begin our study with a gun marked *Cookson*. The *barrel* bears English proof marks, and hence may be considered of English manufacture. The *lock* bears the maker's mark, *I. COOKSON*. Although originally a flintlock musket, the piece was altered to a percussionlock type at some time in the nineteenth century; but has subsequently been restored to its original flintlock form.

Fig. 2 — DETAIL OF FIGURE 1, SHOWING LOCK OF THE COOKSON GUN

The *lock plate* and the *screw plate* are both flat, and thus are similar to those of the military muskets of Queen Anne's War (*1702–1714*); for the convex lock plate and screw plate do not appear on English military muskets until about the time of King George's War (*1739–1748*). The screw plate is in the form of a rather elaborate scroll, and is engraved with an ornamental design, from which circumstance we may infer that the firearm was made primarily for sporting rather than for military purposes.

The *stock* is made of fruit wood, a characteristic notably Colonial. The comb of the stock tends to a crescent shape, and is not concaved where it joins the wrist. The butt plate, where it runs up on the comb, is short. These are characteristics of the muskets of Queen Anne's War. While, as a rule, the design of sporting arms was in advance of that of military arms, Colonial-made arms of both types tended to lag behind the style of

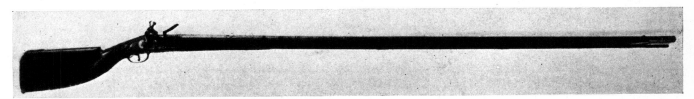

Fig. 3 — MUSKET MARKED *E. C.*

Fig. 4 — HANDY MUSKET, AND DETAIL OF LOCK

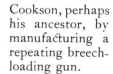

contemporary English makers. The lock and stock of this musket appear to have been made in the Colonies at some time between 1715 and 1740, perhaps not far from the earlier date. The barrel is probably still older and resembles the barrels of the Stuart period.

Turning from internal to external evidence, we find that John Cookson cleaned and repaired the Province arms in 1727, and was paid 51 pounds and 6 pence for his services (*Journal of House of Representatives of Massachusetts, 1727,* pp. 13 and 20).

This item identifies John Cookson of Boston as a gunsmith. He was married to Rachel Proctor in Boston, by the Reverend Cotton Mather, November 2, 1704. The pair had seven children: John, 1706; Rachel, 1707; Eliza, 1708; Obadiah, 1709; Reuben, 1711; Mary, 1712; and Samuel, 1716. John Cookson joined the Ancient and Honorable Artillery Company of Boston in 1701, and served as clerk of the Company from 1722 to 1726. He was chosen constable in 1705, but declined to serve. In 1706, 1715, and 1718, he acted as tithingman. In 1711, he was in partnership with Richard Proctor, probably his brother-in-law, and obtained a chimney-sweeping franchise. The partnership was dissolved about 1715; but Cookson continued to carry on the chimney-sweeping business, at least until 1733. In that year he was one of those who signed the Merchants Notes agreement (*M.H.S.P.,* Series 2, Vol. 17, page 208*). He had a negro man, probably a slave, named Tobie, who did the sweeping. In 1724 Cookson was given permission to build a tomb in the North (*i.e.,* Copp's Hill) Burial Ground.

The following advertisement, which appeared in the Boston *Gazette* of April 12 and 26, 1756, shows that John Cookson was not a mere mechanic, but that he had inventive genius, and sought to emulate an earlier gunsmith named John

* *Massachusetts Historical Society Proceedings.*

Cookson, perhaps his ancestor, by manufacturing a repeating breech-loading gun.

The advertisement reads:

Made by John Cookson, and to be Sold by him at his House in Boston: A handy Gun of 9 Pound and a half Weight; having a Place convenient to hold 9 Bullets, and Powder for 9 Charges and 9 Primings; the said gun will fire 9 Times distinctly, as quick, or slow as you please, with one turn with the Handle of the said Gun, it doth charge the Gun with Powder and Bullet, and doth prime and shut the Pan, and cock the Gun. All these Motions are performed immediately at once, by one turn with the said Handle. Note, there is Nothing put into the Muzzle of the Gun as we charge other Guns.

John Cookson, the gunsmith, died in 1762, willing a large estate, which was divided among his children and grandchildren. He left two married daughters and one son, Obadiah. The latter, by his first wife, had two children, John and Margaret; and, by his second, a son, Samuel. John Cookson left his "gunsmiths tools" to this grandson Samuel. His "smiths shop" he bequeathed to his grandson John. One of these two grandsons is probably the Mr. Cookson whose name appears in connection with a vote of the Selectmen of Boston, passed April 23, 1775, which contains the following item:

On the floor of the Town House a Large chest belonging to Mr. Cookson Containing Gun Barrels, Pistol Barrels, Gun & Pistol Locks and other Gunsmith Wares with sundry Gunsmith tools (Boston *Record Commissioner's Report,* Vol. 29, p. 329).

Little is known of Samuel Cookson, except that he was a gunsmith in Boston in 1775, and may have been the Cookson who was a clerk in the Boston Custom House in 1776, and who removed to Halifax with the British Army, when Boston was evacuated, in March, 1776 (*M.H.S.P., Series 1, Vol. 18, page 266*).

The gunsmith's trade may have been inherited for generations in the Cookson family, for, as early as 1586, there was a gunsmith in England named John Cookson. One of his pieces, a repeating flintlock gun, is illustrated in the United States Cartridge Company's *Catalogue,* opposite page 17, where its history is given.

Fig. 5 — GEM MUSKET, AND DETAIL OF LOCK MARKED *GEM*

Fig. 6 — Rambotte Musket, and Detail of Lock Bearing Maker's Name

II. The E. C. Musket

This musket has a rather massive stock of the type used on seventeenth-century English military matchlock muskets; but, as we have already noted, this type of stock continued to be made in Massachusetts and Rhode Island even as late as the middle of the eighteenth century. The wood is American walnut.

The lock bears neither maker's name nor proof mark, facts strongly indicative of Colonial manufacture. The lock plate and the screw plate are both convex, and the screw plate is in the form of a rather elaborate scroll ornamentally engraved. The tail of the butt plate is too short for a typical English musket of a period as late as King George's War, and in shape its finial resembles the finials of Queen Anne's War. Nevertheless, we must bear in mind that the persistence of archaic forms in the Colonies would make it possible for a Colonial butt plate of this type to have been made as late as 1740. The embryo acorn finial of the trigger guard would seem to indicate manufacture about this time, although there is an escutcheon plate on the wrist similar to the escutcheon plates of the 1763 muskets, but somewhat more elaborate. Of course this escutcheon plate may be a later addition.

The barrel, which is five and one-half feet long, and very similar to the barrel of the Cookson gun, bears early English proof marks and the maker's initials *E. C.* under a crown — a common device on English barrels of the later Stuart period. Its use may, of course, have been continued into the time of the early Georges.

III. The "Handy" Musket

The so-called "Handy" musket has no proof marks, and is doubtless Colonial-made throughout. The stock, which is made of maple, distinctly shows French influence, being much lighter, more graceful, and more delicate than the contemporary English stock. Both the lock plate and the screw plate are flat, an archaic form for an English military musket of the King George's War period, but characteristic of the French military muskets in use at this time. The screw plate is without the scroll drop behind the second screw, which appears on nearly all English muskets of this period and for a century before, but which is not present on contemporary French muskets.

While the lock plate is long, and, in general, similar in shape to the lock plates of Queen Anne's War muskets, it is fastened by only two screws, after the Georgian fashion, instead of by the three screws characteristic of the Queen Anne muskets. It seems, therefore, representative of the transition locks of the reign of George I. The piece was, perhaps, made as early as 1720, though the fence on the pan would seem to place it as late as 1740. The earlier dating, however, is supported by the lack of a connecting arm from the pan to the head of the frizzen screw, unless a French model had been copied in this respect.

There is no butt plate, and, in fact, there never was any on this butt, which, of course, is a strong indication of Colonial manufacture.

IV. The Gem

A musket marked *GEM* in a cartouche on the lock plate offers many difficulties. The stock, which is made of American walnut, and, hence, is presumably of Colonial manufacture, is of the archaic English seventeenth-century type, manufactured in Massachusetts and Rhode Island during the first half of the eighteenth century. The lock, which was originally a dog lock — and hence savors of the period of Queen Anne's War — has a gooseneck hammer, the development of a later period. In the back of this gooseneck hammer, however, is a notch for the dog, indicating that the dog and the gooseneck hammer were used at the same time, although the dog is not now on the lock. The screw hole is plugged.

At first glance this lock would seem to have been a typical Queen Anne dog lock which had subsequently been altered to carry a gooseneck hammer, so notched that the dog might be retained and used. However, the locks of Queen Anne's War were fastened by three screws, while this lock is fastened by only two, according to the practice of the middle Georgian period. There is no evidence of a hole for a third screw that may have been discarded. This reduced number of screws, together with the hybrid form of the hammer and safety device, seems definitely to place the manufacture of the lock later than the time of Queen Anne, and to indicate that it was one of the transitional — or what might even be called experimental — forms of lock that were made in the reign of George I.

There is no screw plate on this firearm; but the absence of this plate does not give any hint as to the date of the piece, although it strongly indicates Colonial manufacture.

The trigger guard, which ends in the fully developed acorn finial, was evidently made after 1745, much too late a date for the lock. Hence, this guard is unquestionably a subsequent addition, as are the ramrod ferrules as well. The trigger is evidently a later addition; and it seems probable that the pan, with a rather high fence and with

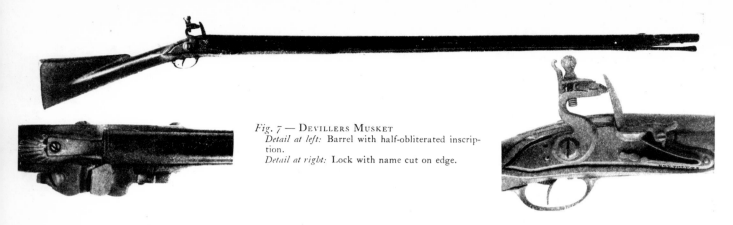

Fig. 7 — DEVILLERS MUSKET
Detail at left: Barrel with half-obliterated inscription.
Detail at right: Lock with name cut on edge.

the extension arm to the head of the frizzen screw, was made many years later than the lock. Innumerable pans burned out and were replaced.

The butt plate, where it runs up on the comb of the stock, resembles the butt plates of the 1745 muskets, but it is much thinner at the heel than those butt plates. In general, the barrel is similar to those of the later Queen Anne period. Indeed, the musket seems to be a synthesis of the best parts of a number of different discarded muskets, perhaps assembled during the Revolution. No proof marks appear on either lock or barrel. The lock, as an example of the transition period of George I, is of especial interest; and the thickness of the metal used in the lock points very strongly to Colonial manufacture.

V. THE RAMBOTTE MUSKET

The musket with a lock marked with the maker's name *RAMBOTTE* offers another interesting problem. The absence of proof marks on lock and barrel are *prima facie* evidence of Colonial manufacture. The stock is birch and is a rather heavy copy of the English military type of about 1745. The tail of the butt plate is short, as are those on the English muskets of the time of Queen Anne. Yet it is not really identical in design with them; for it is rather larger, or broader. The escutcheon plate is of the usual top-shaped form, but crudely made. The lock plate has only two screws, which would seem to place the manufacture of the lock considerably later than the reign of Anne. The screw plate is, in general, convex like the English plates of King George's War, but is flat where it is pierced by the screws, a very unusual peculiarity, which may be attributed to French influence, for the entire surface of French screw plates of this period was flat.

The lock plate is curved down back of the hammer like the English lock plates of the King George's War period; but the extension arm connecting the pan with the head of the frizzen screw, which is so characteristic of English muskets of this period, is not present. It is, however, present on the French muskets of 1717 and 1728, but not on those of 1746, according to Sawyer. Its absence from this lock may well be the result of French influence. The name Rambotte has a decidedly French flavor, but whether Rambotte was a Frenchman, or whether he merely copied certain points from a French musket, is at present an unsolved riddle.

The most probable conclusion as to this lock is that it

was made in the American Colonies during King George's War, and that the maker was acquainted with both the English and the French muskets of the period. Indeed, it seems likely that he copied an English military musket of the period from 1730 to 1745, but that his familiarity with French arms resulted in a visible French influence in the treatment of many of the details.

VI. THE DEVILLERS MUSKET

A very interesting gun is one marked, on the lock, *H. DEVILLERS*. Since neither lock nor barrel bears proof marks, and the stock is made of maple, it seems safe to conclude that this piece is of Colonial manufacture throughout. The barrel, which is typical of the English military barrel of the period, is stamped with a now almost obliterated ownership inscription, of which the following letters can still be deciphered:

M. . . . . . . A DRAG 1742.

This lock is marked *H. DEVILLERS*, on the beveled edge of the lock plate below the frizzen spring. The letters seem to be cut, rather than stamped, and the name may be that of the owner rather than the maker. The lock plate is flat, like those of the French muskets of the King George's War period, and not convex like the English muskets of that time. The metal of the lock, however, is much thicker than that used on either English or French muskets, and may be accepted as a sure indication of Colonial manufacture.

The screw plate is flat and of scroll form, a French rather than an English characteristic of this period. The butt plate, too, is more ornamental than is usual with English butt plates, and savors decidedly of French design. The hammer is of the flat gooseneck type, similar to those of the French 1746 muskets, and not like the convex hammers of the English pieces. The trigger is straight like the triggers of French muskets, and shows no trace of the J shape, so characteristic of English triggers. The trigger guard also shows French influence, and the stock itself is lighter than English stocks, and tends toward the French type. The ramrod pipes, on the other hand, show more English influence than French, but are clearly of Colonial workmanship.

This musket seems to be a rather elegant military piece, perhaps designed for an officer. Unquestionably made in the Colonies, perhaps by H. Devillers, or some other French immigrant, about the beginning of King George's War (*1739*), it clearly shows indebtedness to both the French and the English muskets of the period. The gunsmith seems to have been acquainted with the military arms of both nations, but to have been more partial to, or at least better acquainted with, French arms. The name Devillers suggests French origin, and the theory that he was the maker of the piece is strengthened by the appearance of the gun itself.

COLONIAL AND REVOLUTIONARY FIREARMS

By R. L. DOWLING

Honorary Curator of Arms, Fort Ticonderoga Museum

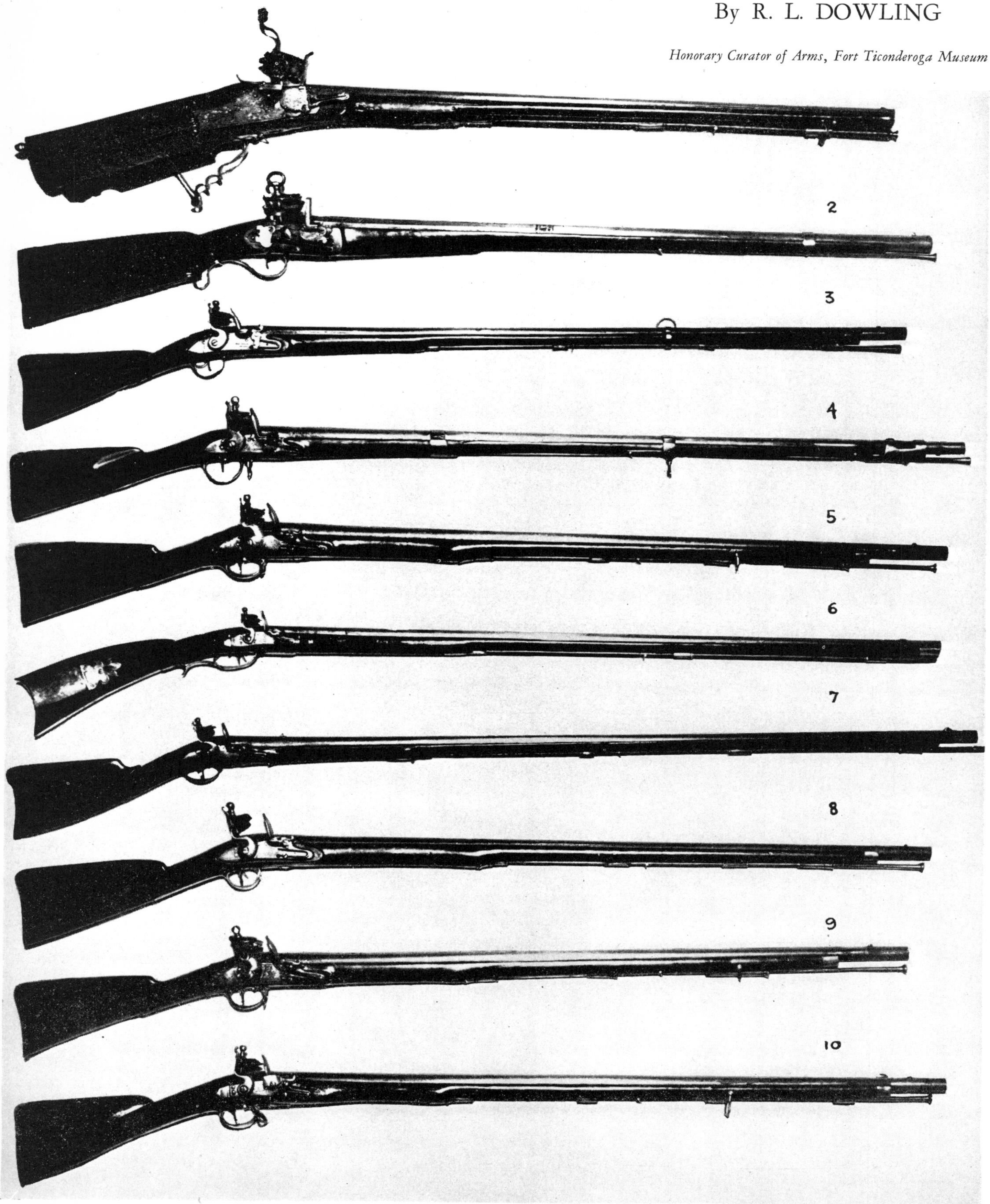

2

3

4

5

6

7

8

9

10

Fig. 1 — Arquebus (*fifteenth century*); type used by Champlain in 1609

Fig. 2 — Spanish snaphance (*sixteenth century*); the first practical gun used in the colonies

Fig. 3 — Charleville musket, model 1717; adopted by the French Government as its first standard infantry arm

Fig. 4 — Charleville musket, model 1763; extensively used by the Continental Army during the American Revolution

Fig. 5 — British infantry musket (*American colonial period*); a flintlock, known as the Brown Bess or Tower musket

Fig. 6 — Kentucky rifle (*pre-Revolutionary*); originated in Pennsylvania; famous for its range and accuracy; continued in use to mid-1800's

Fig. 7 — Dutch goose gun (*dated 1764*); note length of weapon and heavy stock

Fig. 8 — Committee of Safety musket (*Revolutionary period*); note similarity to British infantry musket used in the Revolution (*Fig. 10*)

Fig. 9 — British infantry musket (*Revolutionary period*); slightly shorter than earlier models of same weapon (*Fig. 5*); neck of hammer reinforced

Fig. 10 — Hessian musket (*Revolutionary period*); relic of wars of Frederick the Great; outmoded in Europe, but used by Hessian troops in America

Photographs by John Dowling

THE first type of hand firearm used on this continent was probably the fusee or matchlock, which took its name from the method of discharging. It was a muzzle loader with an extremely heavy barrel and cumbersome stock, and an average caliber of from .70 to .90. The lock had a priming pan on the outside fitted with a sliding cover. In place of a hammer there was a long, slender, curved shank on the outside of the lock plate which rotated about 60 degrees on a bearing some three inches forward of the pan. The upper end of this shank was fitted with a screw clamp in which was placed a few inches of rope previously treated with saltpeter. One end of the rope was ignited and blown until a red coal was formed. The mainspring held the clamp end of the shank above and forward of the pan in which the priming powder was placed. After sliding back the pan cover the trigger was pulled and the shank fell of its own weight, allowing the burning rope to come in contact with the powder in the pan. The resulting flash communicated through the vent hole, in the side of the barrel directly next to the pan, and discharged the load. Weapons of this sort were not very satisfactory in the walled cities of Europe, and much less so in the American wilderness. The coal on the end of the rope was likely to be blown away by the blast from the vent hole; rain would stop all shooting; and it was impossible to make a surprise night attack because of the burning rope.

An improvement over the fusee was the muzzle-loading wheel lock or arquebus. The pan and its cover were retained but the burning rope was discarded. The lock was fitted with a revolving wheel held in a bearing against the side of the lock plate. It was turned clockwise by a removable crank and held against the pressure of the mainspring by a simple catch. Another spring held one end of a movable lever against the edge of the wheel with considerable force. The contact end of this lever was fitted with a screw clamp into which was secured a fragment of flint or pyrites. When the trigger was pulled it released the wheel, which turned rapidly in counterclockwise direction. The stone in contact with the edge of the wheel threw a shower of sparks into the pan and discharged the weapon. A forked staff was required in aiming both the fusee and the wheel lock. With such a wheel lock Samuel de Champlain was armed during his historic battle in 1609 with the Iroquois Indians, near the present location of Fort Ticonderoga, New York. Wheel locks evidently originated about 1515 in Nuremberg, Germany. The arquebus is believed to date from the mid-1400's (*Fig. 1*).

Ammunition was often carried in a bandolier over one shoulder. Fastened to it were hollow wooden containers each holding a charge of powder; the priming powder (of better quality) was carried in a separate container. The usual load for the fusee and the arquebus was a charge of black powder and several lead bullets.

The snaphance, the next marked improvement in firearms, was the first practical gunlock used in the colonies in early times (*Fig. 2*). Its main points of weakness were the slender neck of the hammer and the long frizzen hinge. The principle of its mechanism was so similar to that of the flintlock that a very slight change produced the latter. The locks of both were more practical than those of previous models and less likely to get out of order.

The snaphance and flintlock were both fired by the action of flint in the jaws of a falling hammer, striking against steel and throwing sparks into a priming pan. The mainspring of the snaphance was usually on the outside of the lock plate. In the flintlock the mainspring was on the inside; the frizzen, or steel against which the flint struck, was equipped with a spring. This device was primarily to give sufficient resistance against the blow of the hammer to produce sparks when the flint made contact with the steel, and to retain the base of the frizzen over the pan to secure the priming. In the flintlock the frizzen was so made that its base became the pan cover. Thus the pan was opened by the action of the falling hammer at the instant of contact between flint and steel, and the resulting sparks fell into the priming powder discharging the weapon.

These weapons were superior to previous models in the improved design of the stocks as well as of the locks, and looked less like a club. The stocks were still heavy, compared to present-day standards, but the forked staff of former days was eliminated. Flintlock muskets were the standard service arm in America from about 1700 to the time of the Mexican War in 1845–1847. They were smooth bore, and accurate shooting with them was impossible beyond fifty yards. General Grant, in his memoirs (*Vol. 1, p. 95*), said of the smooth-bore flintlock musket then in use, that you could shoot all day at a man two hundred yards distant without his being aware of it. Army tactics during this period called for volley fire at masses of troops and did not require individual accuracy.

Up to 1717 there was no standard model of military musket in Europe, and even in a single regiment guns of various types and calibers were used. In 1717 the French Government adopted the Charleville musket of that year's model as its first standard infantry arm (*Fig. 3*). The barrel was pin fastened, and had in addition a band embracing the stock and barrel one third of the distance from the muzzle to the vent hole. The total length of the musket was five feet, two and one half inches; the barrel length, forty-six and seven eighths inches.

Charleville muskets were manufactured at Saint Etienne, Tulle, Maubergé, and Charleville. They were the standard infantry weapons of the French army from 1717 until long after Waterloo. In accordance with contemporary practice, the French Government sent the earlier, out-moded models of their military weapons for use in their overseas domains. Thus a great many Charleville muskets that were used in the French and Indian wars were of a model much earlier than the date of the conflict — witness, the remains of ancient muskets frequently dug up on the battlefields of the Champlain Valley and the Saint Lawrence.

In 1728, the French improved their muskets by doing away with the pin-fastening method and substituting bands to secure the barrel to the stock. The gun could thus be more easily taken apart in the field for repairs. Various minor changes in the Charleville were made until 1763. The model of that year became famous in America, for it was extensively used in the Continental Army during the Revolution. The total length was reduced to four feet, eleven and five eighths inches, the barrel length to forty-four and three fourths inches (*Fig. 4*). The first Springfield muskets, model 1795, manufactured by the United States Government were exact copies of the Charleville model 1763, except for a slightly heavier barrel (see ANTIQUES, April 1939, *p. 184*). (Pin fastening signifies that two or three lugs projected from the underside of the barrel into cavities in the stock when the barrel was in place; iron pins were then driven through the stock from side to side, passing through holes in the lugs.)

The Charleville muskets were all smooth-bore muzzle loaders and were far superior to contemporary British weapons. The caliber was slightly smaller and the barrel was more accurately made. The bullet was a closer fit in the bore, achieving greater accuracy and distance than the British muskets.

Fixed ammunition was in use at this time. The cartridges were made of paper and contained a charge of powder and a round bullet. The soldier bit them open, poured the contents down the barrel of his musket, and rammed down the ball in exactly the manner of the Civil War soldier a century later. He then filled the pan with powder to prime it. The American troops of the Revolutionary period, however, did not have much fixed ammunition and resorted to the powder horn and bullet pouch instead of the cartridge box.

The British flintlock musket of colonial times was familiarly known as the *Brown Bess* or Tower musket. It was a pin-fastened gun very strongly and honestly made but lacking the finer qualities of the Charleville (*Fig. 5*). Very little was expected of it so far as shooting went, but, as a contemporary critic stated, "it made a good handle for a bayonet." Not long ago I tested the shooting qualities of both French and British muskets with their proper ammunition. Fired from a rest at one hundred yards at a man-size standing figure, the "Brown Bess" musket hit various parts of the target three times out of ten; the Charleville five out of ten. The British retained the goose-neck hammer on their muskets until the Revolution, while the French adopted the flat-faced hammer with reinforced neck as early as 1763.

The gun which is most romantically associated with the colonial period of American history is the so-called "Kentucky" rifle (*Fig. 6*). That name is misleading, because rifles of the type were extensively used by American scouts and frontiersmen long before they heard of Kentucky. For detailed discussion of this rifle, developed by the gunsmiths of Pennsylvania to meet the requirements of woods fighting, see an article in ANTIQUES for September 1932 (*p. 101*). Its distinctive feature was the greased patch, which greatly reduced loading time and increased accuracy of fire. The rifle became the most deadly weapon of colonial and Revolutionary times, and played an important part in the War of 1812. No bayonets were ever fitted to the "Kentucky" (or Pennsylvania) rifle. It remained a sharpshooter's weapon throughout its existence. Some years ago, after trial shots to test the range, firing from a rest at a target two hundred yards distant, I hit the eight-inch bull's-eye ten times in succession. Not bad for a gun over a century and a half old!

During the Revolution the "Kentucky" rifle underwent several alterations. Some examples were made a little shorter than the early models. The greatest change, however, was in the double-barreled "Kentucky." This gun had an over and under pair of rifled barrels secured on an axle at the breech end. After firing the upper barrel, and releasing a spring catch, both barrels were revolved by hand until the under one was on top, where it was secured by the spring catch. Usually only one lock and hammer were used, with two flash pans, one attached to each barrel. The famous marksman, Timothy Murphy, who killed General Frazier at the Battle of Saratoga in October 1777, was armed with such a weapon.

A very peculiar flintlock smooth bore was in general use in those sections of the country settled by the Dutch. In the Hudson and Mohawk valleys there are still to be found specimens of the so-called "goose gun" (*Fig. 7*). These guns were six or seven feet in length, but of very good balance. The barrel was pin fastened and slightly bell mouthed. The stock was carved with scroll work and had a high comb. Because of the unusually long barrel, these guns could fire several round balls or a handful of buckshot to a considerable distance with great force. They were not a military weapon, but proved effective against the Indians because of their long range and strong shooting qualities. They are among the rarest of colonial guns, seldom found except occasionally in scattered and remote sections of the Mohawk or Hudson valleys.

The first military muskets made in America were the "Committee of Safety muskets," which were made by local gunsmiths under contract to the various Committees of Safety. They were intended for the Continental Army at the outbreak of the Revolution, since many of the volunteers had no weapons of their own. While not all of uniform pattern, the guns were close copies of the British "Brown Bess" musket of the time — pin fastened, muzzle-loading smooth bores of about .75 caliber (*Fig. 8*).

The Hessian troops that fought for the British during the Revolution were armed with a smooth-bore flintlock muzzle loader of German manufacture (*Fig. 10*). The caliber was about the same as that of the British musket, but the stock was much heavier. The bayonet had two cutting edges and was shorter than the British bayonet of the period. Many were relics of the wars of Frederick the Great. Some of the Hessian Jaegers were armed with short rifles of large caliber. Compared to the "Kentucky," they were crude and clumsy. In loading, the ball was forced down the barrel by blows of a heavy iron ramrod, a noisy and time-consuming operation which resulted in inferior shooting.

In the 1770's the British brought out two breech-loading rifles, one of which, the invention of Major Patrick Ferguson, 71st Regiment of Highlanders, saw service in this country during the Revolution. The other, known as the Willmore rifle, was apparently never used in America. Hence only the Ferguson comes within the scope of this article, though both were ingenious. The first authentic record of the Ferguson occurs in the *Annual Register* of 1776 (*p. 148*). It was used for the first time in the Revolution at the Battle of the Brandywine, September 11, 1777. It is mentioned in Besset's *History of the Reign of George Third* (London, 1803, *Vol. II, pp. 423–4*).

The rifle looked somewhat like the "Brown Bess." Its total length was four feet, two inches. The bayonet was twenty-five inches long, and was of the common socket variety, though it had a sword blade. The breech mechanism of the Ferguson was simple and strong. The ornamental brass trigger guard was secured by a spring catch on the end nearest the butt. When it was released from this catch, and turned around by the front in a complete revolution, a round plug descended at the breech end of the barrel, leaving a cavity on top to receive first the ball and then the charge of powder. The ball fell forward inside the chamber until it made contact with the rifling, where the diameter of the bore was slightly reduced to keep the ball from falling out of its own weight. The plug referred to above was an accelerating screw furnished with twelve threads to the inch which enabled it, by one revolution, to open or close the breech. When the charge was inserted, a reverse motion of the trigger guard raised the plug and closed the breech. This plug, which worked in a vertical direction, constituted the entire breech mechanism. The lock was the common flintlock of the period, but of a finer grade than the regulation musket lock. The rear sight was capable of elevation by means of folding leaves to ranges from one hundred to five hundred yards. Seven shots a minute were claimed for this weapon, which was remarkable speed for that day.

Major Ferguson served with distinction in several campaigns of the Revolution, always in command of his corps of riflemen. He lost his life at the battle of Kings Mountain, October 7, 1780. In this battle, the British riflemen were pitted against American frontiersmen armed with the "Kentucky" muzzle loader, whose straight shooting proved more devastating than the more rapid fire of the breech loader. Strange to say, very few Ferguson rifles were made after the death of the inventor, and they are now the rarest weapons of the period. Their weakness lay in the fact that the barrel was almost as thin as that of a smooth bore, so that the blast of the service charge of powder caused a vibration of the metal commonly known as "whip." Consequently it was impossible to shoot the Ferguson with the exactness of the heavier-barreled "Kentucky," with its smaller bullet and lighter charge.

Revolutionary War Muskets

BY RICHARD KIMBALL SPRAGUE

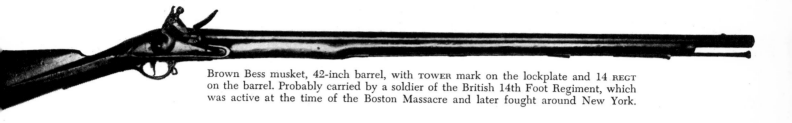

Brown Bess musket, 42-inch barrel, with TOWER mark on the lockplate and 14 REGT on the barrel. Probably carried by a soldier of the British 14th Foot Regiment, which was active at the time of the Boston Massacre and later fought around New York.

Brown Bess musket, 46-inch barrel, marked on lockplate GALTON 1762. Believed to have been used in the Revolution; it carries the number of the 43rd regiment, which saw service in the early years of the war. *Collection of Albert Goodhue, Jr.*

A GREAT DEAL has been written about the long rifle and the part it played in turning the tide of many engagements. The cavalry and the rifle companies stir the imagination, but we should not forget that the bulk of the heavy fighting in the Revolution was done by the common soldier equipped with his smoothbore musket.

The Revolutionary musket was far from being an instrument of precision. At about a hundred yards only some four shots in ten would hit the mark, and even then a good deal of luck was involved. Since the armies fired in ranks and in volleys, however, accuracy did not matter so much. The musket was a cumbersome affair, weighing thirteen pounds or better with a bayonet. It might have a barrel length up to 46 inches, with a caliber range from .69 on French muskets to .80 and over on some of the Hessian arms.

The name commonly applied to the British musket, Brown Bess, stems from Queen Elizabeth, who ordered musket barrels browned artificially to prevent rusting. The Brown Bess was used on both sides in the Revolution. It has the stock held to the barrel by sliding pins. Various marks occur on the lockplate, including TOWER, DUBLIN CASTLE, occasionally the name of a private maker, and during the reign of the first three Georges the initials G. R. and a crown. Beneath the flashpan on the lockplate is a broad arrow, denoting government ownership.

During the period of the Revolution the form of the Brown Bess changed very little, except for the length of the barrel. In the earlier models this was 46 inches, then about 1760 or somewhat before it was shortened to 42, and finally in the mid-1770's to 39. The later type saw

limited if any war service, but the first two types were used extensively, especially that with the 42-inch barrel.

Probably the most sought after and the least understood of all Revolutionary arms is the Committee of Safety musket (see article in ANTIQUES, November 1946, p. 322). These muskets were made under contract for the Committees of Safety by known gunsmiths, but very few of them marked their guns, doubtless for fear of British reprisals in case the Colonies lost the war. Some did put on their mark, however, and even added the date. It is from the few remaining examples, and from the specifications of the various Colonies, that we have learned the little we know about these typically American guns.

One of the most important Revolutionary guns was the French musket, model 1763, which later served as the pattern for the first regulation U.S. musket, the Model 1795. In its day, the French musket was considered the finest known. France sent us 100,000 stand of arms after the Battle of Saratoga. Since most of them were made in the armory at Charleville, these guns are known to collectors as "Charleville muskets." They are also referred to as "Lafayette muskets," because the General brought a number over with him when he came.

The French musket differs from the British in that the barrel is held to the stock by iron bands. It is a much sturdier piece, and has a more modern appearance. Its distinguishing markings are CHARLEVILLE in script on the lockplate, surmounted by a D. The barrel is 44¾ inches long, and the piece 59½ inches overall. Its caliber is .69.

A gun about which very little is known is the Dutch musket. Early in the Revolution, when there was a great

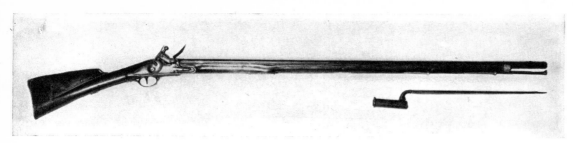

Brown Bess musket, 46-inch barrel, marked DUBLIN CASTLE. Probably used by the 52nd British regiment in the Revolution, active at Lexington, Concord, and Bunker Hill.

Officer's musket, 36-inch barrel, made by the London gunsmith, J. Adams (*c. 1770-1780*), and carried by Robert Peele of Salem at the Battle of Lexington. *Collection of the Essex Institute.*

Committee of Safety musket, 39-inch barrel, made by Hugh Orr of Bridgewater, Massachusetts. Barrel held to the stock with pins as in the Brown Bess. Marked H. ORR on the lockplate, and BRIDGE-WATER *1776* on the barrel. *Collection of Dr. Clyde W. Everett.*

Committee of Safety musket made by Eliphalet Leonard of Easton, Massachusetts, marked on lockplate E. LEONARD IN EASTON, *1776. Collection of Fort Ticonderoga Museum.*

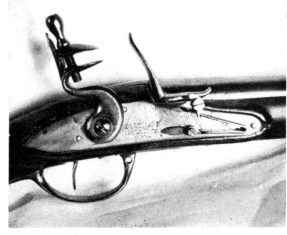

Detail of Leonard lockplate of musket with 48½-inch barrel. The Committee of Safety muskets differed greatly in their measurements. *Collection of Fort Ticonderoga Museum.*

58

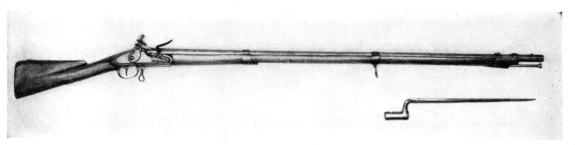

French musket, model 1763, made at the Charleville Armory. A typical specimen, it may well have seen war service in either the American or French armies.

Hessian musket, 41½-inch barrel, the butt having the German or Central European characteristic of an extremely high comb. Colonel Rall's soldiers at the Battle of Trenton are depicted in old prints as using muskets of this type. The three brass barrel bands, which are wide, give the piece a heavy look.

Dutch musket, 41-inch barrel, marked on lockplate THONE, AMSTERDAM. Brass barrel bands, the upper one double. Probably carried at the Battle of Lexington by T. V. Rogers of Rowley, Massachusetts.

Hessian musket of the pinned variety, 41-inch barrel. *Collection of Fort Ticonderoga.*

scarcity of serviceable arms, the Colonists imported a quantity of arms from Holland, but it is not known exactly when the muskets were received. The barrel of the Dutch musket is 41 inches long, and the whole piece has an over-all measurement of 55 inches. It is characterized by a series of brass barrel bands, the upper one double.

The muskets of the Hessian mercenaries who came to America are beginning to interest the student of early firearms. In the series of tiny states which constituted the Germany of Frederick the Great there was little or no standardization of arms. Moreover, many of the guns brought to America had probably seen European service for the preceding thirty or forty years. It appears that Hessian muskets followed both the basic types, the pinned and the banded barrel. The banded Hessian guns which I have examined have brass bands like the Dutch.

In view of the fact that so many Hessian soldiers served in America, it is strange that so few of their muskets are known today. A number have come down to us from General Burgoyne's army, but many of the Hessian muskets must have been destroyed or returned to Germany.

Gradually those interested in the early arms of our country are finding out more about them. Only within the last few years, for instance, the salient features of the British Brown Bess have been listed and described. Many other arms remain to be studied in detail. At some time during the Revolution, particularly in the early years, every known type of musket probably saw service. First came the old fowling pieces used at Lexington, Concord, and Bunker Hill, and then the other types of guns mentioned above. Let us not forget the part they all played in the early history of our country.

Charleville muskets and American arms

BY R. L. DOWLING

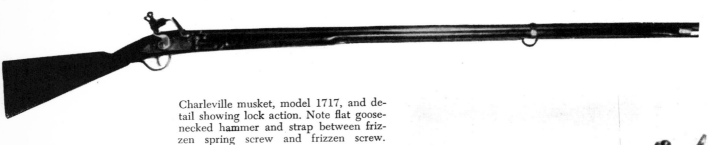

Charleville musket, model 1717, and detail showing lock action. Note flat goose-necked hammer and strap between frizzen spring screw and frizzen screw.

All photographs by J. R. Dowling, from the author's collection.

THE BEST SMOOTH-BORE MUSKETS of colonial and Revolutionary days were the Charleville muskets of France. From 1717 to 1777, they were constantly being improved. French muskets previous to the model 1763 were extensively used by French troops in this country and Canada during the early colonial wars, and demonstrated their superiority over contemporary British muskets, which remained practically the same from early colonial times until long after the Battle of Waterloo. After the embargo of 1774, no British arms were allowed here, except for those in the hands of British troops.

The Charleville muskets were made in St. Etienne, Tulle, and Mauberge, besides Charleville itself. The first one, model 1717, measured 62½ inches, with a barrel length of 46⅝ inches, the barrel being secured by four pins and one iron band situated a third of the way from the muzzle to the vent hole. This model had a walnut stock made with a high comb; round sling swivels mounted on the left side, one at the band and the other in an eye in the stock just to the rear of the side plate; a flat lock

plate, with the rear edge oval; and a thin butt plate secured by pins and a screw. All mountings were of iron. The iron pan had three flat faces and a fence at the rear. An iron strap or tenon connected the frizzen screw with the frizzen spring screw—a unique feature in this lock. The hammer was flat and goose-necked, with beveled edges. The ramrod was of wood.

The next Charleville was the model 1728, the measurements of which were the same as the model 1717. The rear of the barrel was finished off with eight flat faces, the top one extending to within six inches of the muzzle, the others each five inches in length. A rigidity stud on the under side of the barrel extended into a notch in the stock. The barrel was secured by three bands, the upper one with two rings over the barrel and a spring to the rear, the middle one with a projection on the under side to guide the ramrod, held by friction. The lower one, also held by friction, was beck shaped at the bottom. The lock plate, flat-faced with a point to the rear, measured 6½ inches by 2⅜ inches. The hammer was flat and goose-

Lock action of model 1754 Charleville musket. Note flat goose-necked hammer and high comb of stock.

necked, and the jaw screw was notched. The walnut stock, of rather light construction, had a deep comb and a decided drop.

All the fittings of the model 1728 were of iron and of light construction. The iron pan had three flat faces, a fence at the rear, and a tenon to the frizzen screw. The trigger guard was 11⅝ inches long and finished with ball points at the ends. The lower swivel ring was secured by an eye in the left of the stock just to the rear of the side plate, the upper one by the middle band. The ramrod of the 1728 and all succeeding models was of iron.

The next model, the 1746, was much the same as the one preceding, except that the rear of the barrel was octagonal, the rear of the lock plate convex, and the muzzle band shorter.

The model 1754 was a great improvement over preceding weapons. The total length was reduced to 56 inches and the barrel length to 41 inches, with a uniform weight of 10¼ pounds. Officers' guns were still further reduced to 7 pounds, with a total length of 54 inches. Oval sling rings were placed under the stock, one at the trigger guard and the other at the middle band. The muzzle band was greatly lengthened, and all three bands were spring fastened. The hammer remained flat-faced and goose-necked.

The next model, the 1763, has been called the Lafayette musket, owing to the fact that he supplied several thousand to our forces at his own expense during the Revolution. This model was selected as the pattern for our Springfield muskets, model 1795. The length was 59⅝ inches, and the barrel, which was 44¾ inches long, was secured by iron bands, all spring fastened at the rear,

with sling swivels placed as on the preceding model. There was a flat face on each side at the rear. The lock plate was 6¼ inches long and flat-faced, and the hammer was flat with a reinforced under jaw that was much stronger than the goose-necked varieties. The regular bayonet for this musket was in advance of its time; it was of the contemporary socket variety with a three-sided blade, but it was secured by a locking band.

Only minor improvements were made in the models following the 1763—the 1766, 1768, 1770, 1771, 1773, and 1774—and very few if any were used here. But the model 1777 was the best smooth-bore musket of its day. It had a caliber of .69, and its superiority was due in part to the greater exactness of the caliber and the closer fit of the bullet. The total length was 60 inches and the barrel was 44⅝ inches. This weapon was used by the French infantry in the Yorktown campaign.

In this model there were five short flat surfaces at the breech end of the barrel, which was secured to the stock by three iron bands with springs to the rear. Oval sling swivels were secured to the under side of the middle band and in an eye just forward of the trigger guard. The lock plate had an oval surface with beveled edges forward; the hammer was oval, instead of flat as in previous models, and had a reinforced under jaw; and the frizzen was made with a slight bend forward at the top.

Two features of the model 1777 Charleville were adopted in U. S. muskets. The cheek recess, 3⅜ inches by 2 inches, on the left side of the stock was used in the U. S. musket model 1812; and the improved pan of brass, set at an angle tilting forward, with no fence at the rear, was adopted in the U. S. musket model 1822.

Charleville musket, model 1763, and detail showing lock action. Note reinforced under jaw of flat hammer.

Lock action of model 1777 Charleville musket. Note round face of hammer and bend at top of frizzen.

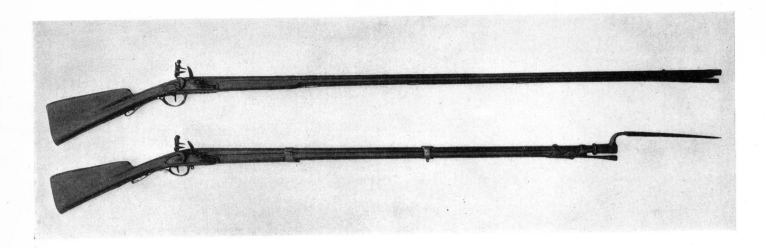

French Officers' Shoulder Arms

By Charles D. Cook

THE farmer-patriot soldiers of New England looked with a sort of awe mingled with esteem upon the brilliant and polished French officers of Rochambeau's army, who, poised by the culture and schooling of the Old World, were equally at home, whether at the court of the French King, in an American farmhouse, or on the field of battle. On the other hand, the Frenchmen esteemed and respected the wholesome honesty, the uncomplaining self-sacrifice, the indomitable will and physical endurance of the Yankee volunteers. Mutual admiration developed firm friendships among these men from two diverse races. So it was that, when the time came for our French allies to leave Providence for the return journey to their native country, various tokens in souvenir of martial fellowship were exchanged by parting comrades. The tokens left by the French soldiers ranged from expensive, artistically wrought dress swords and firearms to such humdrum personal objects as shaving bowls. Americans in return doubtless bestowed similar treasures.

Not only did the French officers and soldiers exchange gifts with their personal friends, but all along the line of their march to the port of embarkation, they yielded to the requests of admiring and grateful Americans for small keepsakes in memory of the allies from overseas. Doubtless the more homely donations, such as the shaving bowl given by Lafayette to Colonel Parker of Scituate, Rhode Island, were made in direct response to requests from admiring citizens of the new country, who felt specially favored in the possession of something intimately associated with the person of a brave and noble foreigner.

The oft-told story about Rochambeau at the Waterman Tavern in Coventry, Rhode Island, will be remembered by many. As he was about to depart from the place, the proprietress begged him to leave some souvenir by which she and her associates might remember his visit. Doubtless they expected a piece of jewelry or perhaps some ornament from his uniform. Picture their surprise when the general drew his sword and slashed a deep cut in the beautiful hand-carved mantelpiece that adorned the fireplace in the front of the house, the while exclaiming, "That will remind you of my visit." To this day the mark of the French sword is proudly exhibited to visitors, who often come hundreds of miles to see it. It is hard to view Rochambeau's sword flourish as a gesture of gallantry. Perhaps, however, had we known his landlady we should realize that in hacking at the mantelpiece of the house instead of at its owner, the French

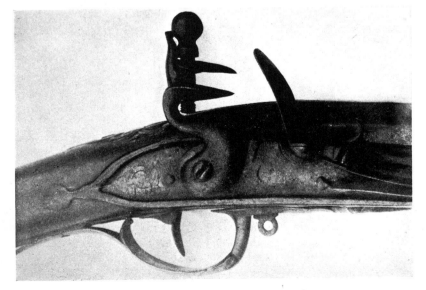

Fig. 1 (top of page) — FRENCH FIREARMS (*period of the American Revolution*) Right view of fowling piece and musket. Both weapons by Cassingnard of Nantes. *Illustrations from the author's collection*

Fig. 2 (left) — MUSKET DETAIL While the mechanisms of the two arms are the same, workmanship on the sporting arm (*shown opposite*) is carried to a much finer finish than is observed on the military weapon

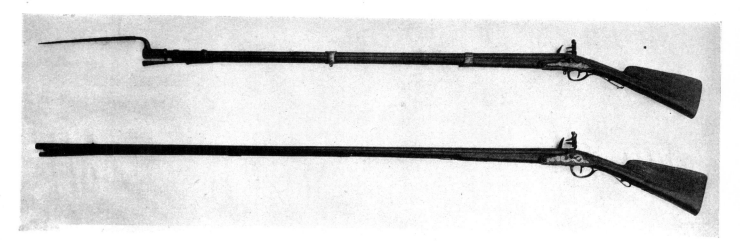

commander displayed rare generosity and admirable self-control.

One of the most pleasing of the gifts presented by French officers to their American confrères is a pair of beautifully wrought firearms, consisting of a serviceable military musket and a gentleman's sporting gun or fowling piece. They were made by the French gunsmith Cassingnard, and represent the best workmanship of their day. One of them was handed down in the Westcote family in Scituate, while the other was cherished for many years as a family heirloom in East Greenwich.

Unfortunately, the name of the French officer who owned these weapons is not recorded, nor has the name of his American friend been preserved in the family traditions. Of course, he may have presented one gun to one friend and one to another, but since they are companion arms, it seems far more probable that they passed together to some very dear friend, not to be separated until, at the death of the recipient, they were taken over by heirs representing two different branches of the family. At any rate, after being apart for years, they are at last happily reunited on the walls of the gun room in my home.

The fowling piece is five feet, six inches long, with a barrel fifty-one and one half inches long, and a calibre of nine sixteenths of an inch. For a distance of eleven inches from the breech the barrel is octagonal; and for the remainder of its length it is round, with a flat top. The stock is of handsome French walnut,

splendidly carved above the escutcheon plate. The sight is of silver, and the ramrod pipes, trigger guard, and other mountings are of brass, engraved.

The musket is four feet nine inches long, with a barrel forty-one and one fourth inches in length and a calibre of eleven sixteenths of an inch. The bayonet lug underneath is one and a half inches from the muzzle, and the front sight is part of the muzzle band. For nine inches from the breech, the barrel is octagonal; and round, with a flat top, the remainder of its length. The stock, like that of the fowling piece, is of handsome French walnut, carved as is the fowling piece. The mountings and bands are of brass, engraved. The butt plates of both specimens bear the same carving, which is of a military design. The musket is marked *Cassingnard* on the lock plate. The fowling piece is similarly marked on the barrel, with the additional inscription *Cassingnard Nantes* on the lock plate. The similarity in shape of the stocks and trigger guards is conspicuously noticeable.

Charles W. Sawyer, an authority on the firearms used by the French, says in discussing the French model *1754* musket, on page 26 of *Firearms in American History*, "A small edition of this musket was issued for the officers, to weigh 7 lb.; total length 4 ½ ft.; mountings engraved. Even a general wore a gun on his back, whatever his rank or country."

I have, in fact, an old print of Washington thus accoutred.

Fig. 3 (top of page) — LEFT VIEW OF MUSKET AND FOWLING PIECE
The overall length of the musket is four feet and seven inches; that of the fowling piece is five feet and six inches

Fig. 4 (left) — DETAIL OF FOWLING PIECE
The finish is finer than that of the musket, quite aside from the employment of engraving in one case and its nonemployment in the other

UNITED STATES MUSKET MODEL 1795

By JAMES L. MITCHELL

THE MODEL 1795 MUSKET was, as all collectors know, the first flintlock firearm made at any United States Armory. Arms of this model were not, however, the first made for the Federal Government. Upon recommendation of President Washington and by authority of Congress, appropriations were made in 1794 for the purchase of 7,000 flintlock muskets. These muskets were received from Germany and England over a period of years up to 1801. How they were marked we do not know. It is almost certain that they were marked not with the United States eagle or a date, but probably only with the letters *U.S.* to signify Government ownership. This is a reasonable conclusion as the Continental Congress in 1777 resolved that arms be marked in this manner, and many Revolutionary firearms existing today bear this mark. Shown in Figure 1 is what is undoubtedly one of these 1794-purchase muskets. It is of clumsy construction with very heavy bands and fittings, but following closely the lines of the 1763 Charleville musket. The lock is etched *U.S.*

Figure 2 shows a musket made at Springfield Armory. It is, in my opinion, one of the earliest muskets made here, possibly in the first year of manufacture, 1795. It is similar in construction to the 1794 musket of Figure 1. The lock-plate is stamped with a very long-necked eagle, which looks to the left with both wings raised to a halfway position. This eagle is much more primitive in appearance than those on later lockplates. The barrel of the gun is stamped *U.S.* in accordance with the existing law, also with an eagle's head and the letters *V* and *P,* proof marks which are used for the first time on these models. There is no date, however, on the tang of the butt plate, and as it is not rusted, there undoubtedly never was. This also indicates very early manufacture, as in my belief the first musket to be dated at Springfield was of the 1799 manufacture. In several years of collecting and checking other arms collections, I have yet to see an earlier date than this, with one exception only. This was an arm where the date had obviously been recut from 1799 to 1796. If any collector has a musket bearing an earlier date than 1799, I should greatly appreciate being informed of it.

Some authorities hold to the belief that the earlier musket locks were not stamped with the eagle but were plain. However, there seem no grounds for this belief. The young republic at that time was proud of its eagle emblem, which was incorporated in the Great Seal in 1782 and the badge of the Cincinnati in 1783. It is true that the eagle was probably not used on muskets purchased abroad prior to 1801, but it is almost inevitable that it should have been used on those made at a national armory where much correspondence right from the start in 1795 must have carried the Great Seal.

In 1889 the Ordnance Department in a letter to the commanding officer at Springfield Armory asked for information on earliest use of the eagle stamping, in order to fight Whitney's contention that it was that manufacturer's property. The answer is as follows: "In the Armory Museum the musket of Springfield Armory manufacture having the oldest date (1799) upon it, has an Eagle and 'U.S.' stamped upon the lock plate. The French and Queen Anne arms also have the 'U. S.' stamped upon them. No record has been found concerning the date or the order for stamping the Eagle and 'U. S.' upon the arms. The first Eagle stamps that appear upon the books are 5 taken up June 11, 1799 on the 'General account of stores in the Armory Department,' as purchased of Thomas Sargeant, and 2 as fabricated in the first quarter of 1800.

FIG. 1 — FOREIGN PURCHASE MUSKET *(1794-1801).* Only mark is *U. S.* etching on lockplate. Barrel, 44½ inches in length.

FIG. 2 — UNDOUBTEDLY one of the first muskets made at Springfield Armory. Very primitive type of eagle stamped on lockplate. Barrel, 44⅞ inches in length. Comb of stock has been trimmed by some former owner.

FIG. 3 — SPRINGFIELD SHIP'S MUSKET. This type arm with little or no comb and barrel length of 42 inches is without doubt the arm referred to by Lieutenant-Colonel Whiting in his report on Springfield Armory in 1809.

The date ('June 11, 1799') may not have been the date of receipt, but of payment for the stamps, as the cash book has the following entry June 11, 1799, No. 59: 'To cash paid Thomas Sargeant for lead pots, Eagles, etc., $7.41' The voucher cannot be found, as all the cash vouchers prior to 1806, if duplicates were made, are thought to have been sent to Washington to replace those burned. (See Secretary of War's letter of October 11, 1806, asking for information as to a deed which he thought had been destroyed at the time the War Office was burned.) Arms made prior to 1799 may have had the Eagle stamped or engraved upon them."

Without a doubt all muskets made at both Springfield and Harper's Ferry were stamped with the eagle, but the first date must have been 1799. This last observation seems to be borne out also by the fact that even Springfield Armory had no dated musket prior to 1799. If there had been muskets bearing an earlier date, it is probable Springfield would have had one and in that event could have proved an earlier use of the eagle.

In my opinion the Model 1795 musket was made at both Armories until the next model was adopted, that of 1812. It is almost certain that there is no such arm as the Model 1808 which is many times assumed to be a distinct model. Contract arms were authorized in 1808 when Congress appropriated $200,000 annually for arming the militia. While they were different in some respects from the Model 1795, they are all practically the same. The main difference was the rounded trigger guard, and some believe this feature first appeared on the 1808 contract musket, but I have one dated *1806* and have seen another of 1807 with this type of guard. The change in trigger guards, non-detachable pans, straight projection on the top of the hammer instead of the curl were merely steps which we today would call streamlining, as virtually all the modifications cut the cost of the finished musket.

Most of the Model 1795 muskets had a 44¾-inch barrel, though some are found with a barrel length of 42 inches. There is no comb on the stocks of these arms, and in this feature, they follow closely the appearance of the arms made after 1816. Although we have no definite proof, they were most probably made for naval use and are the ship's muskets referred to by Lieutenant Colonel Whiting in his report to the Government on the Springfield Armory following an inspection made in 1809. He shows a total of 1,625 of these arms called ship's muskets ". . . being 3 inches shorter than the common size" in store. The manufacture of this musket was not confined to Springfield: I have one of this type made at Harper's Ferry (*Fig. 3*).

That these early muskets, of both Armories, are very scarce is true. I have in my collection or have seen several of the following years of manufacture: 1799, 1801, 1802, 1803, 1807, and all of the years following this last date. I have never, however, seen any of 1800, 1804, or 1805, and have seen only one in very poor condition dated *1806* which is mentioned above. I do not, however, mean to imply that there are none.

Why are they so scarce? Secretary of War McHenry in 1800 ordered that the bayonets of these arms were to be soldered permanently to the barrels to strengthen them

as in the process of manufacture they were made thin. The bayonets were made with a half socket instead of the usual round socket. About 15,000 or considerably more than half of the entire production of Springfield muskets from 1800 to 1807 were made in this way until Secretary of War Henry Dearborn ordered this procedure discontinued. All of these muskets were in store in 1809 when Lieutenant-Colonel Whiting made his report. In 1811 Secretary of War William Eustis wrote to Benjamin Prescott, Superintendent at Springfield as follows: "What would be a just price for sighting, smooth-boring and polishing the barrels, making new bayonets and putting them on, of those muskets to which the bayonet is soldered; and at what rate the old bayonets should be valued, if taken in part payment. Also be pleased to state what would be a just price for cutting off the barrel and stock of those to which it would be necessary, brazing a loop to the under side of the barrel and lowering the bands and band springs." It can be seen that the problem of putting in serviceable order these muskets with an impractical bayonet had presented itself to the authorities, and cutting them down seemed to be the only solution. On July 3, 1813, Secretary of War John Armstrong advised Prescott that in no case were the arms to be cut shorter than 3 feet 4 inches, and then again John Chaffee, Military Storekeeper at Springfield, advised Colonel Decius Wadsworth, Commissary General of Ordnance, that the short muskets were made by cutting off 12 inches of the barrels of the muskets which had bayonets soldered on. Another letter dated June 7, 1815 from R. Lee, Superintendent, to Lieutenant-Colonel Bomford of the Ordnance Department states that six or eight thousand of these arms had been cut off to 2 feet 9 inches. Here we have two different barrel lengths mentioned, and in an attempt to correct an already existing fault, the value of the muskets to the Government had decreased by this lack of uniformity. About July 1815 it was decided to sell these arms, and Callender Irvine, Commissary General, in a letter to Acting Secretary of War Dallas said he had been advised by Lieutenant-Colonel Bomford that it had been determined to sell "all of the unsuitable and defective arms at Springfield" and that a Mr. Crammond of Philadelphia had offered to purchase them. In this letter he admits that the muskets were of an indifferent quality.

The balance of the early arms made at both Armories were recognized to be of such poor quality that Tench Coxe, Purveyor of Public Supplies, in 1809 recommended that sub-standard muskets to the number of 10,-000 be sold. Years later, in 1848, the Ordnance Report shows that many more arms of this period then worn out in service, were sold for as little as 13 cents.

Fig. 4—Butt Plate of Springfield musket, which shows date *1799*, the year of manufacture. This year is undoubtedly the first stamped on any Springfield musket.

Fig. 5—Springfield Armory Musket Lockplates (except No. 1, which is from musket shown in Figure 1). No. 2, Lockplate from musket in Figure 2, showing very early eagle. Lockmaker's initials, *S. P.* No. 3, Lockplate from musket dated *1799*, lockmaker's initials, *A. T.* No. 4, Lockplate from musket dated *1801*, lockmaker's initials, *J. G.* No. 5, Lockplate from musket dated *1803*, lockmaker's initials, *W.* No. 6, Lockplate from musket dated *1806*, lockmaker's initials, *A. T.* No. 7, Lockplate from musket dated *1808*, lockmaker's initials, *F. B.* No. 8, Lockplate from musket dated *1810*, lockmaker's initials, *C. B.* Locks show several of the many types of Eagles used.

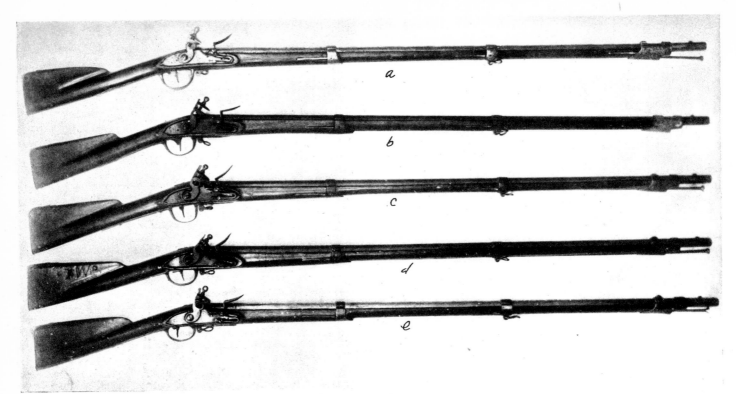

Fig. 1 — POST-REVOLUTIONARY MUSKETS MADE FOR THE STATE OF PENNSYLVANIA
The first four, of American make, are marked with the often misinterpreted initials C P. *a*, by Henry; *b*, by Lether & Co.; *c*, by Miles; *d*, by Evans; *e*, contemporary arm marked U S

Continental Property versus Commonwealth of Pennsylvania

By CHARLES D. COOK *and* HOWARD M. CHAPIN

MUSKETS marked C P are highly prized by collectors as assured souvenirs of the American Revolution. The initials C P have been accepted as standing for *Continental Property*, and pieces so marked have accordingly been identified as belonging to the equipment of the American troops who participated in the conflict between England and the Colonies. Indeed, this engaging belief was shared by one of the writers of this article at the time when Mr. Sawyer, in his valuable book *Firearms in American History* (*p. 121*), added the weight of his own authority. Mr. Sawyer's statement has been repeated by subsequent writers; and one reason for the present pertinence of these notes is the fact that a recent catalogue of guns definitely asserts that the muskets marked C P were Continental property carried by American soldiers during the Revolution.

Just when or why we became suspicious of the current interpretation of the initials C P we need not here explain. It is sufficient that we began a scientific investigation of the whole question and that our search led us eventually to the archives of the State of Pennsylvania at Harrisburg.

Here were found the *Articles of Agreement* made and signed November 15, 1797 between Thomas Mifflin, Governor of the Commonwealth of Pennsylvania, in behalf of the said Commonwealth, of the one part; and Thomas Ketland and John Ketland of the City of Philadelphia in the said Commonwealth, Merchants, of the other part. According to this contract the two Ketlands agree to supply the Commonwealth of Pennsylvania with "ten thousand stands of arms . . . of the fashion or pattern of the French Charleville Musquet . . . and to be stamped or marked near the breech with the letters C P."

From this important document it is evident that the initials C P stand for the words *Commonwealth of Pennsylvania* and were placed on muskets made during, or subsequent to, the year 1797. The inevitable corollary is that muskets thus marked cannot have been used in the American Revolution. The Ketlands were to receive $10.25 per stand for these arms, which furthermore were to be made in England. To this end Thomas Mifflin, Governor of Pennsylvania, agreed to "procure letters from the Executive of the United States to their minister in London to obtain permission from the Court of London for the shipment of the said ten thousand stands of arms and will cause the permission for that purpose to be delivered to the agent of the said Thomas Ketland and John Ketland."

The specifications for the muskets as given in the contract will be of interest to collectors:

. . . the length of each barrel to be three feet eight inches, and to receive a ball of the size of eighteen to the pound; each barrel to undergo the same degree of proof as is now in use for the proof on those made for the service of the United States, and to be stamped or marked near the breech with the letters C P; the locks to be upon the best construction, double bridled on a flat plate and marked with the letters aforesaid; the mounting Iron with the bands and swivels and spring to each band; the ramrods to be of well tempered steel, the bayonets to be fifteen inches in the blade made of steel well tempered and polished, the stocks to be made of well seasoned walnut, the length of the butt of the musket to be fifteen and a half inches from the breech end of the barrel to the heel plate; the side pins, the breech pins and trigger to be case hardened; the weight of the musquet and bayonet thus compleated not to exceed eleven pounds.

The agreement itself was the outcome of an act of the General Assembly of Pennsylvania, passed March 8, 1797, and advertised in the *Independent Gazetteer* and other Pennsylvania newspapers in April and June. The announcement calls for twenty thousand stands of arms, and states that the muskets are to be "marked near the breech with the letters U S."

The other ten thousand stands were apparently to be supplied in

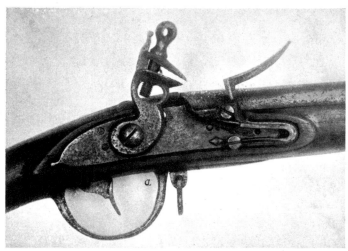

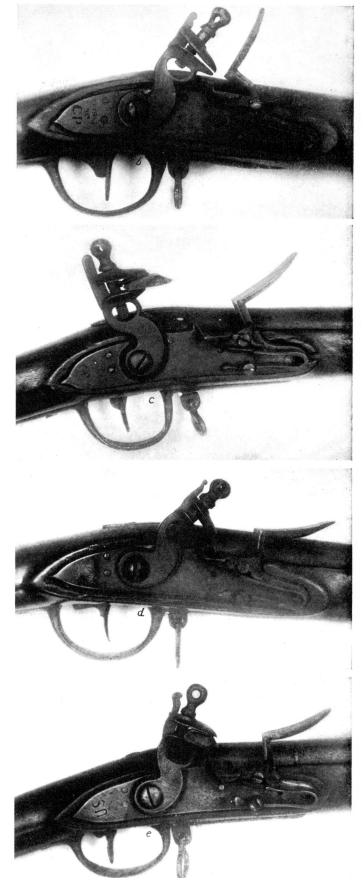

Fig. 2 — Post-Revolutionary Musket Locks

Details of the arms shown in Figure I. *a*, by Henry; *b*, by Lether & Co.; *c*, by Miles; *d*, by Evans; *e*, contemporary lock marked U S

smaller lots by American firms — a theory sustained by the fact that many of the muskets marked C P bear also the name of some American gunsmith. Four of the C P muskets in the Cook collection are native products. One of the locks was made by Miles, another by Evans, a third by Henry, and a fourth by Lether & Company.

Thomas Miles was a Pennsylvania riflemaker, Stephen Evans established the Mount Joy Forge at Valley Forge in 1742, while William Henry, Senior, was a riflemaker at Lancaster, Philadelphia, and Nazareth, Pennsylvania. Born in 1729, Henry, at the age of sixteen, was apprenticed to Peter Roeser of Lancaster, Pennsylvania. He began to manufacture on his own account in 1750, served as armorer in Braddock's ill-fated expedition, and is described by Sawyer as the "most celebrated gunmaker of his time." He employed fourteen men at Lancaster, and later, in 1808, his son William became government contractor.

The barrels of three of the muskets described above are proof-marked with the letter P beneath a liberty cap. It will be remembered that, on October 27, 1775, Robert Towers was directed henceforth to stamp the mark P on all Philadelphia-made muskets that he proved for the Continental service. On the Miles, Lether, and Evans locks the C P occurs in the rear of the hammer; but on the Henry lock it is stamped under the pan. The Henry lock is also marked with an inverted fleur-de-lis, probably a proof mark, and the barrel carries two proof marks. The barrel of the Miles gun is stamped *47* and *Co 14* with *Pa* below.

This Pennsylvania gun contract of 1797 sheds fresh light on the affairs of the famous business house of Ketland. John and Thomas Ketland are described in the document as *merchants and residents of Philadelphia*, although heretofore they have always been considered as an English firm of gun merchants or gunsmiths. Pollard lists them as gunsmiths at Birmingham, England:

Ketland merchants 1740–1832
T Ketland 1750–1829
Ketland and Walker 1750–1829

Some collectors have even gone so far as to insist that the Ketlands were merely jobbers and merchants, and that they never made arms, but merely assembled them, or even bought them outright from others. It is said that Francis Bruel of Philadelphia, while in England, tried to locate one of their factories, but, being unsuccessful, concluded that the elusive pair contracted for parts, and either sold them or had them assembled into the finished arm. There is, in the Cook collection, a sporting arm with curly maple stock, whose lock is marked *Ketland & Ci.*, while, stamped in the rear of the hammer, appear the words *United States*.

Of course the C P muskets are not exact replicas of the French Charleville of 1763. They merely follow the general style of those arms, with such modifications as were caused by the contract specifications, the whims of different makers, or other exigencies of manufacture.

THE 1814 UNITED STATES CONTRACT RIFLE

By JAMES L. MITCHELL

EVERY SO OFTEN A FLINTLOCK RIFLE that differs from all identified models turns up to baffle collectors of firearms. Such a weapon was the subject of a query published in *Arms Collector* for June 1938. The writer, a well-known Pennsylvania dealer in firearms, said that he had recently acquired a most interesting variant of the Model 1817 United States military rifle, but that it differed from that model in so many respects that he was seeking information about it. He said that even a leading authority on United States shoulder arms, of whom he had made inquiry, was unable to shed any light on its identity.

Now the mystery has been cleared up. The rifle in question is not a variant of the 1817 Model common rifle; quite the opposite is nearer the truth. This rifle is the Model 1814 contract rifle made, to the best of my knowledge, by two contractors only, H. Deringer of Philadelphia and Robert Johnson of Middletown, Connecticut. With its identification we add another United States model to those already known.

We have, hitherto, accepted the second series Harper's Ferry rifle as the Model 1814. Harper's Ferry started making rifles in 1803 and continued the manufacture through 1807, making only 146 that year. Production was resumed in 1814 when 1,600 rifles were made, continuing through 1820. With only minor variations the same rifle was made during this entire period. The greatest deviation was that the first-series rifles had 33-inch barrels, while the second-series barrels were 36 inches in length, with the exception of the 1814 production when most of the barrels were 33 inches.

Late in 1812 Callender Irvine, Commissary General of Purchases, advised the Secretary of War that it would be necessary to enter into new contracts for arms at once as many of the existing contracts would expire uncompleted by November 1813. Early in 1813 the Secretary of War stated that $500,000 remained unexpended out of the appropriation for arming the militia, and ordered Irvine to enter into contracts with individual contractors for arms. Rifles, considered necessary for guarding the Northern frontiers, were found to be lacking as they had all been issued. Irvine, losing no time, directed Marine T. Wickham "to set his inventive faculties to work" on a rifle for issue to riflemen for use against cavalry, as well as to mounted riflemen. Obviously the Harper's Ferry rifle with its half stock, key fastened, was not adapted to such service. By July 1813 Wickham's rifle was submitted to General John Armstrong, Secretary of War.

Designed with a full stock and bands like a musket, this rifle, according to Irvine, would throw a ball every shot into a flat crown at a distance of 200 yards, was equipped with a saber bayonet. Later, when production was being arranged for, it was decided to dispense with the bayonet. However, there is in my collection a Johnson rifle of this model complete with the usual musket type of triangular bayonet. Marine T. Wickham, it should be observed in passing, was apparently one of the few Government Inspectors who remained in favor throughout his term of service. The office of Government Inspector was held by John Nicholson, a Revolutionary gunsmith, until he died in 1806. Thereafter, other appointees followed one another in rapid succession, replaced usually for failure to give satisfaction. Many of the woes of the Purveyor of Public Supplies, to whom these inspectors reported, were recounted to William Eustis, then Secretary of War, by Tench Coxe; he recommended that an individual be hired from one of the Armories to act as inspector. This was obviously good judgment, and James Stubblefield, superintendent of Harper's Ferry, was approached on the subject. The result was that Marine T. Wickham, Chief Armorer, was appointed Inspector early in 1811, and in February 1812 was installed in charge of the Armory on the Schuylkill. From here he supervised the making of many pattern rifles, muskets, and pistols, which were used by national armories and contractors alike to guide their production. One of Wickham's devices which is evident on many of these models is the stud retainer for the barrel bands, and this type of retainer was used on the 1811, 1813, and 1816 pistols made by North, on one model of 1812 Springfield musket, and on this rifle.

Late in 1813 Irvine asked for the return of the rifle from Secretary of War Armstrong, with the observation that it equalled in all respects those made at Harper's Ferry and could be made at less expense. January 19, 1814, Irvine wrote Wickham that the Government intended to raise three additional regiments of riflemen and rifles must be obtained with the least possible delay. He instructed him at the same time to make one or two more rifles corresponding to the one in his possession, as he intended to send one East and the other to Virginia to found contracts upon. Obviously these two locations did not mean Springfield or Harper's Ferry, as contract arms were not produced by these establishments. Undoubtedly he had in mind one or more of the many contractors in New England, and the Virginia Armory.

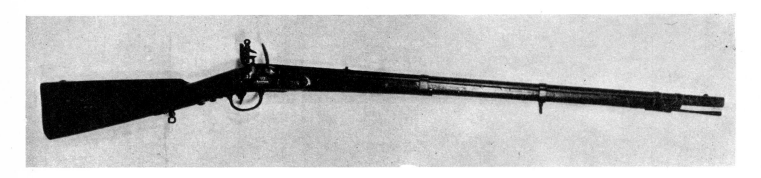

FIG. 1 — MODEL 1814 CONTRACT RIFLE OF JOHNSON'S MANUFACTURE. Lock marked *US/R.* Johnson. Barrel length 33 5/16 inches; marked on top flat at breech, *J. D. Johnson* and *Middletown*; marked on left flat at breech *P* and *Conn.* Has stud band retainers and finger grips in rear of trigger guard; oval iron patchbox in stock which was carried over to Model 1817 Common Rifle. Equipped with brass head, steel ramrod.

One pattern rifle was sent to Governor James Barbour of Virginia in February 1814, with the expectation that a contract could be made with the State Armory, as Irvine said "at $14.00 or at most $15.00 each" complete with bullet screw, screw driver, and wiper. Probably this price was not sufficiently attractive to result in a contract; to the best of my knowledge no rifles of this model were ever made in Virginia.

Another rifle, without doubt, went to Deringer of Philadelphia as a model, because a contract was made with him on March 17, 1814, for 2,000 rifles at $17.00 each. Trouble developed with Deringer in the fulfillment of this contract. In November of 1814 Irvine threatened his Sureties with action because, while Deringer's schedule up to that time called for 980 rifles, only 51 had been delivered.

In the meantime Irvine had written to Perkin, Inspector of Arms for the New England district, to forward a list of contractors whose arms he had inspected, and who in his opinion would be interested in furnishing arms to the Government. Acting on the information received, he wrote November 11, 1814, to Robert Johnson of Middletown, Connecticut, saying that he was prepared to enter into contracts for arms and offering a pattern rifle to be sent to Middletown in care of Perkin or to be held in Philadelphia for personal delivery to Johnson. On January 4, 1815, Irvine advised Wickham that he had a prospect of getting some rifles made and wanted another pattern rifle, asking whether one of Deringer's manufacture already in production, would not answer the purpose. That the reply was affirmative is indicated by the fact that late in January Irvine called upon Wickham to "hurry Deringer with the pattern rifle as it is much needed at Middletown."

This pattern rifle, which is now in my collection, Johnson used as a pattern for the manufacture of his rifles under a contract dated November 23, 1814, for 2,000 rifles at $17.00. It was not regular production, however, as indicated by markings.

When Irvine instructed Wickham to make the pattern, he told him he could use any rifle or parts of rifles in stock. That he used Model 1803 Harper's Ferry barrels is apparent. The barrel of the pattern rifle just mentioned coincides with the Harper's Ferry barrel in all dimensions, in shape, position, and type of front sight. In all examples of the 1814 model the barrels are half octagonal and half round, as in the Harper's Ferry model. The full-length stock and barrel bands were originally intended to give added support for a bayonet.

Johnson's factory was located on Lower Pameacha Creek in Middletown, Connecticut. According to existing records, he had only twenty-five to thirty hands working in the factory, and their production was limited to about a thousand rifles a year. We do not know how many rifles were eventually made and delivered by either Deringer or Johnson, and it is probable that neither contract was completed. This possibility, and the fact that the contracted number was only 4,000, makes this model a rarity among the United States rifles.

Fig. 2 — Model 1814 Pattern Rifle (*right side*). Made by Marine T. Wickham and sent to Robert Johnson of Middletown, Connecticut, to follow in manufacture. Complete with oval patchbox, brass-head ramrod, and stud retainers, and finger grips. Specifications as given for Johnson rifle apply to this pattern, except for markings. Stock bears the initials of Deringer's inspector, *G. F.*, and also Wickham's initials, *M. T. W.*, under a *V*. Lock is engraved *M. T. W.* in script under *U. S.* On left flat of breech of barrel (*Fig. 3*) appear the word *Pattern*, the initials *M. T. W.* again, as well as *P* and *U. S.*

The illustrations are from the collection of the author.

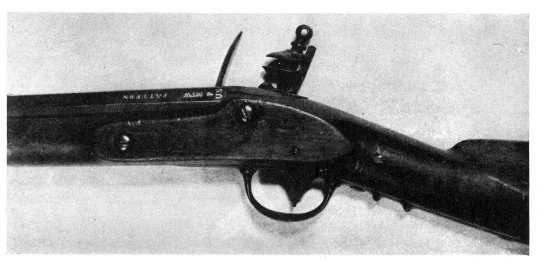

Fig. 3 — Model 1814 Pattern Rifle (*left side*). This shows all of the markings on the left barrel flat.

Our Martial Pistols

By CHARLES WINTHROP SAWYER

Illustrations by the Author

UNCLE SAM first began to manufacture pistols in his own armories about five score years ago. That goes back to the beginning of the nineteenth century; and for the purposes of this article that period offers an excellent starting place. Between those early pistols and our present ones there are points of similarity, strange as it may seem; just as there are certain points in common between political conditions then and now. So, today, the subject of our martial pistols is an apt one. Let us, then, go at it thoroughly, and inspect the whole lot of our martial pistols from first to last, because we can learn something even from the antique ones. The inventor and the ordnance officer may yet obtain good from them, and the civilian will obtain even more.

First we shall attempt to view our antique pistols educationally: next to classify all our martial pistols into three groups — the pistol-clubs, the obsolete repeaters, and the modern repeaters. Through inspection, both individually and in groups, the out-of-date arms will yield us considerable of value. Then, having considered the past and the present, we may anticipate the future.

Antique arms have certain sentimental or spiritual attributes by reason of their age, and their romantic adventures through association with picturesque people and events of by-gone days. It is good for us to yield to their enchantment, to let them stimulate our dormant poetic tendencies and allow them to create for us clean mental pictures. Moreover, to know antique arms well, we must know also the men and manners and machinery contemporary with them. They are, therefore, in a mild and easy fashion, educational stimulators.

Besides these gentle attributes, ancient arms have hard and practical values hidden until displayed by an expert. Consider, for instance, their testimony against minor historical lies and for forgotten arts. As to the former, the old arms stand for fact and truth, gainsaying the anachronisms of modern illustrators, costumers, sculptors, novelists, and historians *ad infinitum*. Anachronisms are lies and—though unintentional—are little less misleading and harmful. Consider these instances:—

Historically viewed, it is unfortunate that an admired, celebrated, and much visited statue of a Minute Man is provided with a kind of gun not in existence in 1775. The public, if discovering this error, might justly challenge also the Minute Man, for, if the gun is wrong, why is the

man right; and, if both are wrong, what good is the statue? In a widely read historical novel the apparent purpose of which is to portray vividly and accurately the period of the Forty Niners, one of the characters "quickly drew his long blue Smith and Wesson." We are not edified, but are pained by the fact that he was too quick by many years.

An eminent historian has reduced the worth of his dissertation upon the War of 1812 by equipping an American Army Officer with a "heavy Colt." This absurdity shakes one's faith in the whole story. The same authority calls the battle of New Orleans an artillery battle. These two bits of information, as important in their place as any others in the whole book, would make anybody question history. When we inspect modern pictures for their educational value, we find anachronisms too numerous to count. As a single instance of many kinds of such errors, look at the Thanksgiving numbers of our leading periodicals displaying elaborate cover pictures of the Pilgrim Fathers turkey hunting with Model 1836 U. S. army pistols, Eureka Air Guns, and Merwin & Hulbert revolvers.

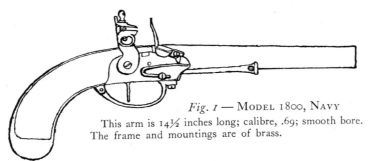

Fig. 1 — MODEL 1800, NAVY

This arm is 14½ inches long; calibre, .69; smooth bore. The frame and mountings are of brass.

Antique arms bear positive as well as negative testimony. They are, in themselves, evidence of forgotten arts. To these specimens of our ancestors' inventive power and handicraft the arms engineer refers for mechanical secrets and for chemical effects long ago forgotten but now again valuable. The average man believes that we know all that our ancestors knew and more. The arms engineer, however, finds that the armorers of old knew and practiced, not only all the fundamentals of quantity production and interchangeability, but also used a vast deal of valuable technical method, which has since been lost. Many an arms manufacturer of the present day, here and abroad, unable to meet increased cost and reduced sales, has been saved from failure and set again on a firm business base by an arms engineer who knew old arms as well as modern ones, old-time short cuts, and the twists of the trade, by which the old-time arms makers saved themselves when in similar precarious situation.

In the matter of lost details, take coloration of metal as an instance. The average blue-black finish of modern pistols is obtained with heat and charcoal. The process is comparatively expensive. But we know that nearly a century ago the official United States pistol maker, Simeon North, obtained a similar color on parts of some of the pistols he made. We know prices then and now, and realize that his method must have been an inexpensive one. So we apply

Fig. 2 — MODEL 1804, ARMY

Marked *Harpers Ferry, 1806.*
Length, 15¾ inches. The 10-inch octagonal barrel is rifled, and is calibre .54; to carry a half ounce ball. A few were made each year during 1804 to 1806, and were issued to non-coms of rifle companies. This is the earliest rifled military pistol issued by any government as a regulation arm. In essentials of design this model corresponds with our contemporary rifle, the Model 1800 rifle, and is of the same calibre, to carry the same size of ball. The iron ramrod has a brass end, cupped to fit the ball. A greased patch was used: and, with a small powder charge, — say 15 grains — in the hands of such expert marksmen as were the officers of our ancient rifle regiments, the pistol insured considerable accuracy within 50 yards. Unfortunately, the accumulation of powder residue put it out of commission after a few shots. Accordingly after 1806, during the flint period, our government issued smooth bores.

to one of Mr. North's pieces of colored metal our smattering of chemistry, metallurgy and microscopy, and find that the result he secured was produced quickly with a single inexpensive chemical. Adopted again, time and money are saved. Illustrations might be multiplied indefinitely. While information of this sort cannot be obtained from antique arms m e r e l y by reading about them, nevertheless a good deal of interest and value may be gained by the reader from text and picture, particularly where various arms are classified into groups, which will be the method employed in these discussions.

GROUP I

Group I includes all of the flint-lock period and the first of the cap-lock period. The arms which compose it are associated because they are a fighting unit. They are all *pistol-clubs*; designed as such; built as such; and, excepting the Model 1804 pistol, much more valuable as clubs than as pistols. They are all close-combat arms. As pistols they are more deadly at close range than modern ones. On the other hand, beyond arm's length they are, as pistols, of little use. They are all muzzle-loaders and single shooters. They were issued in pairs, permitting two shots in the beginning, or one shot held in reserve.

Excepting Model 1804, the pistols of this group are smooth bores of large caliber. Nominally the charge was about 30 grains of powder with a spherical bullet nearly the size of the bore. Such a charge was the actual one only when it was issued as fixed ammunition; — that is, powder and bullet

wrapped together into a paper-covered packet. Service ammunition was more commonly issued loose, in the form of a half pound of powder in a flask or horn and a lot of loose balls and buckshot. When the soldier had lost, or fired, all his lead he pulled off his buttons and fired them, — or fired pebbles or dirt. On shipboard, pistol ammunition was frequently made from broken glass and crockery, rusty nails, or bits of brass and copper; these would otherwise have been wastage from the cook's galley and the carpenters' and gunners' quarters.

Group I furnishes the following data for consideration:

1. Early sea-service arms were, to the utmost extent possible, built of brass or bronze to avoid rust and economize time spent upon keeping them in order.

2. Until the middle of the nineteenth century the spherical bullet of large caliber was preferred for close-combat arms to the pointed bullet. It had maximum shocking power.

3. During the spherical bullet period, the smooth-bore pistol had preference over the one of rifled bore. Warfare conditions entailed then a maximum of hand-to-hand fighting, in which the smooth-bore pistol and the spherical bullet gave best results. Correct for today. And how about ball-and-buck, and miniature shrapnel, also for today?

4. Antique American military pistols had loaded and metal-capped butts and a total length ample to give power as a club. Empty, the pistol was still a very formidable weapon. Our modern pistols, empty, are insignificant.

5. Simplicity, cost, speed of manufacture. In Group I the number of separate parts to a pistol averages 32. A Colt .45 automatic has about twice as many parts. Simplicity is as desirable now as then. The loss of an old-time pistol cost the government about one-third as much as that of a modern one, and three new ones to replace it were made in the time now required to make one modern piece.

Within Group I there is a stride from flint-lock to cap-

Fig. 3 — MODEL 1806, ARMY, NAVY

Marked *Harpers Ferry, 1806.* Length, 16¼ inches; calibre .54; smooth bore, taking a half ounce ball. This type was issued to any branch of the service. Like the model 1804, this pistol had certain details of external design conforming to those of the Model 1800 rifle.

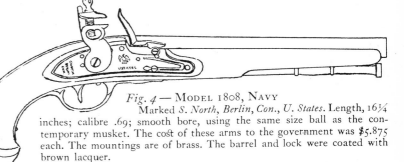

Fig. 4 — MODEL 1808, NAVY

Marked *S. North, Berlin, Con., U. States.* Length, 16¼ inches; calibre .69; smooth bore, using the same size ball as the contemporary musket. The cost of these arms to the government was $5.875 each. The mountings are of brass. The barrel and lock were coated with brown lacquer.

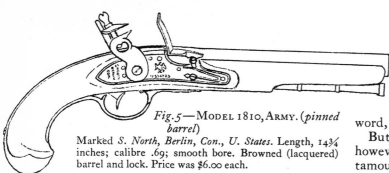

Fig.5—MODEL 1810, ARMY. (*pinned barrel*)
Marked *S. North, Berlin, Con., U. States.* Length, 14¾ inches; calibre .69; smooth bore. Browned (lacquered) barrel and lock. Price was $6.00 each.

lock. Our last flint military pistol was the Model 1836. It terminated a stagnation period which was not of nineteenth century duration merely, but went back several hundred years to the beginning of firearms. The stagnation was due to the inability of inventors to find a means of producing explosion with certainty under the handicaps of wind and rain. The copper cap overcame this defect. It is interesting, and possibly of value, to observe that the inventor of the percussion system did not have this end in view, and that the system, as he designed it, was imperfect in this respect. The system felt its way along, was advanced by successive inventors, and culminated successfully as the result of the application of many bright minds. Our next military pistol which will be radically different from our present ones, will also require the application of many minds during a series of years before it will achieve full power.

The development of the United States pistol from 1800 to 1843 is shown in the illustrations of pistols and the technical discussion accompanying them.

It is, perhaps, worth observing that conditions today, in

the beginning years of the twentieth century, are not so very different from conditions in the beginning of the preceding century, when the United States began to manufacture its own weapons. "Disarmament" is not a newly invented word. Five score years ago it was on many tongues. Recent experience has led us to substitute another word, "reduction," which is safer.

But the arms engineer feels strongly that "reduction" however desirable, shall not be allowed to become tantamount to stagnation. For a long time the development of the modern automatic pistol has been virtually at a standstill; from a military standpoint further improvements in the existing weapon are likely to prove valueless. The first step in a genuine advance will probably be in the complete discarding of the pistol of today, and the designing of one in terms of the new conditions which modern warfare has imposed.

There have in the past occurred similar periods of stagnation, each followed by a swift leap forward. Foreign governments are working night and day to discover the probable landing place of the next leap, and are employing their ablest scientists to make it both sure and long. They are probably discovering that what the present-day pistol has gained in certain aspects of speed and precision, it has lost in the direction of general availibility at close quarters. It has lost in other respects. This, however, is not a dissertation on the proprieties of future army pistols, but on the development of the pistols now in use. The complete series of these articles should make this fairly clear.

How old points of excellence are often lost in gaining new points of excellence, should likewise become apparent.

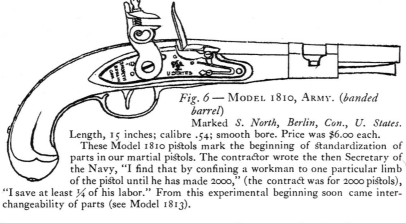

Fig. 6 — MODEL 1810, ARMY. (*banded barrel*)
Marked *S. North, Berlin, Con., U. States.* Length, 15 inches; calibre .54; smooth bore. Price was $6.00 each.
These Model 1810 pistols mark the beginning of standardization of parts in our martial pistols. The contractor wrote the then Secretary of the Navy, "I find that by confining a workman to one particular limb of the pistol until he has made 2000," (the contract was for 2000 pistols), "I save at least ¼ of his labor." From this experimental beginning soon came interchangeability of parts (see Model 1813).

Fig. 7 — MODEL 1813, ARMY
Made by North. Those first made were marked with the old stamp. Those made after 1813–14 bore the new address of the factory, *Middletown, Conn.* Length, 15¼ inches; calibre of those first made .69: of the later ones .54.
In the contract the weight was specified as not to exceed 3½ pounds. The contract was for 20,000. The price was $7.00 each, including a stated number of spare parts, and also bullet screws and screwdrivers.
The contract also specified that "the component parts of pistols are to correspond so exactly, that any limb or part of one pistol may be fitted to any other pistol of the twenty thousand." This contract marked the beginning of a revolution in the manufacture of our military arms.

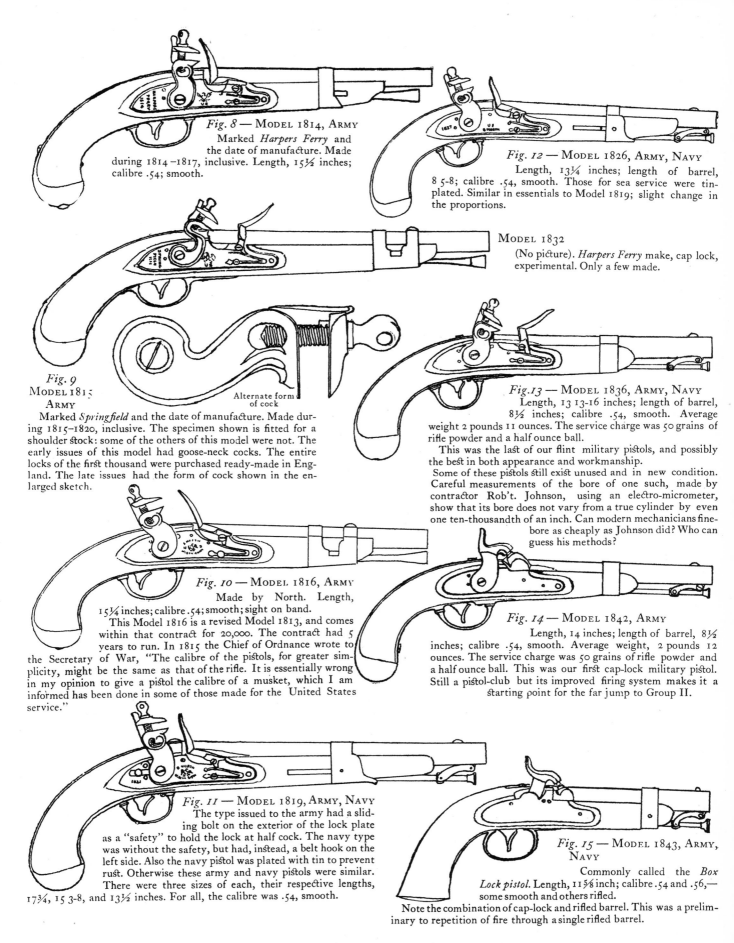

Fig. 8 — MODEL 1814, ARMY

Marked *Harpers Ferry* and the date of manufacture. Made during 1814–1817, inclusive. Length, 15½ inches; calibre .54; smooth.

Fig. 9
MODEL 1815
ARMY

Alternate form of cock

Marked *Springfield* and the date of manufacture. Made during 1815–1820, inclusive. The specimen shown is fitted for a shoulder stock: some of the others of this model were not. The early issues of this model had goose-neck cocks. The entire locks of the first thousand were purchased ready-made in England. The late issues had the form of cock shown in the enlarged sketch.

Fig. 10 — MODEL 1816, ARMY

Made by North. Length, 15¼ inches; calibre .54; smooth; sight on band.

This Model 1816 is a revised Model 1813, and comes within that contract for 20,000. The contract had 5 years to run. In 1815 the Chief of Ordnance wrote to the Secretary of War, "The calibre of the pistols, for greater simplicity, might be the same as that of the rifle. It is essentially wrong in my opinion to give a pistol the calibre of a musket, which I am informed has been done in some of those made for the United States service."

Fig. 11 — MODEL 1819, ARMY, NAVY

The type issued to the army had a sliding bolt on the exterior of the lock plate as a "safety" to hold the lock at half cock. The navy type was without the safety, but had, instead, a belt hook on the left side. Also the navy pistol was plated with tin to prevent rust. Otherwise these army and navy pistols were similar. There were three sizes of each, their respective lengths, 17¾, 15 3-8, and 13½ inches. For all, the calibre was .54, smooth.

Fig. 12 — MODEL 1826, ARMY, NAVY

Length, 13¼ inches; length of barrel, 8 5-8; calibre .54, smooth. Those for sea service were tinplated. Similar in essentials to Model 1819; slight change in the proportions.

MODEL 1832

(No picture). *Harpers Ferry* make, cap lock, experimental. Only a few made.

Fig. 13 — MODEL 1836, ARMY, NAVY

Length, 13 13-16 inches; length of barrel, 8½ inches; calibre .54, smooth. Average weight 2 pounds 11 ounces. The service charge was 50 grains of rifle powder and a half ounce ball.

This was the last of our flint military pistols, and possibly the best in both appearance and workmanship.

Some of these pistols still exist unused and in new condition. Careful measurements of the bore of one such, made by contractor Rob't. Johnson, using an electro-micrometer, show that its bore does not vary from a true cylinder by even one ten-thousandth of an inch. Can modern mechanicians fine-bore as cheaply as Johnson did? Who can guess his methods?

Fig. 14 — MODEL 1842, ARMY

Length, 14 inches; length of barrel, 8½ inches; calibre .54, smooth. Average weight, 2 pounds 12 ounces. The service charge was 50 grains of rifle powder and a half ounce ball. This was our first cap-lock military pistol. Still a pistol-club but its improved firing system makes it a starting point for the far jump to Group II.

Fig. 15 — MODEL 1843, ARMY, NAVY

Commonly called the *Box Lock pistol*. Length, 11⅝ inch; calibre .54 and .56,—some smooth and others rifled.

Note the combination of cap-lock and rifled barrel. This was a preliminary to repetition of fire through a single rifled barrel.

III The Work of Regional Gunsmiths

As the need for firearms increased in North America, a new craft began to develop in the colonies to supplement the supply of imported arms and to repair older weapons that had been broken or needed renovation. Because Lancaster County, Pennsylvania, was the frontier to the West early in the 18th century, German gunsmiths settled there and catered to the trade heading into the wilderness. Other frontier communities surrounding the Lancaster area began to develop their own gunsmithing industries, and, as the westward expansion began to grow, the gunsmiths in Pennsylvania flourished. Soon regional characteristics appeared on weapons as the European-trained craftsmen began to express their own creativity, producing rifles that were soon to become the envy of the world.

The early Pennsylvania rifle—frequently called the Kentucky rifle since the popular mind conceived of all the frontier west of Pennsylvania as "Kentucky"—was immensely successful. Its fame spread to other areas of Pennsylvania, and eventually to Maryland, Virginia, and North Carolina later in the 18th century. By the beginning of the 19th, versions of the Pennsylvania rifle had reached England, New England, New York, Tennessee and Ohio. According to the late Joe Kindig, Jr., the finest examples of the Pennsylvania rifle were made between the end of the Revolution in 1783 and the year 1815, the period that he terms "the golden age of the Kentucky rifle."

Some of the best golden-age Pennsylvania rifles rival in craftsmanship the finest quality furniture and silver of the same period. Collectors of the Pennsylvania/Kentucky rifle attempt to acquire examples from this period, often seeking the work of individual makers and counties whose unique characteristics appeal to them. Many collectors seek the earlier rifles which, though not as sophisticated, may offer greater historical association. Others may look for regional characteristics which require acquisitions that quite possibly date later than the golden age, but are compensated for by the unique qualities of a particular area. Many Virginia and North Carolina rifles, for example, are equal to the best Pennsylvania specimens and are eagerly sought by collectors.

Fine examples from Maryland, New York, Ohio, Tennessee, and New England were also produced, but usually date from the 19th century. During the first quarter of the 19th century, Maryland gunsmiths produced some superb rifles which are highly prized by the collectors who specialize in this field.

As a rule, New York rifles date from the second quarter of the 19th century and have not received the same recognition that the earlier Hudson Valley (New York) fowling pieces have achieved. Many of these Hudson Valley fowlers date from early in the 18th century and are usually stocked in curly maple, extending at times over six feet in length and possessing massive butt stocks. Often ornately carved, many of these fowlers are made up from parts of Dutch muskets that were brought to America by early New York Dutch settlers. These fowling pieces are always associated with the Hudson Valley Dutch settlers, and their early period, extreme length, and dramatic architecture have made them highly desirable to collectors.

Tennessee rifles are usually well made. Long, full stocked with slender lines, they are void of profuse decoration, while Ohio rifles are normally highly ornate with large numbers of silver inlays. Both are being studied and collected by an increasing number of students of regional firearms.

Rifles made in New England can date from the 18th century, but most of them were produced in the first half of the 19th. Worcester County, Massachusetts, was the most productive area, and the cherry-stocked rifles, with delicate silver wire decoration and horse-head patch boxes, are becoming increasingly popular with collectors. During the last quarter of the 18th century, Worcester County gunsmiths also produced long and slender fowling pieces that have always been prized. At an earlier date Massachusetts gunsmiths produced heavy club-butt fowling pieces that resemble those from the Hudson Valley. These have always been highly regarded and are quite rare. Other New England areas, such as Goshen, Connecticut, produced exceptional early fowling pieces and muskets during the last half of the 18th century, but examples of this work, although highly thought of, are quite scarce today.

As the United States expanded westward, so did the many craftsmen needed to support the settlers. Gunsmithing moved further west to the Great Plains, where a new style of rifle was required. A half stock version of the Kentucky rifle became exceedingly popular because it could easily be carried on horseback. It featured a large bore, and a short, heavy barrel, so that it could efficiently kill the plains buffalo or the grizzly bear. St. Louis is thought of as the primary center of production for these rifles, which were popular throughout the second quarter of the 19th century.

CHARLESTON GUNSMITHS

By BEATRICE ST. J. RAVENEL

THIS ATTEMPT at a check list of the gunsmiths who worked in Charleston, South Carolina, before 1861 has been arranged alphabetically and by centuries. It is to be hoped that the growing regard for American-made weapons may cause more of their work to be identified. Besides the gunsmiths, many merchants sold firearms, for large quantities were imported, but their names have not been included. The following data have been gleaned from contemporary documents — directories, wills, inventories, newspapers, and other records. I gratefully acknowledge the assistance of Emma B. Richardson of the staff of the Charleston Museum.

SEVENTEENTH CENTURY

Anthony Boureau, a French Huguenot, came to Carolina in 1686. He was listed as a gunsmith, March 10, 1696/7, when he was "made free of this part of this Province," *i.e.,* naturalized.

John Jones or Johns (died October 1699) was in Carolina as early as April 16, 1694, on which date he helped to appraise the estate of Nicholas Townsend. In Townsend's inventory, as well as in his own will Jones made his mark. September 26, 1699, one John Alexander left the ministry of the Presbyterian Church at Charles Town fifty pounds, to be "at yᵉ Discretion & Managemᵗ. of John Jones gunsmith & robert ffenwick." October 8, 1699, Johns (the form in which the name was then written) "late of the City of London," made a codicil to a will which he had left in England and appointed two executors resident in Carolina, who were instructed to send the residue of his estate to England to be divided between his wife, Frances, and his partner, John Hawkins, gunsmith. Johns was dead by October 10. No record has been found to show that Hawkins was ever in Carolina.

Augustus Mesmin, like Boureau, was among the French Protestants "made free of this part of this Province," March 10, 1696/7.

Nicholas Townsend (died 1693 or 1694) termed himself "locksmith" in his will, made July 20, 1693, and recorded April 6, 1694. By this, he may have meant *lock-filer*, but it is likely that he combined more than one trade, as was the case with several later gunsmiths. The inventory of his estate shows "1 rench for guns," "old Gun Locks & 2 gun barrells," and "5 guns at 5ˢ. each," as well as a variety of tools and metals. The total amounted to only £90/15/10¼. Books, inkhorn, and "Speckteckles'" go to show that, unlike Jones, he was literate.

EIGHTEENTH CENTURY

John Ballantine was mentioned in the will of his father, Patrick, made September 15, 1720. He was working in 1725.

Patrick Ballantine (died 1720) was a householder.

Buchannon was working in 1796.

David Burger (died September 24, 1804) was a native of New York, who lived in Charleston about thirty years before his death; "during that time he supported the character of an honest, industrious man." (*Times*, of Charleston, September 27, 1804).

Hugh Crawford was working in 1776, when he advertised for two "Queen Anne's flat muskets," missing from his shop.

Pierre François Des Verneys (died 1799 or 1800) was a Frenchman. The 1790 directory listed him as "Devernay Peter F."

John Dodd (died 1770) was working as early as 1764. Jeremiah Theus, the portrait painter, was among the witnesses to his will.

Gideon Faucheraud was termed gunsmith when buying land in 1708. Other documents called him planter.

Thomas Floyd, clockmaker and gunsmith, came from England by 1767.

Daniel Henderson came from London by 1798. He was a gunsmith, bell-hanger, and maker of iron balconies. In 1804, he brought "from Philadelphia one of the first Gunsmiths in that state" as an assistant.

Anthony Jankofsky, "late of Surinam," advertised in 1777. He was also a locksmith and metal worker. He was present at a meeting of the German Friendly Society in 1783.

Benjamin Massey was dead by July 1736.

John Massey (died May 13, 1736) was a clockmaker, printer, and gunsmith. In 1716/7, he was appointed tutor and guardian of Benjamin Massey, then a minor.

Philip Massey (died 1739) was working "At the Sign of the cross Guns" by 1736. He left his estate to his wife, Jane (Hopkins) Massey, whom he had married on January 20, 1733. After his death, she advertised "all sorts of Blacksmith's Work" (ironwork), and with the aid of one James Lowry, smith, continued the business as late as 1741. It is uncertain how much she personally had to do with gunsmith's work, though she advertised in 1741 for persons whose guns were in her custody to take them away and pay the "charges of mending, which several have neglected."

John Milner (died 1749) was working by 1734. He bequeathed a "negro Fellow Prince, a Gunsmith," with other property, to his son John.

John Milner, son of the above, was paid by the province of South Carolina in 1758 for mending and cleaning the public arms and furnishing scabbards to the bayonets. He was listed in the 1790 directory.

Thomas Peacock was working in 1750.

J. L. Ransier was listed in the 1790 directory.

John Scott (buried March 27, 1759) from London, was working in 1740. The province bought goods from him in 1758 to give as presents to the Indians.

NINETEENTH CENTURY

Ralph Atmar Jr. (sometimes incorrectly written Atmore), goldsmith, engraver, and gunsmith, was working by 1800. He imported English gun parts.

Francis Beauchee, "black & gun-smith" was working in 1807.

Joseph Beaudrot was working by 1852.

Benjamin Bicaise was working by 1831.

P. Bicaise was working by 1849.

Edward Bowers was working by 1855.

John E. Bowers was working by 1837.

J. M. Breffeihl was working in 1831.

Colongin was listed in the directories of 1819 and 1822.

William Conner was working by 1852.

George Dogarthy served his apprenticeship under David Burger and went into business for himself in the spring of 1802. He was listed in the 1806 directory.

Augustus Dufort was working by 1855.

James Gowdy was working in 1801.

William Gunn (occasionally written Gun) was termed a blacksmith by the 1790 directory. That of 1801 and several subsequent directories called him gunsmith, as did his will, made June 3, 1811, and proved July 17, 1813.

Benjamin G. Happoldt was working by 1852.

J. H. Happoldt won the Silver Medal (first prize) for rifles at the South Carolina Institute Fair of 1852. Examples of his work are known.

John M. Happoldt served his apprenticeship under John Schirer. He was in business for himself as early as 1826. In the *Courier* of May 1, he assailed Francis D. Poyas concerning an improved method of crooking gun stocks. Happoldt was still at work in 1859.

Thomas Henon or Hennon was listed in the directories of 1807 and 1809.

John G. Hobrecker was working by 1806 and as late as 1816.

Hobrecker & Rho are listed in the 1807 directory.

John V. Holmes, in business by 1838, worked into the 1850's.

Samuel Ingles served his apprenticeship under John Schirer and was his foreman for "upwards of ten years." In 1832, he went into business at Georgetown, South Carolina.

C. McAllister was termed gunsmith in the *General Business Directory* of the 1855 directory.

Michael McNearney, termed "gun cleaner" by the 1855 directory, may have been a gunsmith.

John David Miller (dead by 1816) was primarily a gold and silversmith. Silverware and miniature cases made by him survive. He was working as a goldsmith as early as 1781 and as a gunsmith by 1806.

John Moison or Moisson was in business by 1813. John Moison, jun., who may have been the same man or his son was listed in the 1819 directory.

L. Moisson was listed in the 1831 directory.

George H. Moore appeared in the 1837/8 directory.

Joseph Mordecai was at work by 1809. His house burned in the fire of July 5, 1819.

John Mosian was listed in the 1852 directory.

James Nicholson (died September 20, 1836 at Abbeville, South Carolina), was termed gunsmith by the directory of 1809, at which time he and John Schirer had the same address, but he was probably not a craftsman, though he may have owned an interest in the business. Other records and directories show that Nicholson was an attorney at law who owned considerable property, including the beautiful house which is now Ashley Hall School.

Francis D. Poyas was in business by 1825 and worked into the 1830's. Dueling pistols made by him are in the Charleston Museum's collection.

James Poyas, Jr. was working in 1822.

Frederick Roessler was working by 1855.

John Schirer (died about 1827) was a native of eastern France, who was in Charleston by 1806. In 1819, while at work, he was severely shocked by lightning. In 1825, he advertised a method of crooking gun stocks by steam. His name is often incorrectly written Shirer.

Mary Charlotte Schirer was John's wife. After his death, she advertised in the *Courier* of March 27, 1828, that she would continue his trade, "at the old stand, and as extensive as before," with the aid of workmen. In the 1829 directory, her name is followed by "gunsmith shop."

A. Vocelle was working in 1852.

Argyle Williamson (died September, 1807) was a native of Richmond, Virginia.

William Wylie was working in 1806.

CONNECTICUT GUNSMITH

By J. R. MAYER, M.D.

MEDAD HILLS was born in the town of Durham, Connecticut, April 22, 1729. His father was Benoni, his grandfather Joseph, and his great-grandfather William. September 16, 1632, when the *Lyon* eighty-four days out of Bristol dropped anchor off Boston town, William Hills, erstwhile freeman of Roxbury, disembarked and became a colonist of New England.

Father Benoni was a toolmaker and gunsmith of Durham. In 1741, when Medad was a lad of twelve, he moved to Goshen and set himself up in business. It is quite likely that the son was apprenticed to the father. That he became a smith of competence is evidenced by the fine musket dated 1758 which he made and signed for Noah North (*Fig. 1*).

Benoni Hills had another apprentice, John Doud, who likewise made his mark as a skilled craftsman. John started working in the Goshen shop as a boy. Enterprising and ambitious, he soon mastered the art of gunsmithing and opened a new forge on the west side of East Street in partnership with Ebenezer Norton. The new shop had two rooms; in the west one Doud forged the locks and barrels; in the east room Norton stocked them. Lewis M. Norton is quoted in Hibbard's *History of Goshen* (Hartford, 1897) as saying:

I well remember an old oak stump standing on the knoll east of my house, which was fired at by Mr. Doud to try his guns. The stump was much cut to pieces to save the bullets.

The outbreak of the Revolution found Medad Hills and John Doud in an excellent position to handle the vast expansion of gunsmithing necessary to the colonies' defense. From Hibbard we learn that the business in the town of Goshen was very large, up to twenty-eight blacksmiths being employed forging barrels and locks. The dearth of labor and material was so acute that it became necessary for the farmers to make their own tools. In 1776 Hills held a contract to supply muskets to the local Committee of Safety, of which

Ebenezer Norton, Doud's partner, was a member. Most of the guns made at Goshen were received at Hills' establishment on the west side of Whist Pond. Edmond and Miles Beach were the arms inspectors during 1776 and 1777.

In the Connecticut archives there are four documents each dated February 24, 1776, acknowledging the delivery of a total of forty guns, forty bayonets, and forty belts made by Hills and delivered by Colonel Charles Burrel to the sixth, eighth, first, and second militia companies. Each company received ten stands of arms. Luther Stoddard signed for the sixth, Titus Watson for the eighth, David Downs for the first, and John Stevens for the second. The receipts are all in identical hand excepting the signatures. We transcribe one of them:

Received at Canaan Feb. 24, 1776 Col. Charles Burrel Ten new government arms, ten bayonets and ten belts (said arms made by Captain Medad Hills) for the use of the sixth company under the command of the said Col. Burrel.

Rec'd Luther Stoddard.

Hills' military career appears to have begun late in life. October 3, 1769, at the age of forty, he was elected ensign of the Goshen Military Company under Captain Edmond Beach. In 1771 he was designated lieutenant. After the outbreak of the war, commissions came in rapid order. Two days before Christmas 1776, the citizens of Goshen, Torrington, and Winchester raised a volunteer company for the "defense of the Country" as suggested by the Assembly at Middleton. Hills was chosen captain. A few days later the Assembly "made and constituted" the company a distinct

FIG. 1 (*above title*) — NOAH NORTH'S MUSKET (*1758*). Made by Medad Hills. *From the author's collection.* Medad Hill's signature is reproduced as the title. It is from a petition dated June 13, 1776, to the General Assembly, asking for the establishment of an inoculation station one mile from Goshen to protect the inhabitants from the smallpox, which at the time was spreading through the northern army. *From Connecticut Archives, Connecticut State Library.*

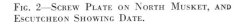

FIG. 2—SCREW PLATE ON NORTH MUSKET, AND ESCUTCHEON SHOWING DATE.

FIG. 3 — MEDAD HILL'S SIGNATURE ON NORTH MUSKET.

regiment, the seventeenth, and named Hills major. Five months later in 1777 he was lieutenant colonel of this regiment of militia. During September 1779 he saw service in and around Peekskill, New York. October 27 of the same year he asked permission of Governor Trumbull to resign his commission because of an "obstinate Rheumatic Disorder." Hills' original communication to Trumbull, which is in the Connecticut State Library, is a well-written, polished letter bearing the stamp of a gentleman of culture.

An examination of the extant Hills papers convinces one that Medad was unquestionably a man of substance and a citizen of importance in his community. His signature appears in various public records (*Fig. 1*). Hills was one of eleven children and had five of his own by Hannah Strong, whom he married at the age of twenty-two. In his active career he was successively craftsman, manufacturer, contractor, soldier, and patriot—in short, a real Connecticut Yankee. He died April 9, 1808.

Noah North's gun is a typical long-barreled musket of the period. It might properly be called an all-around shooter, equally efficient for hunting, home defense, or war. Its curly-maple stock and brass mounts are thinned at the grips from years of service. Rust, oil, powder, and sweaty hands have compounded the mellowness of antiquity. From end to end it measures 68 inches. It weighs 9 pounds. The barrel, 52¼ inches long, is round except at the muzzle, where for 3½ inches it is slightly flared. This terminal portion has five upper flat surfaces. The .60 caliber bore is smooth. The sights are brass, the rear one notched, the fore one knife-like. Attachment to stock is made by four pins. There are no maker's marks to be seen.

The flintlock has a flat gooseneck hammer with beveled edges and an incised decorative border. The lock plate has a curved face, chiseled with floral scrolls. The flash pan is integral with the plate. The frizzen is not faced and its action with the frizzen spring is bridled. The only remarkable thing about the internal assembly is the absence of a reinforcing bridle for the tumbler. As in the case of the barrel, no marks are to be seen. The lack of marks is a distinguishing feature of firearms of early American manufacture.

The brass mounts are decorated with floral scrolls and ornamental borders. The tang of the butt plate (*Fig. 3*) is marked *Made by Medad Hills at Goshen*. The escutcheon (*Fig. 2*) bears the date 1758 and the numerals 44, the latter perhaps the number of a provincial regiment. The year 1758 was one of spirited British resurgence during the French and Indian War. Jeffrey Amherst had taken command, Louisburg fell, Fort Stanwix was built, and Washington with Forbes captured Fort Duquesne. The screw plate bearing the name *Noah North* is shown in Figure 2. There are three plain cylindrical ram pipes. The ramrod is restored.

It seems more than probable that the Noah North who owned this musket was that influential citizen of Torrington who represented his town in the state legislature for many years. He was also selectman of the town and deacon of the church. Born at Kensington, January 10, 1733, he came with father Ebenezer to Torrington when a child. March 25, 1756, he married Jemima Loomis who bore him five children and died eight days after the birth of Mary, December 19, 1767. Four years later Noah married Elizabeth Humphrey. He died March 4, 1822.

Note. The writer wishes to thank Miss Arline G. Finley of the Connecticut State Library and Miss Florence S. Hellman of the Library of Congress for help in finding sources of information.

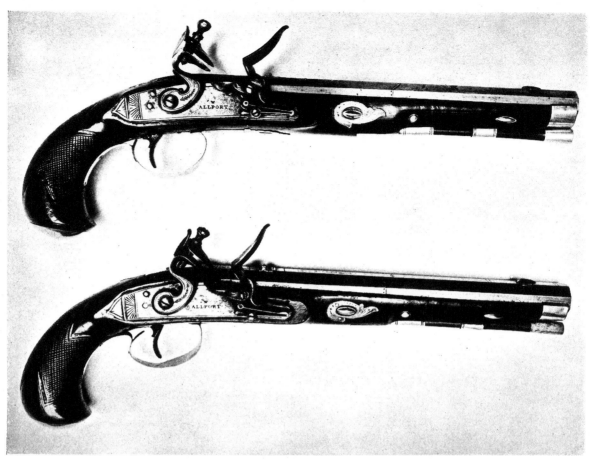

Fig. 1 — Pennsylvania Pistols (*Revolutionary period*)
Marked on barrel, *P. Kunz;* on lock, *W. Allport.* Smooth bore; 40 calibre. *Length: 14 inches.*

Guardians of the Liberty Bell?

By Charles D. Cook

IN STRONG contrast to the muff pistols which I discussed in Antiques for December, 1929, is a brace of American pistols also in my collection, which were made by P. Kunz, a Pennsylvania riflesmith. These are certainly no midgets. Fourteen inches long, smooth bore, and of 40 calibre, they unmistakably proclaim their purpose and their power. Their stocks are of finely figured curly maple, toned to a rich hue with that deep reddish choke-cherry stain characteristic of the old Pennsylvania German wood finish. Back of the breech plug they are inlaid with six geometric ornaments in a light-colored fruit wood.

The mountings are of silver, probably beaten or rolled

from the coinage of their day. The locks, marked *W. Allport*, were doubtless made in England and forwarded to the Colonies; for it was a common practice for Colonial gunsmiths to import the finely made locks of well-known European houses. The front and rear sights, however, are typical of the Kentucky rifle sights of the Colonial and Revolutionary periods and are specially characteristic of P. Kunz's work.

But besides being particularly neat examples of Pennsylvania gunsmithing, undoubtedly made to please the fancy of a connoisseur of arms, these pistols claim distinguished associations. At one time they belonged to John Jacob

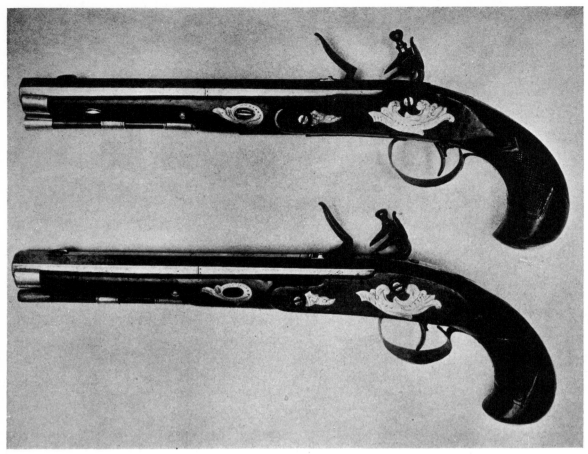

Fig. 2 — PENNSYLVANIA PISTOLS (*reverse of Figure 1*)

Mickley, the Revolutionary soldier who guarded the Liberty Bell on its famous trip from Philadelphia to Allentown in September, 1777.

Some of my readers no doubt have learned that, after the Battle of Brandywine, when Philadelphia was about to fall into the hands of the British, the patriots decided to remove the Liberty Bell, together with nine or ten other Philadelphia bells, to a place where they would be beyond danger of coming into the hands of the enemy and of being transmuted into cannon for use against the Continental Army. Mickley was detailed to watch over this removal, which took place with great secrecy in the dead of night.

To make assurance doubly sure, the hallowed Liberty Bell was placed in an old farm wagon, where it lay ignominiously hidden under a huge load of manure, even as the bones of St. Mark, concealed in a basket of lard, were smuggled out of the Moslem East and thus home to Venice.

One bronze bell, however, is a weightier load than the bones of a host of saints. At Bethlehem, Pennsylvania, the Chariot of Liberty collapsed, and its freight had to be transferred to another vehicle, which managed to complete the journey to Allentown. The event is prosaically memorialized in the records of the Moravian Church at Bethlehem (September 23, 1777), by the following item:

The bells from Philadelphia brought in wagons, the wagon of the State House bell broke down here, so it had to be unloaded, the other bells went on.

Arrived at Allentown, the Liberty Bell and its less distinguished companions were secreted beneath the floor of the Zion Reformed Church. Here they remained until the latter part of 1778, when the evacuation of Philadelphia by the British permitted their restoration to their old-time belfries above the City of Brotherly Love.

It pleases me to believe that my handsome pistols were carried by Mickley when he accompanied the great bell in its laborious flight from the British. In any case, they were treasured by succeeding generations of the Mickley family, until Joseph Benjamin Mickley, a great-great-grandson of the original owner, transferred them to John Huston of Philadelphia, from whom I obtained them.

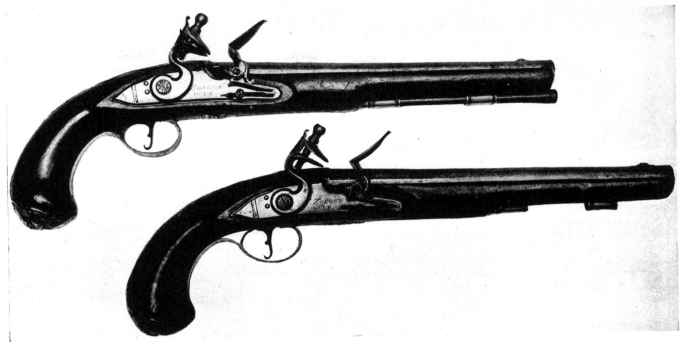

Fig. 1 — Brace of F. Zorger Pistols (*obverse*)

On the Trail of a Gunsmith

By Charles D. Cook

THAT acquisition is not the sole pleasure and aim of the collector is particularly emphasized in my own case in connection with a brace of flintlock pistols, which, a dozen years ago, I obtained from Joe Kindig, Jr., of York, Pennsylvania. These pistols, which have all the earmarks of officers' pistols of the Revolutionary period, are of especially fine workmanship; and all the furniture is of solid silver, although without trace of hall marks (*Figs. 1 and 2*). In the English style of the period, the well-known English acorn finial ornament is shown in relief on the trigger guards, and the British lion's head on the butt plates.

The lock plate is of what might well be termed the old

Fig. 2 — F. Zorger Pistol
Detail of reverse, showing silver screw plate.

Pennsylvania type, and bears the maker's name *F. ZORGER & LF.* The barrels are marked on top, near the breech, *YORK TOWN* (*Fig. 3*). The stocks are of nicely carved walnut, apparently American walnut. All in all, though I could find no reference to an American maker named Zorger, I felt, from the beginning, that the pieces were American made. Nevertheless, many connoisseurs, including one who might well be called the dean of American gun collectors, pronounced the pistols to be unquestionably of English manufacture.

For my own part, though I was not at all convinced by these unsupported assertions, I allowed the question to remain *in statu quo* until,

Fig. 3. — F. Zorger Pistol
Top of upper example in Figure 1.

Fig. 4. — ZORGER KENTUCKY RIFLES
Above, two views of the G. Zorger rifle; below, two views of the rifle marked F. Zorger.

Fig. 5 (Right) — THE ZORGER MARKS
Upper one, that of G. Zorger; lower one, that of F. Zorger.

about six months ago, I obtained a rifle from York. This rifle (the lower specimen in *Fig. 4*) is a Kentucky-type weapon of the Revolutionary period, and has all the characteristics of a Pennsylvania piece. It is beautifully mounted with brass furniture, and has particularly fine relief carving on the stock, which is of curly maple. The calibre is a little over forty-five. Engraved on the barrel, near the breech, in script, appears the maker's name, *F. ZORGER* (see lower mark in *Fig. 5*).

A few months later I was fortunate enough to obtain another similar rifle, apparently of an earlier period, stocked with walnut, but with carving similar to that of the piece just described (upper specimen in *Fig. 4*). The barrel of this second rifle is octagonal for about eighteen inches, and round for the rest of its length — a form that is conceded to be, in general, earlier than the octagonal barrel of the F. Zorger rifle. This second rifle is marked, on the breech, *G. ZORGER* (*Fig. 5*, upper mark).

My interest in these Zorger rifles, having now reached the boiling point, soon culminated in action. I wrote to Mr. Kindig, from whom I had obtained the brace of pistols and the two rifles, and asked him where he had obtained them, and if the old name of York was York Town. He replied that he had obtained all the pieces in the vicinity of York, and that the old name of the place was, indeed, York Town.

Certain that the *YORK TOWN* of the pistols was York Town, Pennsylvania, and that I was now in reality on a hot scent, I again imposed on Mr. Kindig's good nature, and enlisted his assistance in my quest for definite data. He reported that a Frederick Zorger, who lived in Newberry, about ten miles from York, in York County, had left a will, which was probated June 7, 1815. The name of Zorger's wife was Elizabeth; the eight children of the couple were Peter, Matthias, Frederick, Michael, George, Elizabeth, Lydia, and Ann. No clue was found as to the testator's occupation.

I still persisted in my search, and Mr. Kindig obtained for me the services of George R. Prowell, who discovered that York was used, at various times during the American Revolution, as a prison camp, and that the militia of the place was often called out for guard duty. He then referred me to Volume II of the sixth series of Pennsylvania *Archives*, page 710, where Frederick Zorger is listed as on guard duty, March 17, 1778. In many instances, this list, after each soldier's name, notes, in parentheses,

his occupation. Fortunately for my quest, Frederick Zorger's occupation appears as that of "Tennant Gun Smith."

So, combined research has resulted in adding the name of a hitherto unknown American gunsmith to our roll of gunmakers. In conjunction with these notes I am reproducing examples of his work.

Mr. Kindig has called my attention to the fact that Zorger was in York County while the Continental Congress met at York, from Sept. 30, 1777, to June 28, 1778; and makes the following suggestion:

At that time the greatest men in America came to York — both military men and all the Congressmen. I feel sure that your pistols were made at that time for one of the Congressmen, or for one of our military leaders. They are almost too fine for a local citizen or farmer.

I feel that as a general rule the name on the lock means little in a Kentucky rifle, and for this reason: a large percentage of locks appear to have been imported — especially the later ones. You know the type lock plate I mean — usually engraved. I believe that all those marked *GOLCHER* are imported. Also I have seen late Henry's of the same type.

However, there is a typical Pennsylvania lock that I am quite sure was locally made, though nine out of ten of them are unmarked.

Your Zorger pistols have the Pennsylvania type locks on them. I like to see that round groove in back of the hammer and the rest of the plate perfectly plain, no engraving and usually a long narrow plate. If on a Kentucky rifle, such a plate is probably of Pennsylvania make. This type of plate is usually unmarked. However, when marked, I should consider the name (everything else checking up) to be the name of the maker.

While the main object of my hunt, the identification of the maker of the pistols and rifles, has been bagged, there still remain two minor by-problems about which, at present, I have only unsupported conjectures. One of these conjectures is that the letters *LF* after Zorger's name may stand for *Les Fils*, in which case the firm's name would have been F. Zorger and Sons, and the nationality French — either French Huguenot or French Swiss — instead of German as might appear at first thought. Of course *et fils* would be the usual form of the phrase in modern French, not *et les fils*; but the latter form was, without doubt, possible in 1776.

The other conjecture is that the G. Zorger of my second Zorger rifle may have been the father of Frederick Zorger, and that his name was George Zorger. A straw pointing in this direction is the fact that Frederick Zorger named one of his sons George.

The Pedigree of the Pennsylvania Rifle

By Joe Kindig, Jr.

Except as noted, illustrations from the author's collection

THE feathers that adorn the butt of an arrow, though decorative, are not employed for decorative reasons. They have an important duty to perform, that of keeping the missile straight and unswerving in its course from bow to target. To explain just how they accomplish this feat would involve a somewhat lengthy disquisition on certain laws of physics, which I have no intention of undertaking. Suffice it to say that, as the released arrow speeds forward, its feathered end encounters sufficient air resistance to impart a slow rotary motion to the entire shaft. It is this rotary motion which ensures an undeviating flight. The principle involved was known even to primitive man. It holds for metal projectiles hurled by small arms and heavy artillery quite as well as for the bow-flung arrow of the savage; in the case of projectiles, however, the necessary twist is given, not by feathers, but by spiral grooves cut in the tube through which the shell or bullet is forced by an explosion in its wake. They are known as "rifling."

The value of rifling is no new discovery. The earliest gunsmiths were fully aware of it; but they encountered difficulties in giving effect to their knowledge. While it was simple to cut spiral grooves in a metal barrel, it was not at all simple to force a bullet large enough to engage such grooves down the entire length of barrel until it rested upon its appropriate bed of powder. The latter task could be accomplished only by long and hard pounding with ramrod and mallet. This in itself was a slow and tedious performance, rendered even slower and more tedious by the fact that the firing of two or three shots sufficed to foul the grooves with powder residue and necessitate a thorough cleaning of the barrel before loading could be resumed. The amount of heavy deposit generated by the powder of our ancestors was beyond anything to be imagined by the modern marksman; and so was its ability to choke a rifle barrel.

These drawbacks might have been in part obviated had it been possible to insert the bullet at the barrel's breach instead of at its muzzle. Experiments to that logical end were made — plenty of them — but for generations they came to naught. A breach tight enough to restrain the gases of burning powder quickly became fouled into uselessness. On the other hand, a loose breach, while it might be kept clean, was likely to encourage rearward explosions far more dangerous to the marksman than to his target. This apparently irreconcilable situation continued to baffle gunsmiths the world over, until, at the time of the Civil War, the invention of the metal cartridge solved the entire problem and revolutionized the design and manufacture of firearms.

But this was not until the 1860's. For some centuries previous to that epoch, all practical guns were muzzle-loaders — for the most part equipped with smoothbore barrels, which, though unreliable even at short range, presented the great advantage of quick loading. Only in one section of Europe did the rifle enjoy any degree of popularity, namely, in Germany and the contiguous territory where the hunting of the stag and the wild boar was a customary sport.

For such hunting the failings of the rifle were of less moment than its virtues. The stag at bay and the wounded boar could prove dangerous antagonists. Coping with them demanded an accurate, hard-hitting, and deadly weapon. Slow loading entailed no serious consequences to one accompanied by a servant bearing extra arms for emergency use, and the long intervals between the killing of one victim and the sighting of a fresh quarry afforded ample leisure for cleaning. So in Central Europe was evolved a rifle without exact counterpart elsewhere in the world. By way of minimizing the toil of loading with the aid of iron ramrod and mallet, its barrel was abbreviated to a length of hardly more than twenty inches. Its bore was large, seventy-five calibre (three fourths of an inch) or more. Clumsy enough was this weapon, heavy and poorly balanced; but it was reasonably accurate. It is of interest to us as the lineal ancestor of the Pennsylvania rifle.

The story of how this ancestry asserted itself is too long to be told in more than barest outline. In 1681, when William Penn received from the King of England the Province of Pennsylvania in payment of a debt, the shrewd Quaker promptly set about finding ways and means of turning his acquisition into cash. Even after he had persuaded his friends to assume great tracts of territory, he still had a vast empire to dispose of. Much of England's surplus population had already been safely tucked away in the earlier colonial settlements. It was necessary to look elsewhere than to the British Isles for fresh recruits. Realizing that, as yet, the migratory urge had not been communicated to the peasantry of Central Europe, Penn decided to repair so serious an omission. Soon he had inaugurated one of the greatest real estate promotions known to history. At his order, no less than fifty-eight broadsides, pamphlets, and books were printed in English, Dutch, German, and French, and liberally circulated abroad. The roseate picture that they painted was well calculated to play upon the common man's aspiration to become a landowner. And in Pennsylvania there was unlimited land, to be had almost for the asking.

The response, particularly from German-speaking Europe, was almost immediate. The first trickle of Teutonic immigrants was followed by a flood that, for sixty years, poured with undiminished volume into the new region of promise. First Pennsylvania was populated, as far westward as the foothills of the Alleghenies. Deflected by this barrier, the stream of pioneers then made its way southward into Maryland, Virginia, and what is now West Virginia. By 1740 it had crept across the boundaries of North Carolina. It was the men of the next generation who opened up Kentucky and Tennessee. Of this great movement, the life

Fig. 1 — OLD-STYLE WEAPONS
Long, smoothbore fowling piece, such as Penn recommended, and short German rifle of the type brought by many early Pennsylvania settlers. From this type was developed the famous Pennsylvania rifle

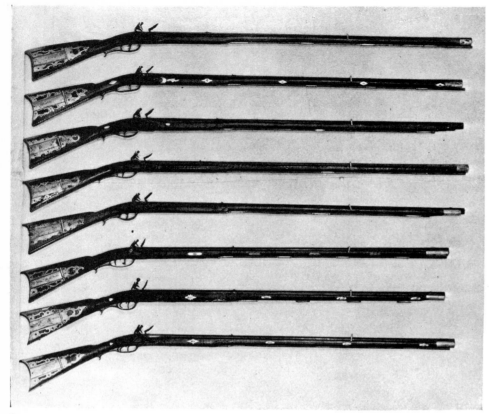

Fig. 2 — PENNSYLVANIA RIFLES WITH CARVED STOCKS (*obverse*)
Showing the variety and individuality of the engraved brass patch boxes let into the stocks. Note also the quality of the wood

history of Daniel Boone affords a striking illustration. Boone was born in Berks County, Pennsylvania, but, when still a boy, moved with his family into North Carolina. Later in life he became the legendary hero of Kentucky.

But I am ahead of my story. In some of the books wherein he disclosed the glories of Pennsylvania, Penn had included specific directions as to the proper equipment of the prospective settler. Among the recommended articles were "good long guns that will throw shot far and well." By this, of course, was meant smoothbore fowling pieces with which either shot or ball could be used. We may doubt that Penn had ever heard of a rifle. In all probability some of the German newcomers obeyed instructions to the letter; others must have armed themselves with the familiar short-barreled rifles of their native country. But neither fowling piece nor stunted rifle was suited to the requirements of a frontiersman's life. The one was woefully short in range, and disastrously inaccurate. The other, on account of the delay incidental to its manipulation, was hardly fitted for use in districts where subsistence depended upon securing plentiful supplies of game, and survival upon outshooting the lightning-like bow and arrow of the Indian.

The necessity for a deadly yet quickly handled firearm was acute. And, since necessity is a prolific mother, she presently brought forth an important invention. The name of her assisting partner is unknown. Enough that, about the year 1720, probably in Lancaster County, some German inhabitant hit upon the idea of employing a heavily greased patch of cloth or buckskin to speed the ramming of bullets into rifle barrels. The method was simple. In loading, the patch was laid directly over the muzzle of the barrel. Upon its centre was placed the bullet, made slightly smaller than the rifle bore. Then with a light hickory ramrod, bullet and patch were slipped down upon the explosive charge.

And just as the greased patch made easy the bullet's downward route, so it sped the return journey by engaging the rifling of the barrel and imparting the necessary twist to the leaden messenger of death. Incidentally, it cleaned as it went and, having thus fulfilled its destiny, finally parted company with its companion bullet at the rifle's mouth.

A beneficent device, the greased patch. Thanks to its instrumentality, the rifle could be as readily and rapidly loaded and fired as a smoothbore gun, and with infinitely greater deadliness. In the hands of a good marksman it could be depended upon to hit a man-size target at one hundred and fifty yards, whereas the side of a barn was fairly immune against the onslaughts of its sister weapon at a hundred yards.

Thenceforth genius, lubricated by the greased patch, rapidly developed a new firearm — a firearm that for the subsequent century and a quarter held sway as the premier weapon of the world. This was the Pennsylvania rifle, a Pennsylvania German product, made almost exclusively in the parent state, and in those regions to the southward that had been penetrated by pioneers of German blood. Essentially a frontier arm, it found its way southward along the valley of the Shenandoah, thence, by slower stages, over the western ranges of Kentucky, where it was the chief reliance of Boone and his companions. In time, following the course of empire and the setting sun, it reached the far-distant coast of the Pacific.

All its early resemblance to its progenitor, the old Central European rifle, speedily disappeared. Its barrel grew long to ensure an improved aim and maximum effectiveness for the slow-burning powder of the day. A richly figured stock of native maple, carved and inlaid, superseded the black-walnut stock common to European practice. In the side of this stock was inserted a fancifully designed brass box to accommodate a supply of greased patches. The bore of the weapon was reduced from seventy-five calibre to a calibre between forty and fifty, thus permitting five charges from the same weight of powder and ball that had constituted a single feeding of the larger calibre arm. This saving of ammunition alone was a vastly important matter, since, while it caused no appreciable diminution of killing power, it added greatly to the mobility of the frontiersman who must carry a full supply of ammunition during long expeditions through the wilderness.

In reducing the calibre of their rifles, the Pennsylvania gunsmiths were fully one hundred and twenty-five years in advance of their time. The bore of the British regulation musket during the Revolutionary War was seventy-five calibre. The American musket of the War of 1812 was sixty-nine calibre. It took fifty years, and the advent of the Civil War, to produce the Springfield fifty-eight calibre rifle. Not until 1873 did the military expert catch up with the early Pennsylvania gunsmith by achieving a forty-five calibre weapon. Incidentally, the World War was fought with rifles of about thirty calibre.

The American troops who faced the British regulars in 1776 were equipped with no regulation arm. They used what they ld find. What would have happened to them except for the intervention of battalions of experienced riflemen from Pennsylvania, Virginia, Maryland, and North Carolina and armed with Pennsylvania rifles would be dismal to contemplate. It was one of these frontier marksmen, Timothy Murphy by name, who picked off General Fraser, moving spirit of the British forces at the Battle of Stillwater, thus not only forcing Burgoyne's surrender at Saratoga, but encouraging French participation in the war.

Yet earlier in the war, while General Howe was still cooped up in Boston, two companies of southern riflemen distributed along the American front wrought such havoc among the enemy troops, particularly among the officers, as to force the British general to institute a special enquiry. When he learned of the frontier soldiers and their deadly weapons, he ordered that a specimen of each be captured. Corporal Walter Crouse of York County, Pennsylvania, was at length entrapped, and with his weapon promptly bundled off to England. There for a time this untamed American, who could kill with every shot at a distance of one hundred and fifty to two hundred yards, was exhibited as a public curiosity.

This somewhat terrifying display produced unexpected results. The already feeble enthusiasm for enlistment among the youth of Britain sank to the zero point. Meanwhile, the government, in casting about for foreign mercenaries, decided if possible to find soldiers accustomed to the rifle. That, perhaps, accounts for the employment of Hessian troops. The theory behind this move was sound enough; but it failed in practice. The Hessian rifles were the ancient contraptions, heavy, dirty, and slow-loading, that had been long since abandoned in Pennsylvania. After a few moments of fighting, without opportunity for cleaning, they could be used only as clubs and, though valiantly wielded in that capacity, were of small avail to their unfortunate bearers.

So the Pennsylvania rifle maintained its supremacy. Later, in the War of 1812, it again proved its extraordinary effectiveness at the Battle of New Orleans. Here, under Andrew Jackson's leadership, two thousand rifle-armed pioneers, backed by a handful of regulars and an improvised horde of pirates, miscellaneous whites, and negroes, utterly defeated eight thousand British regulars, the flower of Europe's fighting men. One by one the unerring Pennsylvania rifles removed the enemy officers until none above the rank of major was left. Turning them upon the advancing soldiers, they mowed down the solid ranks like wheat. The British losses in the engagement were more than two thousand men; our own casualties, including killed and wounded, numbered only twenty-one.

Oddly enough, the weapon that helped so materially to win American independence, and that deserves chief credit for the sole distinguished military achievement of our troops during the War of 1812, has come to be known as the Kentucky rifle. Yet, perhaps, the occurrence is not so odd after all. Romance, rather than historic justice, is accountable for many names in familiar use. The romance of the rifle, in so far as concerned the public, began with the exploits of Daniel Boone and reached its climax

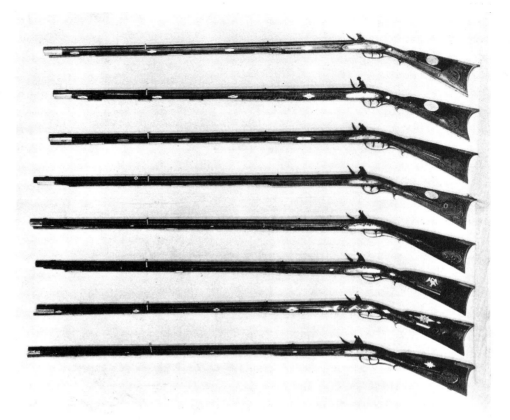

Fig. 3 — PENNSYLVANIA RIFLES (reverse of Figure 2)
Maple stocks whose relief carving often equals the best found on the Philadelphia Chippendale furniture of the period

in the tales of frontier prowess displayed in the Battle of New Orleans. I am illustrating here part of a broadside sheet carrying a long ballad entitled *The Hunters of Kentucky; or The Battle of New Orleans*, evidently issued not long after Jackson's famous victory. Each of its eight long stanzas ends with the refrain:

> Oh, Kentucky,
> The Hunters of Kentucky,
> Oh, Kentucky,
> The Hunters of Kentucky.

Of the stanzas themselves I shall quote only the fifth:

> But Jackson he was wide awake,
>   And wasn't scar'd at trifles,
> For well he knew what aim we take
>   With our Kentucky rifles.
> So he led us up to a Cyprus swamp,
>   The ground was low and mucky,
> There stood John Bull in martial pomp,
>   And here was old Kentucky.

It is not likely that the anonymous balladist was the first to employ the term "Kentucky rifle," but we may hardly doubt that he is responsible for fixing it in the minds of the populace.

The makers of this rifle were, I believe, the greatest of our colonial artisans. While our cabinetmakers worked only in wood, our potters only in clay, our silversmiths chiefly in precious metals, our gunsmiths exercised universal skill. As ironsmiths they wrought barrels and locks, as woodworkers they turned out superbly balanced gunstocks upon whose unyielding maple they carved intricate and lovely designs. In the brass patch boxes and inlaid forms which they wrought to give the final touch of ornament to their creations, they equaled the skill of the ablest silversmiths. Some of them, of course, were inferior to others: but the best were masters who, in producing effective utilitarian tools of offense and defense, at the same time transformed them into works of art.

Rich as they are in historic and artistic association, Pennsylvania rifles have inevitably been coveted by American collectors. While the majority of surviving specimens date from 1830 to 1870, it is the minority, those of the 1750–1820 period, that will engage the attention of the connoisseur.

A word as to their chief points should be appended. These fine rifles are invariably long, especially the earlier ones. About five feet is the length most prized by collectors. The stock, usually of curly maple, extends to within a fractional inch of the muzzle, and hence is known as a "full stock." Later and less desirable examples may boast only a half stock, which supports hardly more than half the barrel. This barrel is normally octagonal and from forty to fifty inches in length. Beneath it is socketed a hickory ramrod. The mountings, almost always of brass, include a long, fancifully shaped patch box let into the right side of the stock. In the period of which I speak the flintlock method of ignition was in vogue. Later rifles are abbreviated in length and employ a percussion lock. (See ANTIQUES for August 1924, pp. 90–91.)

One fascinating characteristic of these early rifles is that no two are ever exact duplicates. Made not in factories, but in small shops by a master and perhaps his one apprentice, they were produced only to order, and in accordance with the specifications of the individual owner, who usually cherished cranky ideas that he insisted upon having embodied in his pet weapon. Hence the endless variety of the particular touches that distinguish one arm from

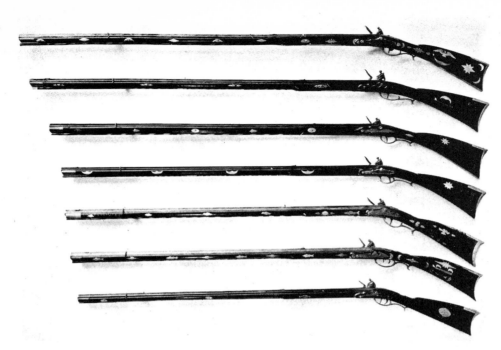

Fig. 4 — PENNSYLVANIA RIFLES, CARVED AND INLAID
In these the carving is incised, the maker's decorative fancy expressing itself chiefly in a wealth of small silver inlays.
From the collections of the Pennsylvania Museum

Fig. 5 — BROADSIDE BALLAD
Issued soon after the Battle of New Orleans. The woodcut portrays the contemporary ideal of the Kentucky marksman with his 'coonskin cap and his long rifle. A squirrel and a wild turkey testify to the deadly accuracy of his aim

another by the same maker. Hence, too, the wealth of ornament that adorns each maple stock. A man's rifle was part of himself. To many a pioneer it meant more than wife and family — it was the chief object of his affection.

Quite naturally, most collectors prefer decorated to plain rifles. The earliest examples have relief carving on the stock. Later, this carving is supplemented by silver inlays. Still later, these metal inlays encroach upon the carving, which is incised instead of in relief and which eventually disappears. But as such details are better illustrated than described, I am picturing a number of Pennsylvania rifles from my own and other collections. I think that they may properly be described as *beautiful*, for they represent, more completely than any other craftsmanly product, the perfect adaptation of form to function, plus that refinement of workmanship and those supplemental touches of individual fancy which betoken the pride of the artist in his work, and his joy in creative accomplishment.

Editor's Note. Mr. Kindig's excellent and stimulating summary of a highly extensive subject suggests interesting food for speculation. It was German ingenuity and fine craftsmanship, released in fresh surroundings and compelled to solve new problems of existence, that finally evolved the Pennsylvania rifle. This weapon was so far superior to any other firearm of its day in speed, accuracy, and range as vastly to increase the effectiveness of the troops by whom it was employed. It is given chief credit for winning more than one battle with the British during the Revolutionary War, and, in some quarters, for the eventual triumph of the American cause. If the latter view is correct, the United States owes a greater debt to Germany than has been realized.

86

Jacob Dickert, Lancaster Gunsmith

BY HENRY J. KAUFFMAN

PENNSYLVANIA RIFLES, which played an important part in the French and Indian Wars, the Revolution, and the War of 1812, were the best firearms of their day. An unusually high quality of workmanship was required to produce them. Each rifle was designed and made by a craftsman skilled in the working of not one medium alone but of all the materials used in making the rifle. He had to be competent in welding and boring barrels, in working and carving stocks, in shaping and engraving brass, and in silversmithing and locksmithing.

It is rather remarkable, in view of the importance of Pennsylvania rifles and the interest in them on the part of collectors, that we have so little information about the men who produced them. Several reasons may account for this. Few eighteenth-century rifles survived the tre-

Two rifles made by Dickert, probably before 1800. Both were originally flintlocks, later changed to percussion type. Although partially obscured, the name J. DICKERT can be deciphered on the top facet of each barrel. *Top* and *center* show two sides of the same gun, with carving on the stock.

mendous demands made of them, not only in supplying the family larder with game but in protecting the family against Indian forays and in several wars. Again, many early craftsmen did not sign their guns. And the earliest rifles were frequently restocked, or at least changed to percussion type, so that many of the original characteristics can now be only a matter of speculation.

In the case of Jacob Dickert, however, a gunsmith working in the late eighteenth and early nineteenth centuries, a good many facts are known. That he was regarded as a superior craftsman is indicated by a reference in the report of Tench Coxe, purveyor of public supplies, to the Secretary of War. He referred to "Jacob Dickert and others" in Lancaster as "regular, able, safe, and capable of securing (say 5000)." It would obviously have been impossible for one maker to produce 5000 rifles, but by pooling their resources the Lancaster gunsmiths were very successful in handling government contracts. Among the others who worked with Dickert were Christopher Gumpf, John Bender, Henry de Hull, and Peter Gonter.

Jacob Dickert was born in Mainz, Germany, on January 9, 1740, and came to America with his family at the age of eight. After spending some years in Berks County, the family moved to Lancaster in 1756. Young Jacob may already have become apprenticed to a gunsmith in Berks County, but if he started when the family moved to Lancaster he could still have completed a five-year apprenticeship period at the usual age of twenty-one.

According to a 1795 advertisement, he must have started in gunsmithing about 1755, since he states that "any person may depend upon being well suited, as said Dickert, by having forty years experience in that line is enabled to give all possible satisfaction."

The spelling of Dickert's name is recorded by various writers as Dechard, Decherd, Dechert, and Dickart. The latter form appears on his naturalization document, which is dated September 24, 1765, but on the guns I have examined, as well as in six church references, three deeds, and a will, it is written as Dickert.

In 1766, with John Henry, Dickert bought land in Manheim Township, near Lancaster, and built a boring and grinding mill. Since there is no record of a mortgage, it is evident that Dickert must have become fairly prosperous by that time. At Henry's death in 1779, Dickert bought his share from his widow for £250.

Dickert married Johanetta Höfer in 1765. Their daughter, Anna Maria, married a Lancaster merchant, James Gill, in 1787. Gill and Dickert combined forces for a time and operated a store "in Queen Street, in the well known dwelling house of said Dickert." The gun-

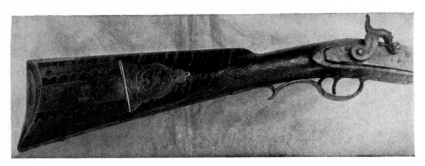

Rifle made by Dickert and Gill early in the nineteenth century (*two views*). This Gill was probably Dickert's grandson, Benjamin, who was classified as a riflemaker in a Lancaster business directory of 1843. The names DICKERT and GILL are on the barrel. The checkering on the small of the stock and the long circular sweep on the lock plate are typical of Lancaster County rifles. *Illustrations from the collection of Joe Kindig, Jr.*

smith line was augmented with a stock of groceries, dry goods, and on one occasion an assortment of large and elegant looking glasses. After Gill's death in May 1796, Dickert continued the business. On August 21, 1799, he advertised in the Lancaster *Journal:*

WANTED

2000 Musquet Locks and Barrels
The subscriber will contract with any person or persons, for any quantity of Locks and Barrels. No locks or barrels will be accepted unless a pattern is first secured from the subscriber.

JACOB DICKERT, Gunsmith

WHO ALSO HAS FOR SALE

A Large assortment of Dry Goods, suitable for the season, as well as a large and general assortment of groceries, which he will dispose of at the most reaonable rate for cash.

The name of Dickert's grandson, Benjamin Gill, who also became a gunsmith, appears with Dickert's on one of the rifles illustrated.

The type of rifle which Dickert and the other Lancaster gunsmiths made is indicated by a letter from Tench Coxe to Dickert and de Huff, dated November 16, 1807:

. . . The rifles I am instructed to purchase are to answer the following description. They are to be common, plain rifles substantially made. The barrel to be three feet two inches in length. The workmanship to be such as to pass strict and rigorous inspection. The calibre as to fit a ball of half ounce weight. The finishing (if the work be good and substantial) will be sufficient if not inferior to those commonly made for ordinary use. The barrels would be preferred round (instead of eight square) from the tail pipe or lower thimble to the muzzle; but of the thickness they would be otherwise, except in the angles, that is to say of the thickness they would be in the flat part or the thinnest part of the octagonal barrels. The price that will be paid for the rifle complete will be ten dollars cash.

In another letter, however, Coxe agrees to a price of $10.2/3 for brass mounted rifles, and $11.17/100 for any rifle with silver star and silver thumb piece.

The specifications of the Dickert rifle in the Alamo may probably be taken as typical: Overall length, 65 inches; barrel length, 45 inches; caliber, .55; weight, 8¼ pounds.

Dickert also made smooth-bore muskets which were an American version of the Charleville firearms secured from France for use in the Revolution. On April 17, 1801, he and Matthew Llewellin contracted with the state of Pennsylvania for 1000 of these, model 1795.

The sticks and patchboxes of the two Dickert rifles illustrated are fine specimens of an early pattern. The relief carving on the stock is appropriately designed for the area, and though the silver star inlay has been lost, the shape of it is preserved. The thickness of the stock at the butt plate, the style of the carving, the cylindrical shape at the small of the stock, and the star inlay indicate that the rifle is of the Revolutionary period or earlier. The patchboxes are typical of those used in Lancaster County by eighteenth-century gunsmiths, but the delicately engraved loops and points on each side of the hinge of the patchbox are peculiar to Dickert.

In addition to his work as a gunsmith, Dickert was active in the community and business affairs of Lancaster. He was one of the subscribers to the Philadelphia and Lancaster Turnpike, the first great highway built in America, which was finished about 1790. The improved transportation from Lancaster to Philadelphia doubtless aided Dickert in disposing of his rifles. When the turnpike was continued from Lancaster to Middletown, Dickert was also one of the managers of that enterprise.

According to the Moravian church records, Dickert served on various church committees, and for more than forty years was one of the Dieners (workers or servers) at the love feasts, one of the most historic and important of the Moravian services. Dickert died in 1822. The final church record states simply that "His death was due to old age." His obituary in the Lancaster *Intelligencer* reads: "He sustained the character of an honest Man, a good citizen, and an Exemplary Christian."

Both sides of a maple full-stock flintlock rifle by Peter Gonter. The patch box and other details show Reading influence; side plate and silver star inlay are typical of Lancaster County. *Collection of Joe Kindig, Jr.*

Maple full-stock flintlock very similar to above, but probably earlier. *Kindig collection.*

Peter Gonter, Lancaster gunsmith

BY HENRY J. KAUFFMAN

ALTHOUGH A LARGE NUMBER OF MEN were engaged in gunsmithing during the Revolution in Lancaster, Pennsylvania—nowhere else in the country was there such a reservoir of gunsmithing experience—military arms bearing the name of an eighteenth-century Lancaster gunsmith are very rare, and they are desirable items for any collection. The close of the war brought a drop in the demand for arms, and many of the less skilled men dropped out of the field. As a consequence the quality of the guns produced locally in the late eighteenth century has led connoisseurs to regard that period as the "golden era of gunsmithing in Pennsylvania."

Recent research among documents of unquestionable authenticity has brought to light some basic facts about Peter Gonter, a little-known gunsmith who seems to have been a good businessman as well as a contributor to this golden era. The records of the Moravian church in Lancaster show that his father was John Peter Gonter, but they do not give the date or place of John's birth. Peter's mother, Susanna Reichard Gonter, was born in September 1724 at Schwenheim, near Speyer, in the Palatinate. They were married on April 21, 1741, and had five sons and four daughters. Peter was one of the sons who survived when the father died, in 1768; another surviving son was probably John Gonter, also a gunsmith, of Lancaster and nearby Reading.

When Peter Gonter was born in 1751 the rifle industry ,of Lancaster County was in its infancy. It is likely that he served the usual seven- to nine-year period of apprenticeship before he was twenty-one. After he became a journeyman he may have continued to work for men who were established in the business; at any rate, he later became a leading citizen in Lancaster—the owner of a gunshop, an innkeeper, and a politician.

In 1775 Peter was meeting with a group of Lancaster citizens who pledged their allegiance to the cause of liberty and freedom and indicated that they would fight for it. In the same year he married Susanna Elizabeth Hagi. Tax records show that about the time Gonter must have been serving his apprenticeship, one Wolfgang Haga was working as a gunsmith in Reading, and this suggests that the surname of Gonter's wife may have been misspelled. Possibly Peter was apprenticed to the Reading gunsmith and then married his master's daughter. In any event, he had interests in Reading: in 1796 he and his wife sold a parcel of land there to Christian Madeira. If Susanna was Wolfgang Haga's daughter, she may have inherited the property; or Gonter may simply have bought it at some earlier time as an investment.

A notice in the Lancaster *Intelligencer* for December 11, 1798, requests the Republican Blues to parade in "compleat uniform" from the house of Peter Gonter. The house probably adjoined the premises on North Queen Street where, according to the papers of the Lancaster County Historical Society, he kept the King of Prussia Tavern. Combining such different occupations as gunsmithing and tavernkeeping was not uncommon at the time: Peter Brong, a contemporary gunsmith, had a board yard, and Jacob Dickert operated a dry goods store in conjunction with his gun shop on North Queen Street.

As early as 1775 Gonter had received £2/12/1 for entertaining riflemen, and in 1799 three Berks County assemblymen lodged with him.

Gonter's stay in the political arena seems to have been brief: he served as borough treasurer only from September 15, 1803, until September 15, 1807. The early years of the nineteenth century must have been busy ones, for at this time he was an active member of a group of Lancaster gunsmiths who were supplying the United States government with arms. Correspondence between Tench Coxe and this group (Peter Gonter, Jacob Dickert, George Miller, Christopher Gumpf, John Bender, and Henry DeHuff) indicates that their products were supplementing those of the armory at Springfield, which had been established in the 1790's. A letter from Coxe, the newly appointed purveyor of public supplies under Jefferson, discusses some of their transactions:

Purveyors Office
Phila. Sept. 6, 1803

Mr. Peter Gonter
Riflemaker, Lancaster
Sir:

I want for the public use of the U.S. six rifles with Silver Stars and Thumbpieces and 42 common rifles to be delivered here as quickly as possible. A vessel sails for Georgia on Saturday or Sunday in which I wish to send them. I should be glad to receive them packed for exportation and transportation by land or water. In regard to prices, I shall expect them for prompt pay on as low terms as you ever supplied them, or lower if you think you can afford them lower. There is another order for 50 rifles which I wish to secure from our Penna. makers. Will you speak to Mr. Dickert, Mr. Getz, and others and let me know what terms you and they will supply them on, and if you can send 50 immediately. They are of the common kind, not silvered.

I am, Sir
Tench Coxe.

Jacob Dickert had been in the gun business in Lancaster for about fifty years, and some sporting guns bearing his name demonstrate the high quality of his craftsmanship (ANTIQUES, April 1952, page 349). Peter Getz, the local inspector of arms, was much better known as Lancaster's finest silversmith. Gonter's participation in this pool of craftsmen indicates that he was sufficiently alert as a businessman to direct his efforts toward manufacturing the common rifle, for which there was a strong market, when supplying the demand for fine rifles did not require all his time.

According to Gonter's will, dated August 19, 1818, and on file in the Lancaster County Court House, his wife received the bulk of his estate—including all rifles and unfinished parts in stock at the time of his death.

Gonter's work cannot be regarded as the best of the period, but all of it was reasonably good and he did make some rifles of high quality, decorated with carving and silver inlays. He made a number of smooth-bore fowling pieces for small game as well as the rifles, which were used for deer and bear. A number of his guns have the irregular eight-pointed silver star inlay on the cheek side of the stock, which other Pennsylvania smiths also used; all are the typically graceful arm of the time.

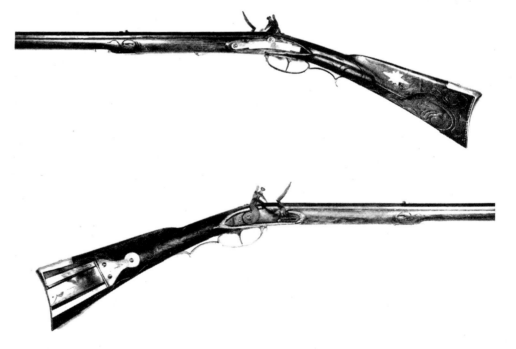

The straight bands on each side of the patch box indicate that this gun was made late in Gonter's career, though the shape of wrist, comb, and butt-plate suggest an earlier period. The incised carving here is not as desirable as the relief carving on other examples; the brass side plate has the characteristic Lancaster sweep. *Collection of Charles Strack.*

Rifling reduced friction between ball and barrel and greatly increased accuracy over that of a smooth-bore. Few guns have survived with the deep rifling shown in this close-up of the muzzle of a Gonter rifle. The dots are for ornament; other gunsmiths used rings, and some combined rings and dots. The ferrule of brass beneath the barrel protected the end of the stock from damage. *Strack collection.*

EARLY OHIO GUNSMITHS

A Partial Check List

FIG. 1 — RIFLE MADE BY LEVI BIDDLE (*1830*). The silver inlay on reverse is more ornate and larger than that shown here, but the eagle depicted on stock is beautifully executed. *This and Figure 5 from the collection of Earl J. Knittle.*

By RHEA MANSFIELD KNITTLE and STUART M. MARTIN

The compilers of this list have used only original sources in obtaining their information. Each name either has been seen and recorded from an early rifle, or has been taken from an early document or historical source. Mrs. Knittle and Mr. Martin had each listed independently more than two hundred and thirty-five names. After eliminating their duplications, the list contains three hundred and sixteen names. — THE EDITOR.

FROM THE TIME of the passage of the Ordinance of 1787 until settlement in Ohio was more or less regulated, the Pennsylvania type of Swiss-German rifle, frequently called the Kentucky rifle in the trans-Allegheny country, proved to be man's best friend. Not only did the frontiersman need this weapon to protect his family and livestock from the depredations of wild animals, but the rifle was necessary also in obtaining venison and wild turkey — the mainstays of the frontier diet. Smaller game was usually bagged by fowling pieces. The accoutrements of the early Ohio hunter, soldier, and frontiersman were a rifle, bullets and bullet mold, pouch, powderhorn or flask, a wiping stick, and a hunting knife.

The long-bore rifle was the most potent weapon of the land forces in this section of the country during the War of 1812. It was used by both white men and Indians. Nevertheless, tomahawks, dirks, butcher knives, and even dueling pistols were put into service during that frightfully bloody engagement. The Indian was often as proficient with a rifle as the white man, and the latter sometimes could wield a tomahawk as effectively as the Indian.

During the slow, danger-fraught migratory movement from the coastal states to this far-western country, it is doubtful if any male over fourteen years of age undertook the long and hazardous journey without at least one defense weapon by his side, and many women, some of them "dead shots," were equipped with a firearm.

PARTIAL CHECK LIST OF OHIO GUNSMITHS

NAME	TOWN & COUNTY	DATE	NOTES
Ager, A.	New Rumley, Harrison	1856-61	
Albright, Henry	Gnadenhutten, Tuscarawas	1800	Made pistols
Albright, J.	Wayne County, near Wooster	1840's	
Albro, H., & Co.	Cincinnati	1847	Made mahogany gunstocks
Andrews, Edward W.	Cleveland Oberlin, Lorain	1826-51 1850-57	
Andrews, P. B.	Cleveland	1840	
Applebay, Alex.	Steubenville, Jefferson	1850	

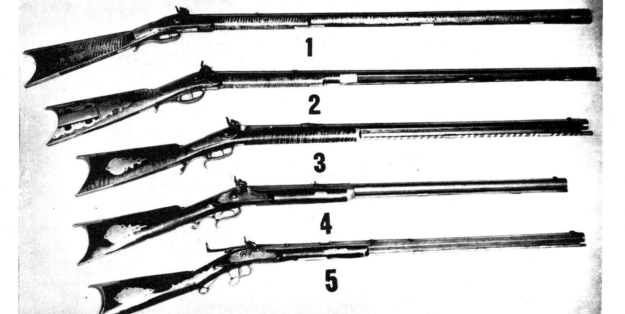

FIG. 2 — *1*, by I. D. Pounds, working 1843-1855. *2*, by J. Albright, working in the 1840's. *3*, by Hugh Weaver, working up to about 1870. Weaver was one of the best gunsmiths in Ashland County. *4*, by Milton Robert Doolittle, working 1857-1897. *5*, Reed of Medina County made this rifle for his son with burl-walnut stock, silver inlays, and patent breech. *Rifles in Figures 2, 3, and 4 from the collection of Stuart M. Martin.*

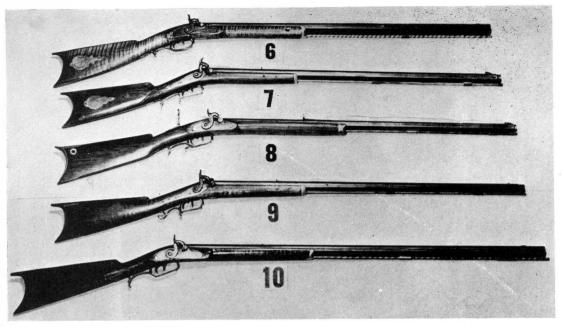

FIG. 3 — 6, by John Rickets; .42 caliber; length, 48 inches; weight, 10½ pounds; barrel length, 33 inches; note tiger-stripe curly-maple stock. 7, by Peter A. Reinhard of Ashland County, the only rifle maker mentioned in the old country history; made rifles ranging from light hunting types to heavy-barrel "slug" guns. 8, by Peter A. Reinhard; his barrels are usually marked *P. A. Reinhard, Ash.Co.O.Loudonville* with two masonic emblems. 9, Captain J. Clutz of Massillon made this rifle about 1860 for General Beatty's daughter who used it in "turkey shoots." 10, by Asa Stildenbauer; barrel marked *A.S.* on top.

NAME & NOTES	TOWN & COUNTY	DATE
Applebay, H. D. & W. R.	Lowell, Washington (formerly Wellsburg, Va. now W. Va.)	
Arnold, Wm.	Cadiz, Harrison	1812-15
Made gunpowder at age of 16. War of 1812		
Augustine, Sam.	Athens County	1853-54
Babbitt, L. W.	Cleveland	1837
Bandle, J.	Cincinnati	
"Gun Co."		
Barnhart, George	Hallsville, Ross	1844
Barnhart, Geo. A.	New Rumley, Harrison	1844-81
Descended from Hessian soldiers who settled in Bucks Co., Pa., after Revolution		
Barnhart, Nehemiah	Hallsville, Ross	1881
Born 1831, son of Wm. Barnhart I		
Barnhart, Wm. I	Green Tp., Ross	1867
Born 1802, brother of George A.		
Barnhart, Wm. II	Green Tp., Ross	1891
b. 1825, d. 1891, son of George A.		
Balser, A. L. & Co.	Cincinnati	1857-59
Battles, C. G.	Wellington, Lorain	
Beach, J. J.	Celina, Mercer	1835-60
Beadle	Maumee Valley	1840
"On Indian Trail"		
Bebout, Wm.	Monroe Tp., Belmont	1858-76
Beddie, Geo.	Sugar Creek Tp., Tuscarawas	1815-71
"Rifles and other firearms"		
Beebe, Richard	Springfield, Clark	1861-64
Beeman, John	Lancaster, Fairfield	1820
Beeman, Martin	Lancaster, Fairfield	1831
Bell, H. P.	Cambridge, Guernsey	
Bevier, James	Plymouth, Richland	1830
Biddle, Levi	Shanesville, Tuscarawas	1830
Bird, A. N.	Kenton, Hardin	1853-65
Bittinger, Peter	Orange Tp., Ashland	1825
Blair, Andy	Belmont County	1802
Sent to Stockade and Fort in Richland County by U. S. Govt.. 1812-17		
Bodenheimer, Wm.	Lancaster, Fairfield	1828
Booth, R. W.	Cincinnati	
Bowman, Wm.	Near Loudonville, Ashland County	1865-91
Worked with P. A. Reinhard of Loudonville		

NAME & NOTES	TOWN & COUNTY	DATE
Brelsford	Zanesville, Muskingum	1850-61
Son of Jonathan Brelsford		
Brelsford, Jonathan	Zanesville, Muskingum	1814
Brenner, Martin	Lancaster, Fairfield	1820-30
Brown, Ira	Cincinnati	1863-65
Brown, J. H.	Dayton, Montgomery	
Bryant, Silas	Cincinnati	1818-21
Buckley, Anton	Cincinnati	1860-64
Buddenhagen, John	Sandusky, Erie	1869-86
Burns, Henry	Lewisburg, Preble	
Burton, L.	Norwalk, Huron	1871-83
Campbell	Fort Washington, Cincinnati	1788
Sent by Federal Govt.		
Campbell, Abner	Hamilton, Butler	1862
Carey, M.	Lexington, Richland	1866-69
Carpenter, Nicholas	Marietta, Washington	1788
First gunsmith in Marietta; killed by Indians 1791		
Cartwright, John	Ottawa	1865
Chase, William	Pandora	1860
Clark, James	Cincinnati	1807-31
Made guns, pistols, daggers		
Clark, John	Canton, Stark	1821-36
Claspill, George W.	Lancaster, Fairfield	1831
Cleveland, W. H.	Cleveland and Norwalk, Huron	1880's
Clutz, Capt. J.	Massillon, Stark	1850
Craig, Andrew	Richland County	prior to 1812
Gunsmith with his brother, David, to the Indians in the "Indian Country," later stockade and fort in Mansfield, War of 1812		
Craig, David (see Andrew Craig)		
Cullman, Charles	Columbus, Franklin	1850-94
Made rifles and shotguns		
Cullman, G.	Cleveland	1840
Cunningham, W. A	Mt. Vernon, Knox	1857-59
D. C. & Co.	Cincinnati	
Made riflelocks		
Danner, Jacob	Canton, Stark	1818 or earlier
Killed the last wolf seen in Stark County		
Demster, B.	Zanesville, Muskingum	
Davidson, F., & Co.	Cincinnati	1850-53
Made gunlocks		
Doolittle, Milton	Homerville, Medina	1857-97
b. 1837 Coatsville, N. Y., d. 1904; came to Ohio 1880; made first rifle at age of 20		

NAME & NOTES	TOWN & COUNTY	DATE
Douglas, Jacob	E. Springfield, Jefferson	1830-40
Douglas, Robert	E. Springfield, Jefferson	1830
Douglass, Thompson	E. Springfield, Jefferson	1850
Dow, Eli S.	Dayton, Montgomery	1874-77
Downey, John	Jackson County	1840-76
Downey, Nathaniel	Jackson County	1869-86
Dunseth, Andrew	Fort Washington	prior to 1790
	Zanesville	1804
Sent by Federal Govt.; also a silversmith		
Eaton	Cincinnati (236 Main St.)	1840-51
Eberle, A.	Cincinnati (545 Vine St.)	1861-63
Eckel, Charles	Cincinnati (518 Vine St.)	1840-60
Eichorn, Charles	Cleveland	1848
Lock- and gunsmith		
Ellsworth, Joseph	Present Richland County	1800
Elwell, H.	Seneca County	prior to 1812
Made gunlocks for Indians		
Ely, A. F.	Mt. Vernon, Knox	1830-56
Enochs, Enoch	Brooksfield Tp., Knox	1830
Made gunpowder for the settlers		
Espich, Charles	Agersville, Auburn Tp. also New Philadelphia, Tuscarawas	1828
Fair, James	Dayton, Montgomery	1872-76
Fensel, Peter	Marysville, Union	1887
Ferree, Joel	Cumberland, Guernsey	1869-70
Fogelsang, John	Richland County	Early
Folger, W. H.	Barnsville, Belmont	1834
From Winchester, Va., "gunsmithing in the wintertime"		
Folk, William	Brian, Williams	1880-90
Folk's Gun Works		
Foncannon, M. B.	Columbus and New Lexington, Perry County	1840-54
Ford, D.	Abbeyville, Medina	1862-65
Fortney, Peter	Chillicothe, Ross	1804
Foster, "White"	Columbia, Williams	1848-69

Name & Notes	Town & County	Date
Frazier, Henry	Brown Tp., Knox	1840-50
Funk, Jacob	Muskingum County	prior to 1812
Armorer, swordsmith		
Furney, William	Mahoning County	1815
Repaired firearms		
G. D. & Co.	Cincinnati	
Made riflelocks		
Gardner, C.	Lima, Allen	1855-61
Gardner, John	Columbus	1866-88
Gaumer, Jacob	Saleto Tp., Muskingum	1811-23
Gibbs, John	Lancaster, Fairfield	1820's
Gillen, Wm.	Jackson, Jackson	1842
Glass, John	Putnam, Muskingum	1814
War of 1812		
Glass, Peter		
Glass, Samuel	Putnam, Muskingum	prior to 1812
Made rifles for War of 1812		
Gorrage, Thomas	Mt. Pleasant, Jefferson	
Grah		
Son of William Grah		
Grah, Wm.	Toledo, Lucas	1877-83
Gray, G. B.	Mt. Vernon, Knox	1867-70
Griffith, John	Cincinnati	1839-65
Contractor with Henry L. Siebert		
Grooms	West Union, Adams	
Gross Arms Co. (Henry Gross)	Tiffin, Seneca	1864-66
Gross Pat. rim fire revolvers		
Gross, Charles B.		
Gross, Henry I	Tiffin, Seneca	1830-34
Two-story log house on Perry St.		
Gross, Henry II	Tiffin and Cincinnati	1830-50
Groves, Isaac	Chillicothe, Ross	1804-18
Guin, James	Data lost	early
Guin, John	Data lost	early
Gump, J.	Upper Sandusky, Wyandot	1852-82
Gwynn & Campbell	Hamilton, Butler	1860
Edward Gwynn and Abner Campbell		
Hackney, Wm. W.	Dayton, Montgomery	1859-69
Hahn, George	Zanesville, Muskingum	1804-64
Hahn, Henry	Zanesville, Muskingum	1804
Halerstroh, L.	Fremont, Sandusky	1866-68

Name & Notes	Town & County	Date
Hall, Daniel	Present Richland County	1800
Gunsmith to the Indians		
Hall, P. E.	Ashtabula, Ashtabula	
Percussion false-muzzle match rifles		
Haquard	Portsmouth, Lawrence	
Harris, Wm.	Seneca County, "near Fort Sandoski"	prior to 1812
First white gunsmith to Indians, "talked Seneca like a Native"		
Haskell, T. R.	Painesville, Lake	
Hattersley, Henry	Cleveland, Cuyahoga	1850-71
Gun Manufactory		
Haynes, Wm. B.	Chillicothe, Ross	
Heaton		
Morgan	Putnam, Muskingum	1814
War of 1812		
Heiser, Lewis	Tiffin, Seneca	1857-59
Rifles and shotguns		
Henry, Moses	Present Ross County	1769
Herman, Peter	Lancaster, Fairfield	1840-71
Herr	Canton, Stark	early
Hetrick, John	Norwalk, Huron	1866-70
"Employed four hands"		
Hetrick, Levi	Lima, Alylen	1888-94
Hobbs, John	Putnam, Muskingum	
Hogg, John	Mt. Pleasant	1812
A saddler who made bullet pouches and belts, War of 1812		
Holmes, Geo. H.	Defiance, Defiance	1860-70
Hood, Geo. H.	Columbus	1847-55
Horton, Moses	Noble County	1818
Sold gunpowder and lead for bullets at trading post		
Hudson, Wm. L.	Cincinnati	1852-64
Made pistols		
Humberger, Adam	Perry County	
Son of Peter II, b. 1806, d. 1865		
Humberger, Henry	Rossville, Perry	
Son of Peter I. Made rifles and revolvers		
Humberger, Peter I	Somerset, Perry	1791
From Pennsylvania		
Humberger, Peter II	Perry County	1791-1852
b. 1775		
Humberger, Peter III	Perry County	1899
b. 1826		
Hunt, David S.	Cincinnati	1850-60
Hunt, Jonathan	Richland County	1806-12
Traded with Delaware Indians		

Name & Notes	Town & County	Date
J. C. M.	Dayton, Montgomery	
Percussion locks		
Jackson, David	Cincinnati	1831
Jacobs, Cornelius	Columbus	1843
Jennings, Richard	Cleveland (1 Broadway)	1840-78
Jones, Joseph	Columbus	1843-48
Jordan, Jerman	Chillicothe, Ross	early
Jughardt, C.	Fostoria, Seneca	1865-69
Kassan, Wm. M	Columbus	1835
Keating & Bell	Vincinity of Cincinnati	until 1826
Ran a powdermill (blown up 1826); also made shot, pistol balls, and holsters		
Kerner	Data lost	
Ketteridge (Kittridge), B.	Cincinnati	1845
Kile, Nathan	Raccoon Creek, Jackson	1817-24
Kimmel, Adam	Canton, Stark	
Only agent in "west" for Colt pistols		
King	New London, Huron	
Kirchbaum, David	Canton, Stark	1850-66
Made shot, pistol belts, holsters		
Lacave, C.	Canton, Stark	1880-83
Leatherman, F.	Dayton, Montgomery	1822
Leatherman, Fred	Dayton, Montgomery	1874-76
Lehman, George F.	Union County	1850-54
Lewis, John	Upper Sandusky, Wyandot, Huntsville	1808 1820
Repaired firearms for Indians		
Libeau, Valentine	Columbus	1827
Lindsley, Wm.	Portsmouth, Scioto	1829
Lingle, John	Clark County	1809
Had powdermill		
McCory	Canton, Stark	
Came from Pennsylvania		
McLeish, Charles	Williamsburg	
McNichols, Joseph	Goshen Tp., Belmont	1828-54
Maize, Henry	Uniontown (now Ashland), Ashland	1828-30
Marker, George	Gettysburg, Drake	1844
Meier	Wooster, Wayne	
Meissner		1880-1902
Son of Charles		
Meissner, Charles	Zanesville (12 S. 6 St.), Muskingum	1840-59

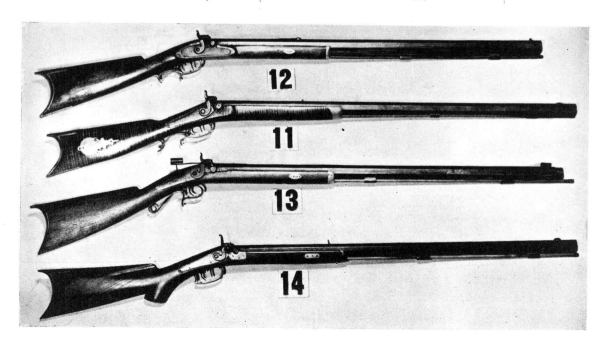

Fig. 4 — 11, by Hugh Weaver. 12, by R. Jennings, working 1869-1873. 13, by O. G. Thayer. 14, by William Bowman; barrel marked 1892; probably one of the last muzzle loaders made in the county; notice pistol grips showing modern trend.

Name & Notes	Town & County	Date
Miller, David	Springfield (209 U. Market St.)	1870-78
Moore, George	Mt. Vernon, Knox	1886-94
Morree (Morrett), L.	Columbus (Friend St.)	1847-48
Musgrave, B.	Ironton, Lawrence	
Neave, C.	Cincinnati	
Neave, T.	Cincinnati	
North, Selah	Stow's Corners, Summit	1835
Nelson, Roger I	Medina-Town, Medina	1825
Nelson, Roger II	Medina, Medina	1858-60
Oblinger, David	Piqua, Miami	1870-88
Oblinger, Walter	Troy, Miami	1869-78
Ohlenhausen	Wooster, Wayne	
Owens, Lemual	Zanesville, Muskingum	1810-20
Packard, Wm.	Elyria, Lorain	1859-60
Parks, Horace	Columbus	1878-93
With Chas. McLeish, 1872-80		
Park, John	Williamsburg, Cleremont	1878-82
Patton, Wm.	Springfield, Clark	1850-68
Perking, Reuben	Belmont County	
Made gunpowder		
Pettit, Andrew	Salem, Columbiana	1835
Pfeiffer, George	Cincinnati (160 Main Street)	1859-60
Piatt	Portsmouth, Lawrence	
Pierce	Liverpool (Grafton), Lorain	
Pomeroy	Canton, Stark	
Pool, Lemon	Springfield, Clark	1874-76
Ports, J. A. (J. E.)	Sunbury, Delaware	1877-82
Potts, Wm.	Columbus	1883-84
Pounds, I. D.	Columbus	1834-55
Made rifles, pistols, and shotguns to order		
Powell, Jacob	Logan County	
Powell, Jacob	"The Indian Country," now Richland Co. Ashland County, and Bowling Green	1825
Made rifles for Indians and repaired same, 1808		
Powell, Palemon	Cincinnati	1839-73
Pratt, Azariah	Marietta, Washington	1787
Also a silversmith		
Pratt, Elisha	Marietta, Washington	1849-54
Priest, Josiah	Cleveland	1840
Reed	Medina County, near Seville or Sterling	1850?
Reinhard (Reinhart) J. C.	Location not known	1840-60
Reinhard, Peter A.	Loudonville, Ashland	1850-90
Usually marked rifles with name, date, and masonic emblems		
Rendyles, Bernard	Steubenville, Jefferson	1852-54
Barrellmaker		
Rexer	Canton, Stark	Early
Rice, Ralsa C. b. 1838, d. 1911	Location unknown	
Rickets, John	Mansfield, Richland	1859-74
Rickets, T.	Mansfield	
Rife, Charles I	Cadiz, Harrison	1800-1812
Rife, Charles II	Cincinnati	1855-56
Righter, J.	Cadiz, Harrison	1800-12
Riley, Edward	Cincinnati	1816-19
Riley, Wm. L.	Watertown, Washington	1840-50
Ritzel	Canton, Stark	1816-40
Ritzel, P. M.	Stark County	1840-53
Probably son of above; made barrels after 1850		
Ross, A. C.	Zanesville, Muskingum	1810-20
Son of Elija Ross; made rifles and pistols		
Ross, Elija	Zanesville, Muskingum	1804-64
b. 1786, Brownsville, Pennsylvania; fine gunsmith and swordsmith		
Rownd	Canton, Stark	1812-64
Safford, Harry	Zanesville, Muskingum	1812
Made swords and dirks		
Schneider	Dayton, Montgomery	
Son of M. Schneider		
Schenider, F. A.	Canton, Stark	1853-57
Made barrels		
Schneider, M.	Dayton, Montgomery	1866-71
Schontz, P. H.	Canal Fulton, Stark	1855-65
Scott, Grant	Zanesville, Muskingum	1804-20
Seewald, Valentine	Tiffin, Seneca	1830
Seibert, Charles M.	Columbus	1851-1915
Seibert, Christian	Columbus (253 S. High St.)	1851-72
Brother of Charles M.; born in Germany		
Seibert, Henry L.	Cincinnati (279 Main St.)	1852-58
Griffith & Seibert		
Seigling, W. C.	Sandusky, Erie	1866-69
Rifles and shotguns		
Seits, Colonel George	Lancaster, Fairfield	1820's
Sells, Benjamin	Georgetown	1835-65
"Curly maple or Sugartree Gunstocks"		
Sells, James		
Sells, M. B.	Georgetown, Brown	1839
Sells, N. F.	Laurelville, Hocking County	1877-82
Shaw, Albert S.	Morrow County	1840
Sheetz	Hartsville, Stark	
Sherman	Portsmouth, Lawrence	
Shirley, Jerry	Cloverdale, Putnam	1870
Shuler, V.	Tuscarawas or Carroll County	
Made rifles and laminated double-barrel shotguns		
Slack	Springfield	
Son of Peter Slack		
Slack, Peter	Springfield (East Main St.)	1859-91
Slaret	Chillicothe, Ross	
Smith, John	Hessville, Hardin	1868
Smith, Lewis	Tiffin, Seneca	1858-59
Smuts	Piqua, Miami	
Sniveley, Jacob	Flint's Mills, Washington	1854-65
Sprague	Loudonville, Ashland	Before 1850
P. A. Reinhard was apprenticed to Sprague		
Statler, Wm.	Logan (Main St.), Hocking	1868-74
Stewart	Bucyrus, Crawford	
Made rifles and revolvers		
Stildenbauer, Asa	Winesburg, Holmes	
Barrels marked on top A.S.		
Sting	Tiffin, Seneca	
Stossmeister, Chas.	Cincinnati	1857-63
Streets, Chas.	Portsmouth, Scioto	1829
Strickler	Dayton, Montgomery	1837
Worked with J. Wilt; made rifle and shotgun barrels		
Strohl, J.	Fremont, Sandusky	1868-70
Stroup, O. M.	Wellington, Lorain	1880-83
Swartz, Abraham	Sugar Creek, Tuscarawas	1850-70
Also an organ tuner		
Taylor, Henry	Jackson Tp.,	1817
First gunsmith		
Taylor, N. B.	Vienna, Trumbull	1840
Teaff, James	Steubenville, Jefferson	1856-91
Father of Nimrod		
Teaff, Joseph	Steubenville, Jefferson	1820's
Teaff, Nimrod	Steubenville, Jefferson	early
A great hunter of bear and deer		
Thayer, O. G.	Chardon, Geauga	
"Creedmore" match rifles		
Thompson, Harry	Fremont, Sandusky	1800
Thompson, Samuel	Columbus and Lancaster	1820-27
Trant, George B.	Thornville, Perry	1877-80
Tyler, N. B.	Vienna, Trumbull	1855-71
Rifle Works		
Urie, Solomon	Orange Tp., Ashland	1818
First winter "killed 40 deer and 8 black bear"		
Van Meter	Chillicothe, Ross	
Venia & Johnson	Toledo, Lucas	1880-83
Vickers, Jonathan	Cleveland	1821
Villwock, Chas.	Toledo, Lucas	1772-82
Vincent, John Caleb	Washington County	to 1900
Born 1841		
Vincent, John	Washington County	1844-82
Born 1809		
Vincent, John	Cleveland	1850
Vogelsang, A. M.	Fostoria, Hancock	1868-69
Wade, Abner	Saleto Tp., Muskingum	1811
Walker, Joseph	Knox County	1804-07
"Tinkered gun locks for the Indians"		
Wareham, David		
Warner, Benj. Franklin	Seneca County, "The Indian Country"	
Native of Conn.; made gunstocks for the Senecas; went with tribe to Fort Gibson, Iowa		
Way, Arad	Canfield, Trumbull, and Middlebury, Summit	1800-1808 / 1812
Made pistols		
Weaver, Hugh	Pleasant Ridge, Ashland	1870

Fig. 5 — "Cross-Bow Gun." One of the few examples extant in Ohio of this frontier weapon, was used against the Indians at the Coulter blockhouse in present Richland County during the War of 1812. Made by hand from soft wood and stained dull, dark red. Several of the adjustable sights are missing. A groove runs the length of pseudo barrel. Sometimes called "Quaker" guns, more or less harmless. A fictitious muster roll was called and voices inside the fort responded, giving the Indians the impression that there were many more persons in the fort than there actually were. These guns were then pushed through portholes and could be used as supports for bows and arrows if the settlers' other ammunition ran low.

Weldon, Robin   Mansfield, Richland   1810
Made implements of war, War of 1812; lived in blockhouse during war

Wertz, Peter   Saleto Tp.,   1811
Muskingum

Whit, J. R.   Seneca County   1812
Bored gun barrels; repaired firearms during War 1812

White, H.   Jackson, Jackson   1851-65
White, J. A.   Jackson, Jackson   1854-58
White, John   New Philadelphia,
Tuscarawas

Wickline   New Ironton, Lawrence
Wilkins, Neil   Zanesville,   1804-20
Muskingum

Williams, John W.   Maumee, Lucas
Powdermaker

Wilt, J.   Dayton, Mont-   1850-54
gomery, and Hamilton
Barrels only

Winniger, Adam   Rockey Fork near   War of
Lucas, Richland   1812
County
Repaired firearms at Beams Mill

Winship, Wynn   Mansfield,   War of
Richland   1812
Worked in Stockade, southeast of public square

Yerian, Frederick   Sharon Tp.,   very
Noble   early

Yerian, John   Sharon, Noble   1879-82

Yerian, L. M.   Cumberland,   1883-
Guernsey   1902

Young, Nathaniel   Fairfield County   1803
Michael   Government
Stockade,   War of
Mansfield   1812
"The Ax-Maker." Made tomahawks and scalping knives for Greentown and Heiltown Indians, 1804

Youtze   Wilmot, Stark

Zartman, Joshua   Newark (77 N.   1852-86
5 St.), Licking

Zeigler, H. D.   Portsmouth, Scioto   1858-65
H. D. Zeigler & Co.

John Hills, gunsmith of Vermont

BY MARIUS B. PELADEAU

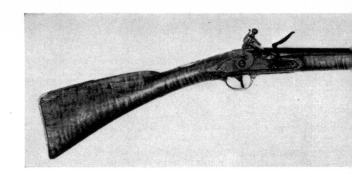

MEDAD HILLS, GUNSMITH of Goshen, Connecticut, was resurrected from the past in an article in ANTIQUES for July 1943 (p. 18), in which the author, Dr. J. R. Mayer, brought out the importance of Hills' production of firearms and his contribution of time, money, and skills to the American Revolutionary cause. Collectors and students of New England arms of that period have long known of the existence of another gunsmith named Hills, said to have worked in northern Vermont during the closing years of the eighteenth century, but he has remained a shadowy figure. This article will show that John Hills of Charlotte, Vermont, was also a gunsmith of importance and skill.

Written records of the eighteenth century concerning the mundane trade of gunsmith are nearly nonexistent, and actual examples of John Hills' work are almost as difficult to find. However, through town and family records and town histories it has been possible to trace the outlines of his life, and to establish his relationship to other gunsmiths of the same name.

John Hills was a brother of Medad, and they were sons of the gunsmith Benoni Hills. Benoni was born in Northampton, Massachusetts, in 1700. With his wife, Hannah, he moved first to Suffield, Connecticut, about 1724 where their first child, also named Hannah, was born. The family then settled in Durham, Connecticut, and there Medad, the fourth child and second son, was born on April 27, 1729. John, next in line, saw the light of day in Durham on December 13, 1732. (Records of Benoni Hills' marriage, and of his nine children, are reprinted in William C. Fowler, *History of Durham, Connecticut*, 1866). In 1740 Benoni moved his growing family to Goshen, Connecticut, where he continued his trade of gunmaking and also became a toolmaker. It is more than likely that both Medad and John were apprenticed to their father and learned from him the interrelated trades of ironmongering, blacksmithing, whitesmithing, and gunsmithing.

John took Jerusha Lewis as his wife on August 11, 1754, when he was twenty-two years old (see the Reverend A. G. Hibbard, *History of the Town of Goshen, Connecticut*, 1897). Shortly before the outbreak of the Revolution the couple moved to Winchester, Connecticut, where John plied his trade as a gunsmith. John was a more restless man than Medad. Like many of his Connecticut neighbors, he saw promise and challenge in the virgin territory then still called the New Hampshire Grants. There a town called Charlotte, or Charlotta, had been granted a charter on June 24, 1762. Six miles square,

with great stands of oak and pine, it lay in the northwestern part of Vermont, in the fertile plain that slopes down to Lake Champlain. The first permanent settlers arrived in 1784, and among them was John Hills with his wife and children.

He practiced his trade in the new town, and participated in local life and government. In March 1787 Charlotte was organized as a township. John Hills was chosen to serve as a selectman and a lister; he also became sealer of weights and measures, and a juryman. In the 1790 census he was listed as the head of a household which included his wife, two girls, two boys over ten, and two over sixteen. Charlotte grew and prospered, and his standing in the community grew with it. On September 15, 1807, his wife died at the age of seventy, and he did not survive her long. John Hills was seventy-two when he died on March 7, 1808, and was buried beside Jerusha in Barber Cemetery, Charlotte.

The eighteenth-century gunsmith had to be a versatile craftsman, able to work with wood, to operate a forge for ironwork, and to cast brass and copper. Building a long arm or handgun was a difficult and time-consuming process, for every component had to be made by hand. Thus the average gunsmith turned out relatively few arms in his lifetime, especially if, like John Hills, he worked without the aid of journeymen or apprentices. Another reason for the scarcity of arms by John Hills today—and indeed of other gunsmiths of the Revolutionary period—is that a firearm was a utilitarian instrument which saw hard service in good weather and bad throughout the year. Although firearms were prized, many were literally worn out.

The long fowler by John Hills illustrated here (Figs. 1-5) is strikingly similar to one by his brother Medad (Figs. 6, 7). Both are extremely long, with a delicacy and grace more often seen in Pennsylvania-made "Kentucky" rifles than in arms of this era made in New England. The two are stocked in a tightly grained tiger maple with a fine "Roman-nose" butt, wide butt plate, and relatively thin wrist.

Both Medad and John had a manner of finishing off the extreme end of the barrel which was apparently peculiar to them: the muzzle is formed by a finely faceted and tapered octagonal section to which the sight is attached. Another distinctive feature of a John or Medad Hills long arm is the tang of the butt plate: it is extended into a long taper, on which the maker's name and location are engraved. A gunsmith's signature on the

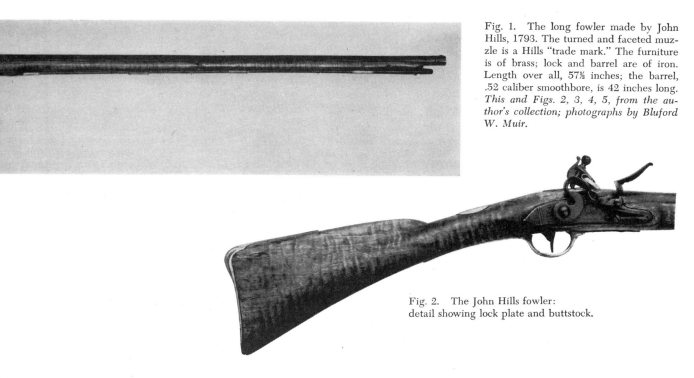

Fig. 1. The long fowler made by John Hills, 1793. The turned and faceted muzzle is a Hills "trade mark." The furniture is of brass; lock and barrel are of iron. Length over all, 57½ inches; the barrel, .52 caliber smoothbore, is 42 inches long. *This and Figs. 2, 3, 4, 5, from the author's collection; photographs by Bluford W. Muir.*

Fig. 2. The John Hills fowler: detail showing lock plate and buttstock.

Fig. 3. Detail showing maker's name and location engraved on the extended tang of the butt plate, the brass escutcheon dated 1793, and the raised shell carving at the rear of the barrel tang.

Fig. 4. Detail showing brass side plate opposite the lock engraved with the owner's name, Rufus Green.

Fig. 5. Detail showing top of the barrel engraved *Vermont*, with ornamental vine.

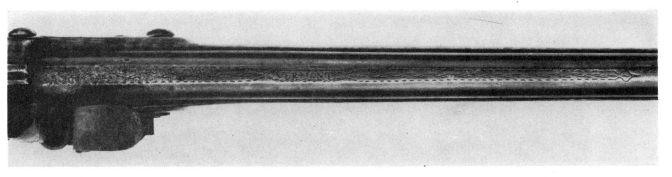

Fig. 6. Medad Hills fowler: detail showing butt-plate tang engraved with maker's name and location. *This and Fig. 7 from the collection of Norm Flayderman.*

Fig. 7. Medad Hills fowler: detail showing side plate engraved with name of owner.

butt-plate tang is most uncommon; usually it appears on the lock plate or on top of the barrel. Still another point of similarity in the long arms of the two brothers is the use of a large, full side plate to bear the name of the person for whom the gun was made.

Medad's fowler is dated 1758 on a brass plate inset at the top of the wrist. John dated his fowler similarly with the year 1793 and indulged in a little decoration besides, engraving a charming rose and vine on the brass wrist inset. The trigger guard is also engraved with a rose. And on the top of the barrel of this gun, made just two years after Vermont was admitted to the Union as the fourteenth state, John engraved the word *Vermont* and a trailing vine. In all cases John's engraving is freer than Medad's. The stock work is also fine. The maple is of an even, tight, tiger grain to the end of the barrel. It is decorated by a shell carved in relief at the end of the barrel tang and by a double molding on both edges of the barrel and ramrod channels. The barrel carries no proof marks and this, along with the faceting at the muzzle, supports the belief that it was not imported but made by Hills himself.

The pistol illustrated (Figs. 8, 9) is the only known handgun by John Hills. Its spartan appearance contrasts with the decorative character of the fowler. The lock is simple and unadorned, the side plate and trigger guard are plain, and the brass bird's-head grip cap is strong and utilitarian. Similar in design to British arms used in America during and after the Revolution, this pistol was a military or semimilitary weapon, probably carried in the War for Independence or in local conflicts by a Vermont militia officer.

It too is well made. The stock is maple, with a slight tiger grain in the forestock. Again the ramrod and barrel channels are decorated by a simple double molding, and the brass side plate, although not engraved, has much the same contour as that on the fowler.

It is hoped that this brief record of John Hills' life and work may help bring to light other examples of his craftsmanship.

For their kind assistance in the preparation of this article I should like to thank Violet W. Vaill, Vincent J. Stanulis, Gunnar K. Holmes, and Mary Waller.

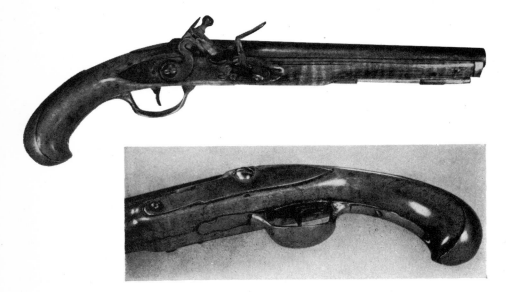

Fig. 8. Pistol made by John Hills, engraved *J. Hills* on the lock plate. Side plate, trigger guard, ramrod pipes, forestock tip, and bird's-head butt cap are of brass; barrel and lock are of iron. Length over all, 14⅞ inches. The .50 caliber smoothbore barrel is 8¾ inches long.

This and Fig. 9 from the collection of Joe Kindig Jr.; photographs by courtesy of George C. Neumann.

Fig. 9. The John Hills pistol, detail. Note similarity in shape of the side plate and trigger guard to those of the long arm.

A Key to Rifle Locks

By T. B. Tryon

Illustrations from the author's collection

A STUDY of the development of Kentucky rifle locks adds interest to the collecting of the famous weapons themselves. The typical custom-built Kentucky rifle — long and graceful, splendidly wrought and decorated — is primarily a weapon of the flint period, though many specimens altered to the percussion system saw service to the end of the muzzle-loading era. However, the lock, most intricate part of the weapon, was not invariably fabricated by the maker of the rifle. The American riflesmith concentrated on the accuracy, balance, and decoration of his creation, and not infrequently procured the lock ready-made, for lockfiling was a trade in itself. Hence a portion of the locks found on pre-Revolutionary Kentuckies were imported from England — product of the professional lockfilers of Birmingham and Wolverhampton.

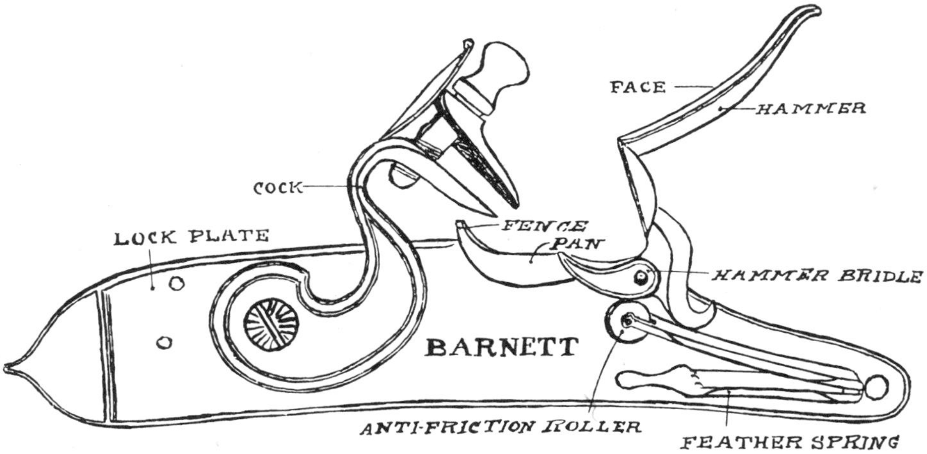

It would appear that the Ketlands, under sundry firm names, were the principal English concern engaged in exporting locks (and finished arms as well) to the American colonies, though the Barnetts undoubtedly figured to a certain extent in this as well as in the African trade. Whether the London Ketlands were independent jobbers or outlets for the Birmingham concerns is not altogether apparent; but the fact remains that locks of sundry styles, grades, and periods, bearing the trade names of the various Ketlands, form the major portion of the locks imported from Europe to America and now found on Kentucky rifles.

Pre-Revolutionary locks of American workmanship may be distinguished by the one or two vertical grooves which invariably appear on the tail of the otherwise severely plain lockplate. Prior to 1790 American plates were seldom elaborately engraved. With few exceptions, the really early American riflesmith placed his name only on the barrel of his rifle, even when he himself had fashioned the lock. Hence it may be stated as a general rule that unless the name on the lock coincides with that on the barrel of a Kentucky rifle, the name on the lock is that of the lockfiler, not of the riflesmith. By the same token, a plate devoid of marking may be accepted as the work of the man who made the rifle. The early American lockfilers, in common with the English craftsmen of the period, adhered to the Continental custom of forging plate and pan separately, and then dovetailing and pinning these parts together.

Locks of about 1740, of either English or American origin, may be distinguished by the absence of the so-called bridle on the internal mechanism as well as on the pan, and by the separately forged plate and pan. The typical cock is of the full rounded *S* gooseneck type.

Locks of this period, though entirely serviceable, were not particularly smooth in action, due to weak support of internal mechanism and hammer pivot pin. To obviate this structural imperfection, locks of the better sort were later fabricated with a bridle over the tumbler, which greatly strengthened the internal mechanism. An extension on the pan, also known as a bridle, was designed to support the pivot pin of the hammer. These improvements, which served to render the lock smooth and reliable in action, appear on locks of about 1760, which otherwise are similar to locks of the preceding period. English locks, especially the more expensive, with both cock and plate filed with oval face, occurred in both periods, but rarely thereafter.

We may safely assume that most of the original locks found on the very oldest Kentucky rifles are of American manufacture. On the other hand, a majority of locks found on rifles of the 1760 decade are of English origin. In 1750 Parliament decreed that bar and pig iron imported to London from the colonies be exempt from duty. It further decreed that no rolling or slitting mills or furnaces for making steel should be permitted in the colonies. These laws were, of course, designed to create a greater demand for the manufactures of Great Britain. The colonial lockfiler's source of steel was, therefore, chiefly scraps salvaged from discarded tools and weapons. In this connection we may remark that, while the hammers of English locks were usually forged from one piece of steel with the face hardened, the hammers of *pre*-Revolutionary American-made

Fig. 1 — DIAGRAM OF BARNETT LOCK (*c. 1770*)

A piece of flint, securely held in the jaws of the cock, actuated by a powerful mainspring, creates a shower of sparks upon striking the vertical steel face of the hammer — the latter being impelled to an oblique position against the resistance of the featherspring, by the force of the blow. Thus the priming powder in the magazine of the pan is deflagrated by the sparks; the resultant flame, being communicated by a train of powder through the vent, serves to ignite the charge in the chamber of the rifle

Fig. 2 — AMERICAN LOCK FROM ROESSER RIFLE (*c. 1740*)

Note separate steel facing on hammer. The pivot pin is introduced from the exterior of plate, while in the following types it enters from the inner side. Vertical groove across tail of plate is indication of pre-Revolutionary American manufacture

locks were forged from wrought iron and faced with a thin piece of steel held in place by rivets, or spelter, or both. It was due to his lack of steel, and to the fact that good English locks were readily procurable, that the American riflesmith found it better to utilize the imported article than to forge and file his own locks, even though he possessed the requisite skill.

With the advent of smooth-working locks, finely filed, fitted, and finished, effort was directed to accelerating the speed of the action. This resulted in the introduction of the antifriction roller on the featherspring, which permitted the hammer to be thrown quickly and smoothly. The better locks of about 1770 carry this improvement. From this time on, furthermore, both English and American lockmakers forged plate and pan in one piece. Such was the type of lock with which the fine custom-built Kentucky rifles made just prior to and during the Revolution were equipped. Even mediocre English locks of this period, attached to inexpensive commercial rifles, are distinguished by the integral pan and plate. These locks, however, are roughly filed and fitted and usually lack many or all of the refinements that characterize the fine locks.

In 1774 the British embargo on munitions of war virtually ended the importation of English locks into the colonies. The trade never regained its former volume. During and following the Revolution, many lock shops were established in the new Republic — principally in Pennsylvania. The Golchers, J. Bishop, and C. Bird & Co. were among the more prominent of the post-Revolutionary American makers who produced strong, reliable locks. Though superior to the majority of English locks imported prior to the Revolution, the American mechanisms bore no comparison to the productions of such master craftsmen of the day as Wogdon, Henry Nock, and Joe Manton of London. To these English artisans must be credited the vastly superior locks which appeared in the last quarter of the eighteenth century. Their improvements, designed to increase the speed

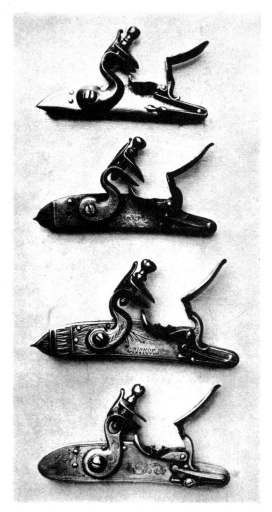

Fig. 3a (above) — ENGLISH, T. KETLAND, LOCK (*c. 1760*)
Note oval face of cock and plate and extension on pan (hammer bridle) designed to add support to pivot pin of hammer

Fig. 3b — ENGLISH, BARNETT, LOCK (*c. 1770*)
Note addition of antifriction roller on featherspring

Fig. 3c — AMERICAN, BISHOP, LOCK (*c. 1790*)
Note ornate engraving of this late period; drains of waterproof pan; and sturdier, straighter form of cock

Fig. 3d — AMERICAN LOCK (*c. 1800*)
From Henry rifle. Note braced underjaw of improved form of cock

Fig. 5a (right) — REVERSE OF LOCK (*c. 1740*)
Note the bridleless internal mechanism and indentation in bolster which marks the dovetail joint of separate pan and bolster fastened to plate by rivet plainly visible in centre of rear portion of bolster. (A screw was sometimes used instead of a rivet, as in the case of a lock of about 1760 shown in the drawing, Figure 6)

Fig. 5b — REVERSE OF LOCK (*c. 1800*)
Note drains on sides of pan; bridle *over* tumbler; integral pan, bolster, and plate; and the fact that the hammer pivot pin (screwhead visible on forward part of bolster) enters from inner side of plate. The constricted opening in the periphery of the pan is somewhat larger than the diameter of the vent and was intended to concentrate the flame at this point, where the priming reaches the train of powder in the vent

and reliability of dueling pistols and to make these weapons virtually rainproof, were later adapted to sporting weapons and ultimately adopted by lockfilers the world over.

During wet weather a waterproof cover of leather or oilskin to protect the idle flintlock from moisture was a prime necessity. Furthermore, if one were shooting in the rain, water had a way of collecting in the pan and wetting the priming almost at the moment when the lock cover was removed. To obviate this situation English masters developed the so-called "rainproof" pan. In this the lock cover was not eliminated, but the pan was so constructed as to permit rain water to drain away without immediately impairing the priming. This improvement, of great benefit to the rifleman who must take deliberate aim, was soon adopted by American lockfilers.

The finest American locks of the 1790's embodied all the successive improvements made in preceding types, with the addition of the

Fig. 4 — DUELING-PISTOL LOCK BY MANTON (*c. 1790*)
Note exaggerated drains on pan and sliding catch on tail of plate intended to lock cock at half bent, known as a *cock bolt*

rainproof pan. American lock plates of this period were ornately engraved. It will also be noted that the cock of the lock pictured in Figure 3c as typical of this period, though of gooseneck form, has become straighter and much sturdier than its prototypes. The graceful gooseneck cock of earlier days was inclined to snap at most inopportune moments. Hence the sturdier shape was adopted by many English lockfilers at a rather early date. It first appeared prior to 1760, became more widely recognized in the 1770's, and is typical of American locks of the 1790's.

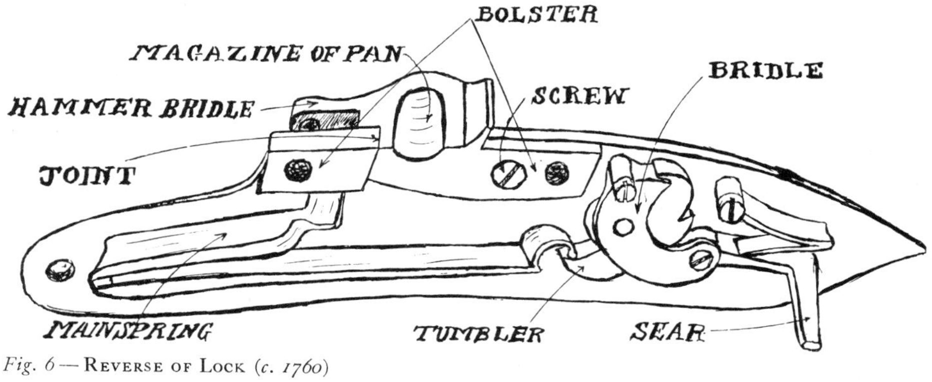

Fig. 6 — REVERSE OF LOCK (*c. 1760*)

But even the improved type of gooseneck was not unbreakable. Hence for the benefit of pioneers and far-roaming hunters many American lockfilers adopted the so-called flat or solid cock with braced underjaw. This virtually unbreakable cock was by no means a fresh invention. It was a revival of a form employed by Edward Nicholson of London in the early 1600's. It appeared in France in the middle of the same century, but did not supersede the gooseneck cock on French martial arms until 1763. Its belated acceptance was due to what the English considered its ungainliness. Not until the close of the century did English gunmaking use it on pistols and sporting arms. However, the finest American locks of about 1800, considered by American riflemen to be the acme of flintlock perfection, incorporated this type of cock with all the improvements of the preceding type. Both gooseneck and straight cocks, the latter in preponderance, were used by American makers to the end of the flintlock period — roughly, 1840.

The elegant custom-built Kentuckies — the only rifles worthy of the connoisseur's attention, incidentally — were invariably equipped with the finest locks available. It is to these locks that the preceding criteria apply. Yet it does not follow that the period of the lock infallibly determines the age of the rifle on which it is found. It must be borne in mind that the latest thing in locks was not always available to the remotely situated American riflesmith. The best obtainable was not infrequently a fine lock of the preceding period. Hence sundry characteristics of the rifle itself must be weighed against the special features of the lock before their equality of age may be assured.

Per contra, a fine rifle, conceded to be early, may, and frequently does, carry a lock of much later period. The large-calibre rifles that saw actual service in the colonial wars often suffered such abuse as to necessitate extensive repairs. The erosive effects of inferior powder, coupled with rust induced by exposure incidental to frontier campaigns, rendered unserviceable many a lock as well as vent and rifling. Under such circumstances, repairs were drastic. Rebouching the vent, rerifling the bore, and replacing the original lock with a new one of a style later than that of the rifle, were the order of the day. Obviously, therefore, the period of the lock is an unreliable index to the age of the rifle on which it is found.

IV Edged Weapons

Edged weapons were as much a part of American history as firearms, but their popularity as a collectable artifact has never reached that accorded guns. One possible reason for this may lie in the fact that swords began to lose popularity as an infantry side arm with the advent of the bayonet during the American Revolution. By the end of the Civil War, the cavalry saber was an almost forgotten weapon.

Swords, spontoons, halberds, tomahawks and scalping knives were all very important tools in colonial America, as well as symbols of rank and stature. Halberds and spontoons were cutting and piercing weapons mounted on long poles. Halberds were quite effective until the beginning of the 18th century when their use was limited to a symbol of rank carried by sergeants and subordinate officers. American-made halberds are usually delightfully-crafted examples of the blacksmith's skill.

The spontoon (or trench spear) was used throughout the Revolution as a defensive weapon, and it was a symbol of rank as well. This shafted weapon became obsolete by the end of the Revolution and was replaced by carbines and fusils in American military service. Some, however, were still carried as symbols in courthouses and in parades. Extremely rare today, pole arms are not available in large enough quantities to afford many collectors the opportunity to add them to their collections. Just as rare are tomahawks and scalping knives of the colonial period.

When Congress asked for volunteers to enlist in the militia in 1775, each man was required to provide himself with a musket and with one of the following: a cutting sword, bayonet, tomahawk, or hatchet. It is not known whether the tomahawk was popular with the infantryman during the Revolution, but it was an important side arm for the rifleman and the frontiersman during the 18th and early 19th centuries, as was the scalping knife. Few collections today include authentic examples of these early American edged weapons, and little has been written about them. Swords, on the other hand, have been the subject of many articles and books.

Swords have served man since the Bronze Age, and as collectables they fall into many categories. Early settlers brought them to America from Europe and England. Many were imported into the colonies during the 18th and 19th centuries, and a few were manufactured there. Most of the blades, however, were imported. The two major blade-producing centers were Solingen, Germany, and Toledo, Spain. Other countries, in-

cluding England and France, induced craftsmen from those centers to settle in their own countries to avoid having to import blades.

Although copied from English and European styles, many brass and iron-hilted colonial American swords acquired delightful characteristics that were unique, often times giving the impression that they can be classified as folk art. Silver swords, on the other hand, were finely-crafted examples of the work of gifted artisans. Except in a few rare instances where crude, unbecoming examples were made, the American silversmith followed the English and European styles as carefully as he did in crafting tankards and teapots. For some unexplainable reason, the silver sword has never commanded the appreciation of the American silver collector bestowed upon other forms of that craft.

A colonial gentleman normally wore a sword, called a "court" or "small" sword, suspended from a belt at his waist. He usually carried this same sword into military service unless he was a mounted officer requiring a heavier-bladed saber. The small sword has a straight blade, usually triangular shaped (although sometimes merely double edged), tapering to an even point, or a colichemarde blade, which is wider at the hilt, suddenly narrowing to an even taper to the point. Many of the hilts were gilt brass, but, when the customer could afford the additional cost, silver was purchased. Imported silver swords were in the majority, but occasionally a local silversmith would fashion the style hilt requested and secure it to a blade that was probably imported. A scabbard, with mountings matching the decoration of the hilt, would be made to fit the blade.

Sometimes silver swords are found without hallmarks, and an attribution of American manufacture has often been too quickly made without documentation. The intelligent collector should be wary of undocumented "attributions."

Those readers who would view colonial weaponry in the Spanish provinces of America will welcome Arthur Woodward's fine article on swords of California and Mexico. Although the subject of Spanish colonial swords does not command nearly as large a collectors' audience as that of the English colonial edged weapons, their history and romance are nonetheless enticing. Knives, too, have always attracted a great deal of collector attention—particularly the large Bowie knife of the 19th century—so it is well that this section of the anthology ends with J. Nielson Barry's splendidly-named article, "The Fine Art of Stabbing."

AMERICAN SILVER-HILTED SWORDS
Part 1
By PHILIP MEDICUS

THE ONE-HUNDRED-YEAR PERIOD ending in 1840 was the approximate span during which the silver-hilted sword was in vogue in America. To a greater degree than any other weapon, it represented the elegance and importance of a privileged class, particularly in the first sixty years of its popularity. But this decorative badge of authority, despite its soft luster and delicate lines, was as deadly as it was beautiful and served as well on the battlefields as in the ballroom. Prior to the Revolution the preference of most of the colonists was for swords from the mother country, but the work of some of our leading American silversmiths is to be found in the hilts of street, dress, presentation, and fighting weapons. Although foreign-bladed, for the most part, these can truly be called American swords because of their completion and service in this country. These silver-mounted swords, very few of which are in existence, afford interest in two distinct fields — early American silver and American edged weapons.

In this article American silver is treated only in its application to American swords; likewise no attempt is made to explore the entire background of American sword history. The many foreign-made silver-hilted swords used in this country are outside the scope of this treatise, which is concerned only with examples assembled and used here. Certain factual data which apply to swords in general are, however, included in this part of the article. Part II will deal more specifically with the parts of the sword made by the silversmith.

Before the Revolution most American silver hilts were punch-marked or engraved with the maker's name but in the years of the war this practice was curtailed as there was a decided risk in placing identification marks on any weapon intended for the use of American patriots. This accounts for the relatively few marked specimens attributed to that period. A mark is a help in determining the period during which a sword was made but it does not enable us to pin it down to a specific year. The shape and style of the hilt are also pointers to its approximate period, as are certain features of its silverworking technique.

In general, style changes followed those of the European silver designers whose products were shipped here and quickly duplicated by American smiths. As with every other type of decorative object, silver hilts reflect the time lag that accompanies a change of style before the new completely ousts the old, and an item may have been made many years after its particular style reached its peak of popularity. With swords we have the blade to consider as well as the hilt, and it is usually very helpful in determining the date of making, except when obvious remounting has taken place. Old blades were often used on new hilts, particularly in

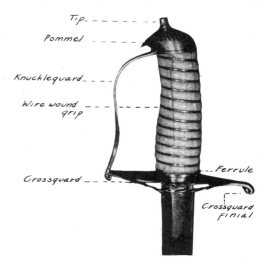

FIGS. 1, 2, 3—SWORD PARTS. Showing the details of construction, and listing the parts used in every sword, and those specialized parts used occasionally.

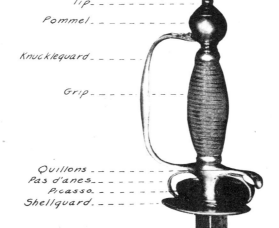

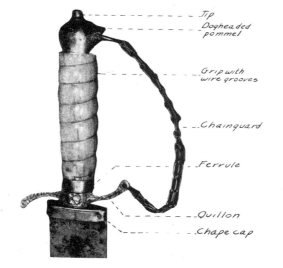

early days in America. However, unless a sword or blade is actually marked with a date, as it rarely is, there is no way of determining the exact year of its making. As none of the swords here illustrated is dated the years given in the captions are approximate.

The first type of silver-hilted sword made in America was the colichemarde which was fashioned more or less along the lines of the European court sword. The court sword was a beautifully made weapon, ornamented with jewels and semi-precious stones, none of which, however, were used with the colichemarde and small-sword types made in America. The so-called small sword, closely resembling the court sword in form, had replaced the heavy and cumbersome rapier in favor when dueling started to become popular in Europe. Strictly speaking, all swords with the court-sword hilt should be termed small swords, but common usage has subdivided them into the court sword, colichemarde, and small sword, more or less following their periods of service. The colichemarde blade derived its name from Count Christoph Philipp Konigsmark, a Swedish swordsman who helped develop the type about 1700. Its feature was the abruptly heavy shoulder of its forte, or upper section, which gave greater rigidity and strength to the thin blade.

Improvement in dueling technique brought

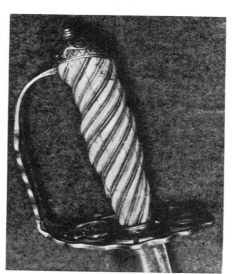

FIG. 4—SMALL SWORD *(1740-1750)*. Unmarked. Attributed to Boston. Ball pommel, untipped; wire-wound grip with ferrule of rigid metal; triangular foreign narrow blade. *All illustrations from the collection of Philip Medicus and PFC Philip Jay Medicus.*

FIG. 5 *(below)*—HANGER *(1750-1760)*. Unknown maker. Spiraled ivory grip; engraved pommel in roundcap form; cupped chape cap; lower knuckle guard and crossguard patterned with openwork and scalloped edge. Blade, 32 by 1⅛ inches, with one narrow and one deep groove; slightly curved.

out the necessity for a blade with a tapering shape for thrusting instead of the colichemarde which fulfilled a cutting and thrusting function; in consequence, the blade became increasingly narrow. The newer narrow-bladed weapon used practically the same hilt as the colichemarde, except for a change in the size of the pas d'anes. The two loops that go by this name had a functional purpose: the index and second finger of the sword hand were inserted in them so that the sword could be more dexterously handled. With the passage of time and the decline in dueling, these loops became increasingly smaller and served only as decorations.

In this country the colichemarde was used soon after its introduction in Europe and it was the first style copied and completed by our silversmiths, around the year 1735. Then came the change to the narrow-bladed types, just as had occurred on the Continent. About 1760 the hanger became increasingly popular, and by 1800 the small sword had become obsolete as far as our silversmiths were concerned. The hanger was a slightly curved modification of the straight-bladed English hanger which, in turn, was evolved from the Continental hunting sword. It was favored by the fighting man because of its compactness and its ability to cut instead of thrust. While cutting was not considered good form in dueling, it was effective in mortal combat. About 1780, the D-guard sword, also adopted from the other side and made in many variations, started to attract the public fancy and, like good businessmen, the silversmiths followed the trend. Here again was a sword for the fighting man rather than for the gentry. And near the 1790's the vogue of the stirrup-guarded sword began.

As far as silver-hilted swords are concerned, these types represent our silversmith's output. At the turn of the century, and even before, the manufacture of Sheffield plated, gold-plated, and fire-gilt plated sword hilts curtailed the demand for the silver hilts. They were made less and less frequently until, about 1840, they became obsolete, with the exception of specially designed presentation models which, while made of silver, in most cases were finished with a gold plating.

With the scarcity of all kinds of fighting equipment, from the early days to almost the end of the eighteenth century, virtually anything that could serve as a sidearm and could stop the enemy was brought into service. Our fighting men had to content themselves with weapons which were far less imposing than the silver hilts but which were their equal in combat. In the field of swords, brass and iron-mounted hangers and cutlasses were favored by seamen, longer bladed weapons for use on land. Many sabers with very long curved blades, classified as types used by the Hessian mercenaries, were used when they fell in the possession of our armed forces. Long and short edged weapons, mounted with brass or iron, with foreign or locally forged blades, were, to the average soldier and sailor, dependable and reliable weapons on which he could always put his faith.

During the Revolution the Committee of Safety issued small quantities of swords and cutlasses, but these issues did not provide enough for all the fighting men and the local blacksmith became an armorer for better or worse. In 1798 the government started placing sword contracts and subsequently American makers began the production of swords on a larger scale but, until that time, swords were a hit-or-miss problem, lacking uniformity of any kind. The better-made swords, used by some of our higher ranking officers, were similar in design to the silver-hilted swords made in this country, but an officer's disposition and purse were a deciding factor in his choice of these weapons.

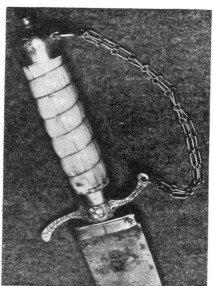

FIG. 6 *(above)*—HANGER *(1770-1775)*. Unknown maker. Beaver- or bear's-head tipped pommel; double chain guard; ivory grip with widely spaced channel; ferrule above surface-engraved quillons; cupped chape cap. Flat blade, initialed *T. D.*, dates about seventeenth century; 26½ by 1 9/16 inches. No scabbard.

FIG. 7 *(right)*—COLICHEMARDE *(1770-1780)*. Made by Samuel Ford; mark on the quillon finial. Ball pommel; wire wound grip; thickened knuckleguard. Triangular foreign blade, two sides concave and the other single grooved; indistinct engraving; 30 inches long. No scabbard.

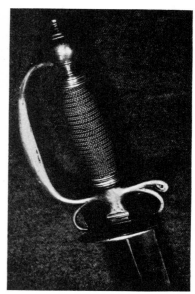

To aid in understanding the details of sword construction and the names of the sword parts, the following listing defines in *Group 1* the parts used in every sword, and in *Group 2* specialized parts used occasionally (*Figs. 1, 2, 3*).

GROUP 1

Hilt. The handle of the sword with varying types of protective construction, extending from the crossguards to top of pommel.

Pommel. Top terminal of hilt, located above grip.

Grip. Section grasped by the hand.

Guard. Entire section covering outer hand, including knuckleguard and crossguard.

Knuckleguard. The curved metal or chain protecting knuckles of the hand.

Crossguard or Quillons. Section protecting the lower part of the hand.

Blade. Cutting or thrusting (or both) part of the weapon.

Forte. The strongest part of the blade, always the upper third.

Tang. Part of blade which runs through the grip and is secured at the top of pommel.

Scabbard. The sheath which covers the blade when sword is not in use.

NOTE: When blade is long and curved the sword is called a saber; when blade is long and straight the sword is called a straight sword. All blades were made with a single edge and a flat back except the types of small sword which were made with more or less triangular blades. All were ground with sharp points although the edges were blunt.

GROUP 2

Tip or Button. Small projection at top of pommel.

Backstrap. Metal strip at rear of grip, running from pommel to crossguard.

Ferrule. Metal band located at base or top of grip.

Shellguard. Shell-shaped extended crossguard used with the small sword and colichemarde.

Ricasso. Section between shellguard and quillons on small sword.

Pas d'anes. The two loops above the shellguard, used only with the small sword and colichemarde.

Groove. The channeling of blade, sometimes called the fuller.

Langets. Small shields parallel to the blade suspended downward from center of crossguard.

Chape cap. Flat or cupped section of metal located under the quillons and serving as a stop for the scabbard mount of the hanger.

Quillon or crossguard finial(s). The decorative outer end or ends of the crossguard.

Grip Band. The decorative center band located on the grip.

The triangular blades of the colichemarde and small sword were usually concave; a few types were flattened on the underside, allowing space for a single narrow groove. Blade lengths varied an inch or so below and above 29 inches. The finest quality of European steel was used for the small-sword blades. Hanger blades were entirely different, as their use was for a cutting instead of a thrusting stroke against an opponent. They were flat, single edged, usually with one narrow deep groove. Hangers used in England had straight blades, those in America were most often curved slightly. They were both locally and foreign made, the former occasionally decorated with a domestic bluing extending halfway down the length. They varied in length from 25 to 33 inches. The majority of the blades made following the vogue of the hanger were foreign, until about 1820 when our makers began producing a better quality of American-made etched, engraved, and decorated blades. In general, more curved-bladed swords have been found than straight, but in the silver-hilted items the numbers are about equal. The two basic grooves in the blade were the deep narrow and the wide shallow. Used alone or in varying combinations with grooves of other sizes, these channels or fullers served the definite purpose of a blood gutter, to use the popular but gruesome term.

The blades of colichemardes and small swords were sometimes embellished with gold inlays or engraved with gold patternings. Locally made long blades have been found with

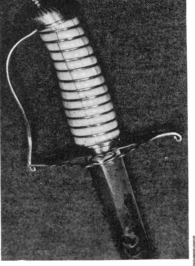

simple surface gilding on a blue ground. But it was from the Klingenthal and Solingen factories in Germany and France that we received, for some thirty-five years after about 1785, some of the most beautifully decorated sword blades ever used in this country. All manner of motifs were executed in gilding, engraving, or etching, or all three. But the decoration usually featured was the American eagle. Sometimes the design used the name of the American importer. All of these blades were single edged, flat backed, both straight and curved, and from 29 to 34 inches long and 1 to 1½ wide.

(To be concluded)

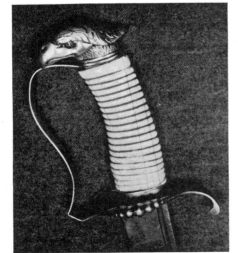

FIG. 8 — SABER (*1780-1800*). Maker unknown. Broad eagle's-head pommel with decided rear crest of feathers, typical of heads of this period. Other characteristic decorations were American Indians, Liberty caps, American flags and shields, cannon and drums. D guard; ivory broad-base grip; small ferrule; branch crossguard with bead decoration. Blade decidedly curved with single, deep, narrow groove; 28 by 1⅜ inches. Scabbard has three mounts, the upper lipped for belt hook.

FIG. 9 (*above*) — STRAIGHT SWORD (*1790*). Maker unknown. Blade with one wide, shallow groove, blued and decorated in gilt with scrolls, Liberty cap, lances with a centering of the American eagle and *E. Pluribus Unum*.

FIG. 10 (*right*) — DRESS SWORD (*1840*). Maker unknown. Shows French influence. Blade has two narrow grooves; slightly curved; 33½ by 1⅜ inches. There is no scabbard with this sword.

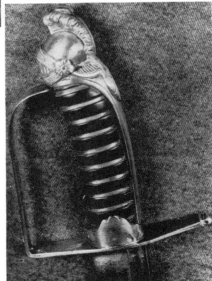

AMERICAN SILVER-HILTED SWORDS

Part II

By PHILIP MEDICUS

THE SWORDS ILLUSTRATED IN PARTS I AND II of this article indicate the relationship of hilt design to other products of the silversmith's art. Comparison of them also reveals the varying treatment accorded similar types of hilts by different craftsmen. In many cases our silversmiths followed the basic European hilt designs of the period in which they worked, but sometimes, particularly in the period from 1775 to 1810, they imparted to these basic designs the graceful simplicity characteristic of early American silver. The illustrations show examples by Jacob Hurd, Myer Myers, Benjamin Burt, William Ball, William Moulton, Hugh Wishart, John Myers, and Richard Humphreys. Judah Hart, William G. Forbes, Pierre Lamothe, Emmor T. Weaver, and Samuel Ford, among others, also made hilts.

Pommels afforded silversmiths the best part of the sword for decorative effects. Each change in sword type or style usually meant a change in pommel design, except for the animal- and bird-headed varieties which had their start with the hanger types and continued to the stirrup-guarded period. Pommels are an important factor, therefore, in determining a sword's age.

The pommels of the small swords were ball-shaped or ovoid. Hangers ornamented with lion and dog heads were favored by the British. The Americans, although using such heads,

were more partial to the eagle-headed designs, a few of which were made during the Revolution for both hangers and long-bladed weapons. A very few hangers have been found with simple disk or cap tops, engraved in shell or floral pattern. The D guard used the eagle-head, crown, or helmeted pommels and, in addition, the urn and another type which, for want of a better name, can only be described as one with squared or hexagon base and pointed dome. With the advent of the stirrup guard, plainer pommels became the order of the day, although some headed varieties were still made. These plain pommels were slotted or cut out to accommodate the upper end of the knuckle guard.

The eagle-headed pommel deserves special comment. Though it developed as a distinctly American type, the French, Poles, and Sardinians, among others, used an eagle-headed pommel long before we made it our own. There has never been any evidence to support the claim that the type was made in this country prior to the Revolutionary War. Some colonial silversmiths made a few hangers and swords on which they used an eagle head, but the eagle was a purely decorative motif like the bird head, lion head, or dog head, not a patriotic emblem. After the Great Seal of the United States was adopted in 1782 the eagle-headed pommel gained popularity which reached a peak from 1815 to 1830. It continued to be used chiefly by the Navy and the many militia and overdressed city guard companies until 1850. The regular Army, while using a few eagle-headed swords, seemed to favor the simpler forms of pommel decoration, such as the urn and the one with squared or hexagon base and pointed dome. With all its popularity, the eagle head was never officially adopted

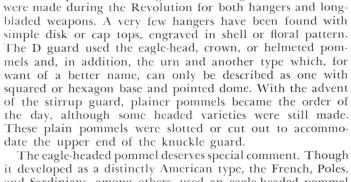

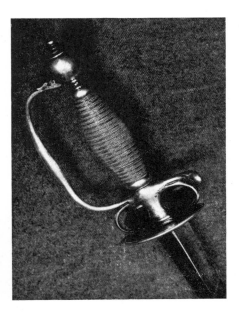

FIG. 2 (*above*)—COLICHEMARDE. Made by Jacob Hurd (*Boston, 1702-1758*). This sword dates about 1750. It is marked on the top of the shellguard. The blade is triangular with gold inlays. The pommel is shaped like a ball and the wire-wound grip is very delicately done. Blade 29 inches long.

FIG. 3 (*right*)—PRESENTATION COLICHE-MARDE. Made by Myer Myers (*New York, fl. 1745-1802*). Marked on upper section of knuckleguard. This sword was presented to Lieutenant David Jones of South Oyster Bay, Long Island by Captain John Hulot of Woodbury, Long Island. It antedates 1756, since the recipient was killed that year at the Battle of Oneida Crossing while serving with General Bradstreet's army. Presentation inscription is on underpart of shellguard. Wire wound grip, swelled knuckleguard. Three scabbard mounts, bottom one of which is a replacement.

FIG. 1.—COLICHEMARDE. Made by Benjamin Burt (*1729-1803*). His mark is on upper knuckleguard near pommel. The grip is wound with twisted and plain wire; knuckleguard center slightly tapered. Blade has decided shoulder, two sides concave, other flattened with single groove. *All illustrations are from the collection of Philip Medicus and PFC Philip Jay Medicus.*

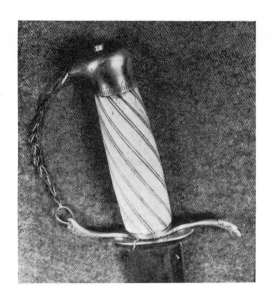

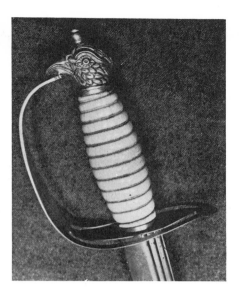

FIG. 4 (*far left*)—BIRDSHEAD HANGER (*1770*). No maker's mark. A practically identical hanger is being shown at the Metropolitan Museum. The only apparent difference is the grooving of the grip. The Metropolitan hanger is hallmarked with initials *DH* and is attributed to Daniel Henchman of Boston (*1730-1775*). Because of unique type of work it seems reasonable to class the unmarked hanger as the work of Daniel Henchman. The grotesque animal heads at the quillon finials are of special interest.

FIG. 5—EAGLESHEAD OR CHICKENSHEAD SABER. Late Revolutionary. Made by William Ball of Philadelphia and Baltimore (*fl. 1752-1788*). Marked inside knuckleguard. Tipped pommel, grooved ivory grip, D knuckleguard increasing in size toward crossguard, which has four plain openings. The slightly curved blade is 31 inches by 1¼ inches and has three deep grooves.

as regulation by any of our armed forces. The early sword eagle heads usually resembled a short-necked and harassed-looking chicken or parrot, but they developed into well-proportioned, impressive decorations with broad heads occasionally adorned with a back crest. There is a feeling of certainty that some of our larger silversmiths carried a stock of blades, silver hilts, and eagle heads, and joined all three to individual order. Many eagle heads have been found that have been die cast and it is presumed that these cast heads were individually chased to order, as the shapes are identical but have been engraved with different patterning.

The belief has been held by some that the eagle-headed pommel antedates the Revolution. A significant argument against this theory is that the eagle mark which appears on early New York and Baltimore silver is not attributed to a date earlier than 1780, and use of the eagle as a decorative motif in American furniture, ironwork, textiles, pewter, earthenware, and various other media did not become general until after the Revolution. It is only fair to state some of the arguments in support of the very early use of the eagle head. In 1776 the full eagle was used on a Massachusetts penny, and in 1777 a full eagle, in appearance similar to the one used on our Great Seal, was a part of the design in one of our Revolutionary flags. It is my belief, supported by others well versed in the study of American edged weapons, that *circa 1780* is the earliest date we can ascribe to the eagle-headed pommel as a purely American sword decoration.

Knuckle guards were made in many vari-

ations of straight and curved lines. The semi-elliptical guard of the small sword and colichemarde was used before the chain guard of the hanger. Some specimens were centrally decorated with multiple bead patterns or with an openwork design, or gradually broadened and receded toward the crossguard section. Other variations broadened immediately below the pommel, widening to a maximum at the center of the crossguard, then tapering to a point at the latter's outer arm. The last style used by our silversmiths, the stirrup-shaped guard, bulged toward the upper section. This widening served two useful purposes, one to afford the swordsman freer finger play, the other to help deflect the blow of an opponent's blade.

Crossguard or quillons — the terms can be used interchangeably — continued the line of the D and stirrup guard, curving in toward the grip or, in some examples, shaped at right angles to the knuckleguard. The quillon finials terminated in disk, animal-, or bird-head shapes in addition to simple rounded or decorative designs. Other examples of the crossguard were made with an extended rounded branch, tapering along the full length and occasionally decorated with heart- and diamond-shaped retaining sections. The quillons of hangers were made with a more or less flattened horizontal S curve and finished with a plain or engraved surface; or, again, were fashioned with pierced or openwork designs in

FIG. 6 (*right*)—EARLY REVOLUTIONARY DOGSHEAD HANGER. The maker is unknown, though it is attributed to New York City. Double chainguard is original. Openwork crossguard with metal insert to prevent silver blackening clothing. Rosewood grip wound with alternating band and strand of silver wire. The scabbard is a replacement using two original mounts, the top one inscribed with initials *JL* (unknown).

FIG. 7 (*far right*)—DOGSHEAD HANGER (*c. 1770*). Made by William Moulton of Newburyport,, Massachusetts (*1720-c. 1793*). It is supposed to have been used by Ebenezer Morgan, an officer of unknown rank, in the Revolution. Marked twice with initials *WM* on both sides of grip on crossguard. Ivory spiralled grip. Blade appears to be of local manufacture.

various patterns, with and without surface decorations, and finished with a scalloped edge on one side while the side nearest the body was smooth. In a few instances the smooth edge was inlaid with a steel insert, to prevent the silver from blackening the clothing.

Over the years, grip styles did not vary as much as other parts of the hilt. Shapes were round, round flat, square, square with rounded corners, and ovoid. A distinctive type used with a very few hangers resembled an inverted cone. Another scarce type was the squared grip made with a center silver band which was decorated with an eagle or other patriotic emblem. The materials used for the grips were ivory, both white and stained green or brown, and bone, horn, and rare woods such as ebony, rosewood, and greenheart. Ivory grips were used before the Revolution and continued for virtually the entire period during which silver-hilted swords were used. Small swords, in the silver hilt group, were always fashioned with a grip made of twisted silver wire finely wound over a wooden base. Broad silver bands, widely spaced and leaving sections of the wood grip exposed, provided another method of finishing a grip. The ivory, bone, and horn varieties were usually grooved with spiral, round, horizontal, and vertical channels, which in all cases except the vertical served as receptacles for twisted silver wire. Checkered, ribbed, rounded, and diagonal patterns, separately or in combination, were carved into the grip material when grooving was not used. Sometimes a metal-decorated ferrule was used at the base of the grip. All these types of decoration also served a useful function — to afford a better hold than a smooth grip would provide.

Scabbards were customarily made of black finished leather, although one very early silver-hilted colichemarde was furnished with a rawhide or parchment covering. Some early scabbards were tooled along their entire length. Usually two or three silver mounts, with simple line or with scalloped edge patterning, set off the top, center, or base. Rings were attached to the top and center mounts for the purpose of securing the encased sword to the belt, waist sash, or baldrick. Some of the top mounts had, in addition, a button or hook used to attach the sword to the frog. Metal scabbards, while used with many swords, were never furnished with the silver-hilted types.

All known specimens of silver-hilted swords made in America do not exceed fifty. The relative scarcity of collectible swords as compared to firearms is understandable. It must be remembered that the blade of a sword could be used for many more useful purposes than a gun or a pistol. Fine steel

was at a premium and many a sword that did effective work on the battlefield was literally beaten into a plowshare or some homely equivalent. One example is a silversmith's tool set made long ago from sword blades, now in the possession of the family of Franchot Tone. In the case of silver hilts, many of the hilts were melted down and made into useful household articles.

There are few American silver-mounted swords on public exhibition. In the Smithsonian Institute at Washington are a hanger that belonged to General Washington and one owned by Brigadier General Montgomery. In the museum at Morristown, New Jersey, is another of Washington's hangers, by Lewis Prahl of Washington. The Metropolitan Museum owns two silver-hilted swords and has another on loan. One is a colichemarde by Edward Winslow (1669-1753), one an eagle-headed straight sword made by Hart and Wilcox of Norwich (1805-1807), and the item lent by Mrs. Florence H. Matthews is a colichemarde made by Elias Pelletreau (1726-1810). The West Point Museum shows a rather late silver hilt (c. 1810), made by William Rose for General Winfield Scott. The New York Historical Society owns an unusual eagle-headed hanger, made by T. Bailey of New York. Its distinction lies in the name *Jonothan Warner*, engraved across the two sides of the beak, probably that of the artisan. It was the property of Major General Henry Dearborn of New Hampshire whose name is engraved across the upper scabbard mount. A dog-headed hanger made by Burger and Pritchard of New York is owned by the Museum of the City of New York. The Garvan collection at Yale University and the splendid museum at Fort Ticonderoga likewise have a few silver-hilted swords.

Note. The information and opinions here expressed are based on present knowledge, which may be revised as unknown specimens of silver-hilted American swords are brought to light. Little has been written on swords, and nothing, so far as I know, on silver hilts. In preparing this article I have turned to Stephen G. C. Ensko for advice regarding silver, and to Captain H. N. Perhan of the United States Coast Guard regarding technicalities of swords. To both I would express my appreciation for their kind and willing assistance in sharing their fund of knowledge.

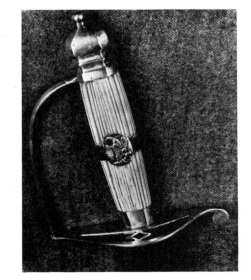

FIG. 8 — DRESS SWORD (1780-1790). Made by John Myers of Philadelphia (fl. 1785-1804). Two marks under crossguard. The ivory grip is banded with eagle emblem, which is similar to that used on the Massachusetts penny of 1776.

FIG. 9 (above)—DRESS SABER (1800). Made by Hugh Wishart of New York (fl. 1784-1810). Checkered ivory grip, broad based. Flat blade, unmarked, probably made by Nathaniel Starr, our earliest contractor.

FIG. 10 (right)—REVOLUTIONARY DRESS HANGER. Made by Richard Humphreys of Philadelphia (fl. 1772-1796). The hanger owned by George Washington had the same type of inverted cone grip, which was typical of French hunting swords.

Sword hilts by early American silversmiths

BY JOHN K. LATTIMER

In November (p. 264) and December (p. 342) 1944 ANTIQUES published a two-part article, *American Silver-hilted Swords*, by Philip Medicus. This was followed in June 1955 (p. 510) by another article on the same subject by Hermann Warner Williams Jr.

THE OFFICERS of General Washington's struggling army wanted their dress-sword hilts to be a bit richer and handsomer than those of their combat swords, which had pommels of heavy brass. Some of the gentleman-officers had inherited court swords styled after those of the European courtiers of the early 1700's. Indeed, they were to see such swords worn by Washington himself; his state, mourning, and other swords, now on display at Mount Vernon, were the products of skilled European sword-smiths and silversmiths.

A handful of American silversmiths had undertaken to make dress-sword pommels as early as 1690, adopting a simple style which had a pristine beauty all of its own. Court swords bearing the marks of Bartholomew Schaats (New York; 1670-1758), Benjamin Burt (Boston, 1729-1805), and Jacob Hurd (Boston, 1702-1758; Fig. 1) illustrate this style. The earlier swords had plain, flat, hand-hammered blades. Others had triangular, hollow-ground blades, brought from Europe, while still others had colichemarde blades, slender triangular ones which widened abruptly for the ten or twelve inches nearest the hilts, in order to provide greater strength. Earlier court swords can be distinguished by the larger rings for the fingers (called *pas-d'ânes*) set just above the protective counterguard (Fig. 1), which reflect the sword construction of the early 1600's when Spanish fencing styles dictated that two fingers be hooked through these rings. Later court swords had smaller rings, because fencing techniques had changed and the fingers were no longer so placed. Still later, the *pas-d'ânes* rings became vestigial in both Europe and America.

Paul Revere's books reveal that he made silver sword hilts, but like many other makers at this time he did not put his mark upon them. Possibly all of them feared reprisals if the British should find this proof that they had made weapons for the rebels.

Lion-head pommels. About the mid-1700's silver sword pommels in the shape of a lion's head began to appear in America on both hunting and military swords, probably reflecting service in His Majesty's army or navy by the young men of the Colonies. This style remained popular until 1776, but even after that the men who owned such weapons did not discard them, so that many an officer in Washington's army continued to carry the British lion on his sword hilt even while fighting

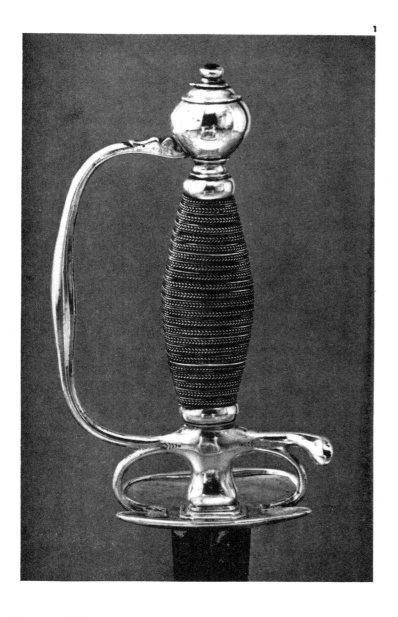

2   3   4

against the King. In fact, lion-head pommels continued to be made to some extent after the Revolution, according to leading authority Harold Peterson. These were ordinarily of hollow construction, with the two shell-like halves soldered together down the mid-line. Some makers carved or stamped the finished lion head in a distinctive manner, sometimes changing the style after some years and continuing in the second style for an additional period of time—a practice which facilitates the dating of specimens made during each period. This was true of William Moulton (Newburyport, 1720-1793), for example, who first produced flattened lion-head sword pommels with distinctively carved ears. Then he changed his style and produced a different type of lion-head pommel, made of thicker silver in a more three-dimensional style easily recognizable by the connoisseur, which was deeply carved to show the hair, ears, and whiskers (Fig. 2).

Because of their general similarity, it seems

probable that large numbers of these shell-like halves of lion heads were made and sold by someone, either in America or in Europe, and assembled by individual silversmiths. (This is probably also true of other parts of the hilt.) Nevertheless, as with all handmade objects, each sword pommel is slightly different from every other. Often the lion carries a small ring in its mouth through which a chain is linked, with the other end secured to the counterguard which protected the hand from slipping down onto the blade and also acted as a guard against counterstrokes. The chain presumably provided some assurance that the sword would not drop from the hand if the sword were to slip from the user's grip accidentally or as a result of a blow. The separate counterguards, an example of which is seen in Figure 2, were often cast of silver, with a smooth edge along the side toward the wearer's leg and fancy serrations on the other edge. The margin worn toward the leg was sometimes inlaid with a strip of iron to prevent light-colored silk trousers from being blackened by tarnish, or to protect the soft silver from wear, or for both purposes.

Dog-head pommels. About the time of the Revolution some makers changed from the familiar lion-head pommels to pommels bearing the heads of dogs. It is not known whether these shapes were new or were created by remodeling the lion's head, but the pommels on this small group of specimens are quite recognizable as dogs' heads rather than lions' and all are sufficiently alike in expression and shape of ears to suggest a single source. However, they are found on swords made by Franklin's engraver-partner David Hall (Philadelphia, w. 1765, d. 1779), as well as on examples by Ephraim Brasher (1744-1810) and John Bailey

---

Fig. 1. Court-sword hilt by Jacob Hurd, Boston, 1702-1758. Note the two large rings (*pas-d'ânes*) at the base, through which the fingers might be hooked. *All illustrations are from the author's collection; photographs by Taylor and Dull.*

Fig. 2. Lion-head pommel by William Moulton (Newburyport, 1720-1793). Note that the margin of the counterguard worn toward the leg is smooth, whereas the outer margin is serrated.

Fig. 3. Dog-head pommel by Ephraim Brasher (New York, 1744-1810). This was Ethan Allen's dress sword.

Fig. 4. Philadelphia eagle-head pommel showing long crest and prominent beak. After 1782.

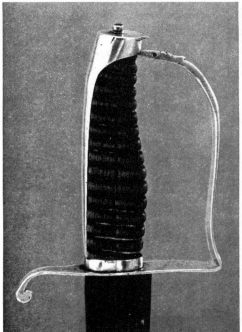

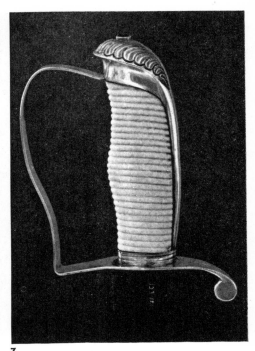

5

6

7

(w. 1762) of New York, so there is no clue as to even a common geographical origin. Ethan Allen's dog-head dress sword, by Brasher, is shown in Figure 3.

Eagle-head pommels. When the American eagle was made our national symbol, about 1782, silversmiths, particularly in the Baltimore and Philadelphia areas, began to make silver sword pommels in the form of eagle heads, using the same technique of two shell-like halves soldered together. Most "Philadelphia" eagles are easily recognized by the crest of feathers projecting from the back of the head and the large, rather bulbous, beak (Fig. 4). These heads are quite long from front to back and are attractive, despite their large size. On some Philadelphia eagle heads the crest is missing, though the rest of the eagle is recognizable as the Philadelphia type.

Baltimore sword makers, such as William Ball (1763-1815), made numerous eagle pommels with a comparatively delicate head which looks more like a chicken (Fig. 5) than a bird of prey. Some Baltimore eagle heads found their way onto swords with blades made by a Philadelphia swordsmith named Prahl, and it is impossible to determine in which direction the sword components traveled to make this marriage possible.

Still other variations of the eagle can be found, some with large beaks and tiny heads, and some with flat crowns suggestive of a rooster. As time went on, eagles became more and more ornate; in the early and mid-1800's they were employed in great quantities on brass-hilted swords.

Cap pommels. Some silver-mounted swords have merely a cap of silver over the end of the handle, with or without a knuckle bow or chain of silver but usually with a silver counterguard bearing the maker's mark. Some of these caps are quite rudimentary, as on George Washington's sword by John Bailey now in the Smithsonian Institution or on the sword by Prahl shown in Figure 6. Some, known to collectors as bird-head pommels (Fig. 7), are curved to suggest the profile of a bird's head. On these the cap sweeps gracefully down the back of the handle in the form of a silver strap.

Distinctive styles. French influence is easily seen in the pommels made by Pierre Lamothe of New Orleans, about 1820 (Fig. 8), and in other known examples as well. As time went on, the trend toward ornateness and complexity became manifest even in the later silver-mounted swords, as shown in the example by Kucher (Philadelphia, w. 1806-1831; Fig. 9). The plumed and helmeted head on the pommel is a motif which became popular after 1800.

Some makers, like Isaac Hutton of Albany (1767-1855), made stylized eagle heads instead of the more usual naturalistic ones. Ward & Bartholomew (Hartford, Connecticut, w. 1804-1809; Fig. 10) and Daniel Dupuy (Philadelphia, 1719-1807) made "pillow" pommels, a style popular both before and after 1800.

After 1776 the triangular European blades of the court swords faded in popularity, and flat military blades of all types were found on

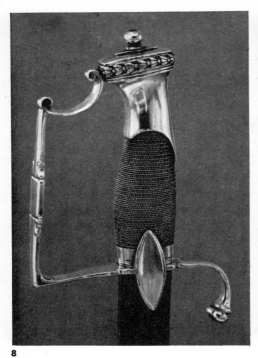

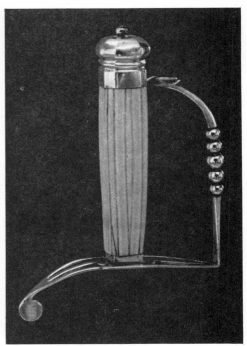

8   9   10

silver-hilted swords. Some are the long, curved blades of horsemen, others the straight blades of infantrymen; some are blued and gilded, some engraved with eagles and stars, liberty caps and scrolls, and shields bearing the words *United States;* some have patently foreign blades and some show the three narrow grooves popular here during the Revolution (Fig. 5). There is no relationship between the silver hilt and the nature of the blade used. In general, however, the blades tend to be smaller and shorter on dress swords than on combat swords, for greater ease in the ballroom or around the council table.

Scabbards. Scabbards are usually of black or russet leather, and those for flat-bladed swords often bear repeated sets of cross marks pressed into the leather on the side opposite the seam. The upper silver band, or throat, of the scabbard, the band around its center, and the protective tip vary from completely plain to fairly ornate, sometimes bearing the initials of the owner, sometimes small trophies of arms, flags, or drums, and sometimes the silversmith's stamp on the throat or on all three silver parts. Indeed, some silversmiths preferred to put their signature on only the throat of the scabbard. John Bailey, for instance, put his name there in script on most of his swords, but occasionally he stamped it on the counterguard or some other portion of the hilt. This was a more sensible location because, as Hermann Warner Williams Jr. has pointed out (ANTIQUES, June 1955, p. 513), when the leather rotted the entire scabbard would be discarded and if there was no mark on the sword proper, identification of the maker would be difficult. Where the silver furniture of the scabbard—the throat, the band, and the tip —survives, it may be sufficiently characteristic of a particular smith to help in identifying his work even if sword and scabbard are both unmarked.

Because so many of our early American leaders had silver-hilted dress swords made by well-known silversmiths of their day, the study of this rare American art form is of interest to historians, military men, and costume specialists as well as to students of American silver.

Fig. 5. Baltimore eagle head resembling that of a chicken; by William Ball, Baltimore (1763-1815).

Fig. 6. "Cap" pommel on a sword by the Philadelphia swordsmith Lewis Prahl (Philadelphia, 1775-1790).

Fig. 7. "Bird" pommel, extending down the back of the grip but with no detailed carving to represent an eagle.

Fig. 8. French-style silver hilt by Pierre Lamothe (New Orleans, 1820).

Fig. 9. Ornate basket-type silver hilt by Kucher (Philadelphia, w. 1806-1831). Foreshadows the more complex hilts of the 1800's.

Fig. 10. "Pillow" pommel by Ward & Bartholomew (Hartford, Connecticut, w. 1804-1809). This type was popular from 1790 to 1815.

American silver-hilted swords

BY HERMANN WARNER WILLIAMS, JR.

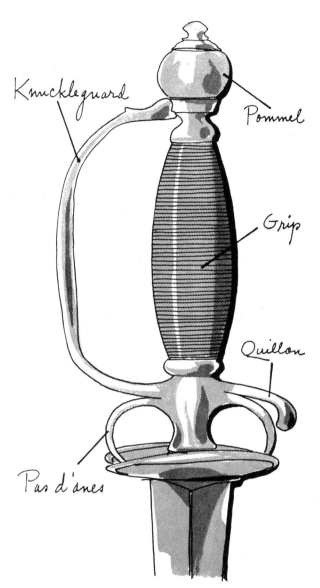

Parts of
the sword hilt
based on construction of the colichemarde.

AMERICAN-MADE SILVER-HILTED SWORDS are typical products of their age, and have the qualities which distinguish other examples of American craftsmanship in silver. Usually collected by arms enthusiasts, these swords are rarely available for study by collectors and students of silver. Only the Metropolitan Museum and Yale have significant collections, so it is especially rewarding when an exhibition brings together examples of this craftsmanship and provides an opportunity to study and compare the work of many silversmiths of the eighteenth and early nineteenth centuries.

Such an opportunity was offered by the recent exhibition *The Sword in America*, organized by the Corcoran Gallery of Art and shown also at the Detroit Institute of Arts. The exhibit gathered together eighty-six examples, the majority of those available from public and private collections in this country with the exception of the many superb specimens in the collection of the late Philip J. Medicus, whose articles on swords appeared in ANTIQUES for November and December 1944.

On the basis of the swords exhibited it appears that the earliest surviving specimens by colonial craftsmen date from about 1725. None of seventeenth-century date have been located. Silver-hilted swords continued to be made until well into the nineteenth century—up to about 1825. After this, they were no longer worn as articles of civilian dress, and only rarely as military accoutrements, when they were usually presentation swords for formal occasions.

Silver-hilted swords reflect the same course of development and adaptation as swords fashioned of more common materials. Chronologically, the first types to be made in this country are the small sword and the colichemarde, which differs from the small sword in the type of blade. These were in vogue from about 1725 to about 1790 in their purest form, and survived until about 1815, in variants. Under such masters as Edward Winslow, Jacob Hurd, Myer Myers, and Timothy Bontecou, the small sword, with its delicately fashioned ball pommel and gracefully curved knuckleguard and *pas d'anes*, is an object of beauty. American-made small swords are normally restrained in their decoration, with little raised or engraved ornament. European silver-hilted swords of the same period are usually richly decorated on almost all surfaces. The small sword was essentially an item of personal apparel of the well-to-do colonial gentleman, although it was also a very efficient weapon. It was often worn by its owner in his capacity as a militia officer in the field in the French and Indian Wars and also in the Revolution—as we can observe in contemporary portraits.

The next large class of silver-mounted swords is the hunting sword. Those made in this country range in date from about 1750 to about 1795. They were apparently more common than the small sword: a larger number have survived.

Hunting swords may be sub-divided into two basic types solely according to the decorative treatment of the pommels. The first and by far the most common is the lion head—obviously derived from the British prototype, many examples of which were probably imported for sale here. William Moulton, John Bailey, Christian Wiltberger, Isaac Hutton, and William W. Gilbert are among the native craftsmen who fashioned fine swords of this type.

Second in number of surviving examples are swords in which the pommel is a flat disk fastened on top of the grip, or a plain cap extending down around the upper part of the grip. It is a sword of this type by John Bailey, but with no silver cap at all, that Washington preferred to use during the Revolution.

A few pre-Revolutionary hunting swords do not fall in either of these categories. There is, for example, the superb one by Ephraim Brasher of New York in the Mabel Brady Garvan collection at Yale, which uses as its pommel an unmistakable dog head. An unusual if not unique feature is two semi-precious stones inset in the eye sockets. Contemporary advertisements also offered swords with dove or hawk heads, but none have so far been located. Then, too, there are a number of others whose pommels resemble such animals as bears, but which actually were in all probability intended by the craftsmen to represent lions.

The popularity of the hunting sword was great. It was widely used as an officer's side arm, although the chains which joined the pommel to the quillons provided but slight protection to the knuckles.

Similar in appearance, but more practical as a weapon, are the short sabers which appear for the first time in silver about 1770. On these the continuous strip of metal forming knuckle bow and quillons is usually pierced with four rectangular slots; they retain the short blade characteristic of the hunting sword. The short saber is found with lion-head pommel as well as with plain cap pommel, but the majority, which were made in the 1790's, have that typically American motif, the eagle.

The first surviving specimens of this new motif—the

Hunting sword, c. 1775,
by William Moulton of Newburyport (1720-1793)
carried by Ebenezer Morgan.
Towle Silversmiths.

Colichemarde, c. 1730,
by Timothy Bontecou of New Haven (1693-1784)
carried by David Day.
Author's collection.

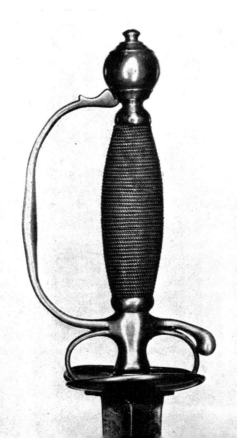

eagle head—are of the early 1780's. This new motif probably became popular because the lion head, derived from the supporter of the royal arms, was not appropriate for the decoration of republican weapons. The eagle heads that are believed to be the earliest are small and exceedingly crude. The few that survive are not much more than knobs with a small protuberance for the beak, and the slightest indication, by engraving, of the details of eyes, beak, and feathers. It was not long, however, before the inherently decorative quality of the eagle was recognized and developed into a handsome and distinctive element. Characteristic of this intermediate type are those made by William Ball, Jr. One type which appears to be earlier stylistically has a short uplifted beak and rounded back to the head. The second, and probably slightly later, type has a ridge or comb at the back of the head, and the beak, while short, is more pronounced.

By 1800 the eagle head was the principal decorative element in American-made silver-mounted swords. It would make identification of unmarked pieces easier if one could distinguish between types on a geographical basis, but unfortunately there appear to be few regional characteristics. The work of New York and Boston smiths, for example, does not show stylistic differences. One can,

however, note a distinct type which was developed in the Philadelphia area. There eagle heads were elongated, hollow, and made of two pieces of comparatively thin metal, with a well-developed beak and a pronounced bulge above the eyes. Details of eyes and feathers are engraved.

A distinct Baltimore style of short saber can also be recognized. This appears in marked specimens by William Ball, Jr., and Joseph Lynch. Both makers used a sheet of rather thin silver to fashion the guard, and pierced it with four slots which, in Ball's work, have rounded ends and, in Lynch's, pointed. The eagle heads used by these makers are grotesque caricatures, highly stylized and, though slightly different in detail, conforming to the same pattern.

Another type of sword, far less common, has an urn-like pommel usually rectangular in form and often with chamfered edges. To judge from the few examples which have come to light, the popularity of this type was limited to the period between 1790 and 1810.

Dating from about 1800 to 1820 are the silver hilts with a plain rounded cap or bird head, sometimes elaborated by a projecting rim. Their simple design follows the standard iron-mounted militia cavalry saber which came

Hunting sword, c. 1775,
by Richard Humphreys of Philadelphia
(active 1772-1796).
Collection of Kendrick Scofield.

Hunting sword, c. 1775,
by Ephraim Brasher of New York
(active 1766-1805).
Carried by Ensign Petrus Wynkoop (1744-1818)
of the First Regiment Ulster County, New York,
Militia in the Revolution. *Mabel Brady Garvan Collection, Yale University Art Gallery.*

Primitive eagle head
on a hunting sword, c. 1780,
by an unidentified silversmith.
Fort Ticonderoga Museum.

into use about 1808 and was made on contract by the Virginia Manufactory, Nathan Starr, and William Rose.

In general, silver hilts were made for individual patrons and thus vary according to the wishes of the purchaser. After 1800, however, a degree of standardization developed. In the exhibition there were, for example, four identical sabers with flat caps and blades by William Rose, two eagle-pommel swords by William Ball in one style, and three in a different style.

In the absence of marks the problem of attribution of American silver hilts is a confusing one. The famous John Bailey, for example, engraved his name on the throat of the scabbard, and if because of the rotting of the leather the scabbard was destroyed, there is nothing to help the scholar distinguish his work from that of such contemporaries as William Moulton. Some of our smiths may have ordered quantities of pommels and other parts from wholesalers, merely assembling the various elements into complete weapons, possibly chasing the pommels, and making the silver lockets and chaps to fit the blade and scabbard.

The marked pieces in the Corcoran exhibition were by the following makers. I would welcome information on other American-made silver-mounted swords.

John Bailey	New York	(1777)
William Ball, Jr.	Phil. & Balti.	(1763-1815)
Timothy Bontecou	New Haven	(1693-1784)
Ephraim Brasher	New York	(active 1744-1810)
William Cario	Portsmouth	(active 1721-1809)
C Chouso	New York	(c. 1770)
John Coney	Boston	(1655-1722)
William Cowell, Jr.	Boston	(1713-1761)
Joseph Draper	Wilmington	(active 1816-1832)
Samuel Drowne	Piscataqua	(1749-1815)
John Edwards	Boston	(1671-1746)
William W. Gilbert	New York	(1767-1818)
Philip Hartman	Philadelphia	(active c. 1813)
Richard Humphreys	Philadelphia	(active 1772-1791)
Jacob Hurd	Boston	(1702-1758)
Isaac Hutton	Albany	(1767-1855)
John Lynch	Baltimore	(1761-1848)
William Little	Newburyport	(c. 1760)
William Moulton	Newburyport	(1720-1793)
John Myers	Philadelphia	(active 1785-1804)
Jonathan Otis	Newport	(1723-1791)
William Rose		
J. Schaffer		(c. 1800)
Robert Swan	Philadelphia	(active 1795-1831)
Geer Terry	Enfield & Worcester	(1775-1858)
Jacob Ten Eyck	Albany	(1705-1793)
Jonathan Warner		(1780)
Christian Wiltberger	Philadelphia	(1766-1851)
Ward & Bartholomew	Hartford	(active 1804-1809)

Short saber, c. 1800,
by William Ball, Jr., of Baltimore
(active 1785-1815).
Collection of Capt. Charles J. West, Jr.

Short saber, c. 1810, by William Ball, Jr.
of Baltimore (active 1785-1815).
*Mabel Brady Garvan Collection,
Yale University Art Gallery.*

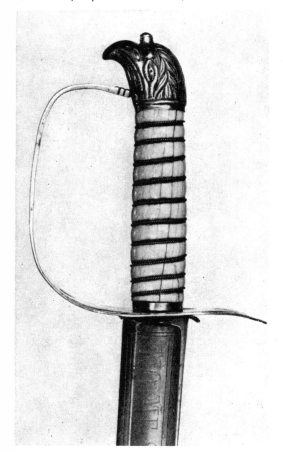
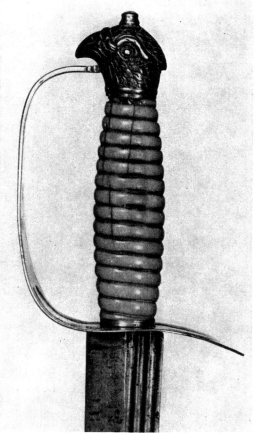

SWORDS OF CALIFORNIA AND MEXICO

In the Eighteenth and Nineteenth Centuries

By ARTHUR WOODWARD

Illustrations from the Los Angeles County Museum

TIME WAS WHEN every gentleman in California owned and carried a sword. These swords fall in two main groups, short swords and long, but since weapons in California were not standardized we may expect to find almost anything in offensive arms used in Alta California from the time of Spanish occupation in 1769 to the arrival of the Americans in 1846. In the main the swords originally brought to California were quite short, frequently wide of blade and very heavy. The *espada ancha* or broad sword *(see Fig. 1,b)* is mentioned as one of three offensive weapons employed by the first military in California (Miguel Costansó, *Diario of the Expedition Made to California* [1769] *in The Spanish Occupation of California*, San Francisco, 1934.) Some swords were of cut-and-thrust style, some were of the single-edged type for slashing only. The latter were sturdily made and served as brush cutters quite as frequently as for action against an enemy.

Short swords *(Figs. 1-7)* might be either straight or fullered, with one or more grooves, or curved and ungrooved. They range in length from sixteen to twenty-eight inches. They were known by a somewhat loosely-used term as *machetes*, though in style at least they differed from the type called machete today.

In describing the weapon carried by the horsemen of Mexico, D. Carlos Rincon Gallardo, the Duque de Regla, Marques de Guadalupe, and the foremost *charro* of Mexico, says: The machete: it is a weapon shorter than the sword, having a heavy, thick blade with sharp cutting edge. It serves the *charro* as a weapon and to slash his way through heavy brush. The hilt sometimes has a knuckle guard and sometimes does not" *(El Charro Mexicano, Mexico, D.*

F., 1939). He continues his description of carrying the machete attached to the saddle and concludes: "Some prefer to carry the sword instead of the machete."

It is only in Mexico that this term machete seems to have been applied to short swords of this type. The hilts and knuckle guards of the Mexican machete-swords of the eighteenth and nineteenth centuries are comparable in most respects to the hilts and guards of other swords used in Europe and America during the same periods. The modern machete carried by the *charro* of Mexico today is, in reality, a sword. It is a lighter, more handsome weapon, than the true machete. Both sword and scabbard are frequently silver-mounted, the blade being slender with blued surface and etched with the Mexican coat of arms and other designs.

In an effort to clarify the Mexican application of this term machete to the weapon which might normally be considered a sword, I visited the Marques in Mexico City, July 1940, and asked him a number of questions on the subject. He explained that when the sword was carried as a weapon of offense during the 1700's and early 1800's by the horsemen of Mexico and California, the blade was made heavier and shorter, more like that of a cutlass, to aid in slashing brush on the trail, the hilt remaining practically unchanged. When the custom of carrying the sword as an offensive weapon fell into disuse through the invention of improved firearms, it became strictly utilitarian and probably underwent certain definite changes, such as elimination of the knuckle guards, broadening of the blade, and discarding of all frills. The machete became the poor man's weapon. He used it to cut cane and firewood. When he

SHORT SWORDS

FIGURES 1,A & 2.

Straight, double-edged blade, 28¾ inches long, 1⅝ inches wide at hilt; fullered with three short grooves 9¼ inches long on each side of the blade. Grip, smooth, unpainted wood 3¾ inches long, 1 inch in diameter. Knuckle guard, of iron with an abbreviated quillon slightly ornamented with simple chasing. Leaf-shaped shell guard—a relatively common feature of these short swords—2½ inches long, 2 inches wide, is elaborately chased in a floral pattern. Original leather scabbard *(Fig. 2)* embroidered in a floral design in blue, yellow, and green hemp thread, now faded. Apparently the sword was slung from a shoulder belt, to judge by the four holes perforating tab at upper end of scabbard.

FIGURE 1

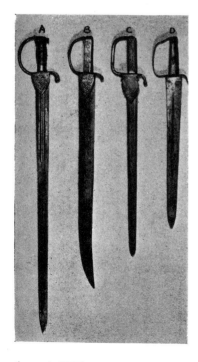

Although the authentic and very interesting history of this sword traces it from 1831, there is no doubt that the weapon dates considerably earlier, probably from the late 1700's. Known as the Avila sword, it was, according to our information, owned by José María Avila, a native of Sinaloa, who came as a boy to Los Angeles with his parents, Cornelio Avila and Isabel Urquides de Avila. José María was a wild, reckless youth, noted for his horseman-

FIGURE 2

ship and personal charm. In 1825 he was elected *alcalde* of the *pueblo*, but was suspended from office because of his autocratic and despotic rule. In a general revolt against Governor Manuel Victoria, who succeeded José Mariano Echeandia, March 8, 1830, Avila was one of the Los Angeles rebel faction. Victoria organized an armed force and marched south to quell the revolt. Avila and the other hot-heads from Los Angeles met Victoria at Lomitas de la Canada de Breita, somewhere near Cahuenga Pass, December 5, 1831. Leading the vanguard of Victoria's men was Romualdo Pacheco. Avila and Pacheco rode at each other with lance and sword. They exchanged blows but accomplished nothing. As Pacheco wheeled and rode away, José María discharged a pistol and killed him. Then Avila dashed into the thick of the opposing forces seeking Victoria, whom he lanced and threw to the ground. As he poised the weapon to give the wounded Governor the coup de grâce, Avila was shot through the spine by one of the Federal force. The bodies of Pacheco and Avila were carried into Los Angeles and buried the next day.

This sword is believed to be the one Avila carried in this fight. Long cherished by his family, it eventually came into possession of Mrs. Isabel del Valle, whose mother was an Avila, and it was presented to the Museum by her daughter.

FIGURES 1,B & 3.

Blade, 23½ inches long, 1¾ inches wide. Square grip, made of two pieces of horn covered with engraved iron side-plates riveted to the tang. This combination of iron and horn is typical of grips of this style of weapon. Iron shell guard *(Fig. 3)*, elaborately chased with a floral

went to war, the machete became a vicious living thing in the hand of a determined man. In drunken brawls it was just as deadly. A man who fought with a machete, cut sugar cane with it, or did a lot of saber-rattling was called a *machetero.*

Oddly enough, it was a North American firm, the Collins Company of Collinsville, Connecticut, founded in 1826, which entered the field of machete-making in 1850, and took the lead from European cutlers in the manufacture of such implements for Central, South America, Cuba and Mexico (*The Collins Company, One Hundred Years of Existence 1826-1926, Spanish ed., Collinsville, Conn. 1926*). The hilts of the first machetes manufactured by this company were modified versions of the sword hilts of the late 1700's and early 1800's minus the knuckle guards. The principal innovations of the European and American matchete-makers of the early 1800's were the use of the eagle- and lion-head pommels surmounting checkered wooden grips comparable to the grips and pommels on cavalry and dragoon swords of the late 1790's and 1800's.

Some of the machetes of the early period retained even the long, thin blades. The machete blades of later days are broader and heavier, widening at the tip and more rounded, sometimes appearing almost blunt. Slightly curved, short quillons are used on three of the Collins models of today. However, the original eagle pommel is now known as *gallo* or rooster, while the dog- or lion-head pommel has become an elephant. Grips are usually of polished horn or hard wood. Quillons are seldom used and knuckle guards have vanished. These are the true work machetes used by field hands.

The well-equipped *charro* in Mexico today seems to be drifting back to the definite sword form, though he still calls his weapon a machete. The knuckle guards are either a solid bow, usually of silver, or a silver chain guard, comparable to those of some of the court swords or hangers of the late 1700's or of the presentation swords of the mid-1800's.

A maker of these beautiful, thin machete blades is Austraberto Aragon, rated as one of the finest metalworkers in Mexico. He operates his shop, La Espada, in the City of Oaxaca. Senor Aragon is a true blade-smith, master craftsman of a dying art. His best weapons are so well made that he can pack them for shipment in circular boxes, the tip of the blade bent to touch the hilt of the machete. The grip and guard are of chased silver while the blade is usually handsomely etched with various pictorial subjects dear to the heart of a Mexican horseman. When Aragon's blades are released from their containers they whip straight out with a satisfying ring of sound metal. His best swords are sold for about 100 pesos or about $20 in United States currency. In California and Mexico of the eighteenth and early nineteenth centuries, the workmanship on the short swords of machete type was not so delicate (*Figs. 1,b and 3*).

The long swords (*Figs. 8, 9*) followed a more conventional pattern than the short, and are in reality less interesting and of less significance. These weapons, which may be called the true swords, cut and thrust only. They are usually double-edged, and are fullered (grooved). They average about three feet in length.

Swords in California were carried at the belt or suspended from a shoulder bandolier which crossed diagonally from right to left across the chest, the sword hanging at the left side. When traveling on horseback, the swordsman carried his weapon fastened to the left side of the saddle skirt, under the leg, hilt to the fore with the knuckle guard down.

The scabbards as well as the weapons are often of special interest. During the eighteenth and early nineteenth centuries virtually all of the leather work used in Mexico and California, from spur-heel covers to saddles, as well as sword and knife sheaths, was elaborately embroidered with hemp, silk, silver, and gold threads. At the missions, Indian neophytes were taught this art. Such items as "*sillas bordadas*" (embroidered saddles), "*mochilas bordadas*" (embroidered saddle covers), as well as embroidered saddle pads, leggings, and so on, are frequently encountered in the manuscript account books of La Purisima Mission from 1806-1834.

In the Los Angeles County Museum are a number of swords which were once owned by the original Spanish-Mexican settlers of Alta California. Similar swords are to be seen in the Museo Nacional of Mexico City; in the Museum of Guadalajara, State of Jalisco, Mexico; in the Governor's Palace, Santa Fe, New Mexico, and in the United States National Museum, Washington, D. C. No doubt many other examples are in private collections.

FIGURE 3

FIGURE 1,D.

The shortest sword in the Los Angeles County Museum collection. Blade, 16¾ inches long, fullered slightly for 7 inches on either side;

motif, as are the side-plates of the grip. A thin, linear meander ornaments blade near back edge.

No data are available regarding the history of this specimen. The backside of the blade is so thick that it is decidedly a clumsy weapon, though it might serve well as a brush cutter, but the lavish ornamentation of shell and hilt indicates that it was probably carried as an offensive weapon rather than as a field tool. It is truly a broad sword as described by Constansó. Two such weapons in the collections of the Museo Nacional in Mexico City are called machetes; there is also one in Guadalajara. *This and Figure 1,c, donated to the Los Angeles County Museum by Mrs. Charles P. Holder.*

FIGURES 1,C & 4.

Double-edged blade only 20 inches long, 1⅛ inches wide; fullered with three grooves on each side extending 8½ inches from the hilt. Inscribed *Fabrica de Toledo* (Made in Toledo) on each side of blade. I strongly suspect that the blade does not belong to the hilt. Grip and guard are characteristic of other swords of this type which were locally made, either in Mexico or possibly at the mission forges in California. Grip is roughly octagonal and made entirely of iron, therein differing from those having horn or wood as basic material. Hilt and shell are rudely ornamented with floral and geometric designs (*Fig. 4*). No historical data available; may be ascribed to late 1700's, early 1800's.

1⅝ inches wide; double-edged; terminating in a rather sharp point. Round horn grip. Knuckle guard, ⅝ inches wide, is a simple piece of flattened iron, ornamented with a few diagonal file marks. The simple, unadorned black leather scabbard (not shown) has a loop for attachment to a waist belt. The weapon, in the Coronel collection, is believed, probably correctly, to have been brought to California with the Portolá expedition of 1769. The design is right, and it is obviously a specimen that has seen long, hard service. The blade may have been shortened by a few inches.

FIGURE 5,A.

Blade, 23½ inches long and a mere ¾ inches wide. Hilt is poorly seated on the tang of the flimsy blade. Iron knuckle guard semi-basket type, entirely covered, grip and all, with light brown leather. On under side of guard is an insertion of undressed cowhide, hair side out. Scabbard, broken in two pieces, is of shiny brown leather with bands of untanned brown cowskin ornamenting the sheath immediately below guard and at tip. Hair-covered panels outlined in fine silver thread, a Spanish-Mexican type of ornamentation with a Moorish ancestry. Round eyelet at proximal end of scabbard was for fastening to saddle or belt.

This rather odd specimen would not be of much service as a weapon. Obtained, like *Figure 1,a,* from the del Valle collection, it is said to have been owned by José María Avila. Obviously it is not the sturdy fighting weapon carried by Avila to his death in 1831. Judging by the smallness of the grip, this weapon was made for a youngster, perhaps Avila in his youth.

FIGURE 4

FIGURE 5

FIGURE 6

FIGURE 7

as a subordinate until about 1814, then assumed more definite leadership of the insurgents. Guerrero was second President of Mexico from April 1, 1829 until February 14, 1831, when he was deposed and executed. Although this weapon may have belonged to Guerrero, more likely it was used by one of his officers during the insurrection. The inscription (*Fig. 7*) *MUERA ESPANA BIBA GUERRERO ano de 1813*, with the word *VIVA* spelled phonetically, supports this probability, unless the sword was made and presented to Guerrero by an admiring smith who was a poor speller.

In general *6,a* and *6,b* are quite similar. Swords of the type were evidently popular during the period of the insurrection. There is one in the Museo Nacional bearing the inscription *Marzo 28, 1810* (Hidalgo sounded his *Grito de Dolores* [call to arms against Spain] in September 1810). Another specimen of this style, in private hands in Mexico City, is inscribed *ABRYL 15* on one side and *ANo DE 1812* on the other.

That such swords were used in California is evidenced by an oil painting in a series of fourteen Stations of the Cross, executed by Indian neophytes at San Fernando Mission between 1800 and 1815. The Indian artists were unfamiliar with any uniformed troops other than the garrisons at the Presidios and the Missions. Hence, when they pictured the Roman soldiers in the procession to Calvary, they garbed them in Spanish military uniforms seen in California and gave the leaders weapons carried by Spanish officers of the day. The sword in the hand of one of the "Roman" officers is of the same style as those shown here.

LONG SWORDS

FIGURE 8,A.

Blade, 36½ inches long, 1½ inches wide, double-edged, has two short, rather broad grooves on each side extending 9½ inches below the hilt. Silver guard, one branch broken. Grip of dark corrugated wood. Blade engraved on both sides with the same group of symbols, not uncommon on Mexican blades of this type: a star-shaped figure, moon and stars, sun—and an arm emerging from the clouds brandishing a sword in the hand, an old heraldic device, termed "the right hand of God."

This sword is alleged to have belonged to Sr. Demecio Dominguez a general in the Mexican army in 1829, though it may be of earlier date. It was presented to the Society of the Native Sons of the Golden West by Florencio Dominguez, a descendant of Dn. Demecio, in 1907.

FIGURE 8,B.

Blade, 36½ inches long, 1⅛ inches wide, unfullered and without inscription. Grip of wood covered with rawhide. The weapon was owned by Don Antonio F. Coronel and probably dates well back to the last quarter of the 1700's. A similar sword in the U. S. National Museum is inscribed *C.IV 1794* (Carlos IV 1794) (T. T. Belote, *American and European Swords in the Historical Collections of the United States National Museum, Bull. 163*, U.S.N.M., Washington, D. C. 1932). Swords of this type were used in California by both civilians and soldiers.

FIGURE 9.

Double-edged blade, 36¼ inches long, 1¼ inches wide, fullered with three short grooves. Grip of wood, covered with russet leather, wrapped with a fine, two-strand, twisted copper wire. Guard is a plain iron strap, iron back plate, and a single iron branch welded to iron knuckle-guard strap. Blade is engraved in spidery block letters on one side: *NO ME SAQUES SIN RASON* (Do not draw me without cause); and on the reverse: *NO ME ENBAINE SIN HONOR* (Do not sheath me without honor). This sword was formerly the property of Don Fernando Sepulveda.

FIGURE 5,B

One of the simplest of the short machete swords, this more nearly approaches a cutlass in form and weight. Blade, 25 inches long, 1½ inches wide. The hilt is made of wood, knuckle guard is a flattened piece of iron with simple down-curving quillon. The top band on the hilt is of iron, the lower one is of brass. The scabbard of this weapon is of dull brown leather. The sword, obtained from Jose G. Moraga of Santa Barbara, California, is utilitarian, the product of some local blacksmith.

FIGURE 5,C.

Blade, 27½ inches long, 1½ wide. Hand grip, probably originally of horn or wood, without plating, has long since disintegrated. Guard rudely made of flattened strips of iron with two branches attached to a quillon. Blade badly rusted and pitted; apparently the weapon was excavated. Probably it was carried into California after 1769.

FIGURES 6 and 7.

6,a, blade, 26 inches long, 1¼ inches wide. Shell bowl has leather lining. Bone hilt, yellow and well polished by many years of constant handling, is ornamented with diagonal and checkered incised marks. It is 3½ inches long. Pommel is copper or bronze. *Owned by Dwight Franklin of West Los Angeles, California.*

6,b, blade 30¾ inches long, 1⅛ inches wide, slightly curved. Inscription on blade (*Fig. 7*). Carved white bone grip, 3¼ inches long. Knuckle guard of iron to which are riveted three curving steel branches, whose lower ends are in turn riveted to a shallow steel or iron bowl, while a short curving piece of steel is riveted to the under side of the bowl to form quillons. Shallow bowl is lined with four small leather pads. *In the Sepulveda-Chapman collection on loan to the Museum.*

Here (*6,b*) one sees the *machete-espada* in its most elaborate form. This weapon is said to have been the property of Vincente Ramon Guerrero, born in the town of Tuxtla in 1782. He served under the *cura* Morelos in the insurrection against Spain

FIGURE 8

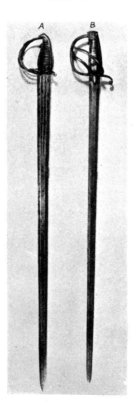

FIGURE 9

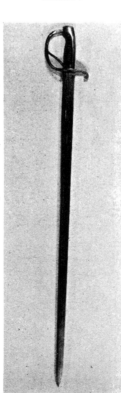

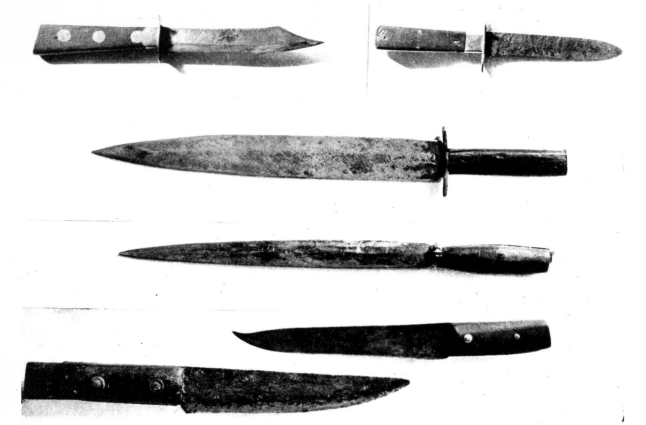

Fig. 1 — AMERICAN KNIVES

The upper left knife is a bowie, *six-inch blade*. Since it is sharpened on one side only, like a chisel, it evidently belonged to an Indian. The knife at the upper right is an American fighting knife, with white metal guard and mountings; plowed up in the "Free States," Fauquier County, Virginia; the original bone, or wooden, part of the handle had rotted off. The weapon showed evidences of having been in the ground for a long time. *Six-inch blade*.

The others, in order, are:

"Arkansas tooth-pick" made from a blacksmith's rasp; this was made at a blacksmith's shop during the Civil War, near where Booth hid, after assassinating Lincoln. *Twelve-inch blade*.

Frontier knife; adapted for throwing; probably belonged to early French Canadian in the old Oregon country; crudely made. *Eleven-inch blade*.

An attempt at a bowie knife; crudely made by a miner in the mountains of Oregon; *blade seven and one-half inches*.

Crude home-made knife; *eight-inch blade*.

The Fine Art of Stabbing

By J. NEILSON BARRY

ALMOST any collection of antiques is likely to include at least one dagger, because the kind of people who used the antiques often, incidentally, owned a dagger or two as well. In the atmosphere of established respectability which permeates the artistic and the ancient, the weapon is like the proverbial black sheep, a sort of very naughty boy in a school of very good children. Yet such weapons are treasured among antiques because they are interesting. People who carried daggers usually had very decided reasons for doing so; and, just as a man is known by the quality of his friends, so, in the old days, the kind

Fig. 2 — INDIAN KNIVES

The larger one is made from a species of slate and was found in Oregon; *seven and one-half inches long*. The small stone is a scalping knife, chipped from obsidian.

of dagger which a man bore constituted his badge of character. This is one of the facts which gives fascination to collecting these weapons.

It is difficult to obtain the authentic history of an old weapon. I am always suspicious of specimens which are advertised as having finished off Caesar, or as once owned by some famous person. Personally, again, I do not care to bring into my home anything which is known to have specifically unpleasant associations. It is the light which they throw upon temperament and character that makes daggers interesting to me.

I was once in a barber shop in the South when the colored hair-dresser informed his assistant that, as two of his friends had

Fig. 3 — POCKET KNIFE–PISTOL.
Shoots .22 calibre cartridges.

just had an altercation, it would be well, in case either of them should drop in for a friendly call, *to watch the razors*. Every one knows the story of the negro, who in purchasing a razor, declined a safety, and insisted upon one of the old fashioned type as he desired to use it for "social" purposes. Now the reason that the southern darkeys prefer a razor instead of a dagger as a weapon is found in their manner of striking a blow. Instead of the straight, forward thrust of the white man, the negro is fond of a sweeping stroke. Hence he finds the shaving instrument admirably adapted to his needs.

It is this same slashing form of striking which has produced the Turkish scimitar. It is equally applicable to the use of the machete, which was originally a knife to cut sugar cane. Old-time sailormen had to pull the ropes to hoist the heavy sails, and thus developed huge muscles in their shoulders and backs, with the result that the cutlass became their weapon. The old broadsword was adapted to a similar style of offensive technique. All such weapons illustrate the cutting stroke. On the other hand, the Roman legions conquered the world by means of the short pointed sword, which was intended to be thrust at the faces of the foe. The rapier of more recent time illustrates the same principle. For closer quarters the dagger, the dirk, the stiletto and the poignard were used with the forward stab. These weapons illustrate the thrusting punch.

In the East Indies a characteristic twist accompanies the stab, and this process has resulted in the development of daggers with a peculiar shape. Just as David, when preparing to fight Goliath, selected a weapon in keeping with his temperament and ability, so the individual and the race illustrate their characteristics in the kind of arms they employ.

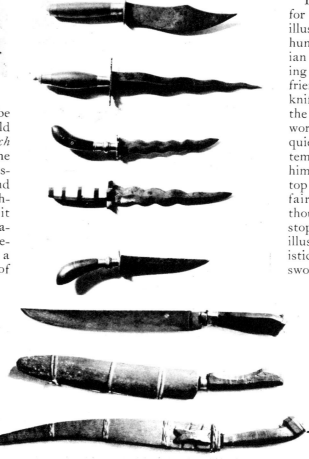

Fig. 4 — PHILIPPINE DAGGERS

a. Shaped in imitation of bowie knife, but not in line with handle. This is due to the characteristic twisting method of stabbing. Handle of horn of the water buffalo; iron mounted. *Blade, seven inches.*

b. Brass mounted; handle made from horn of water buffalo. *Blade nine and one-half inches.*

c. Brass mounted, wooden handle. *Blade six and one-half inches.*

d. Its form indicates an attempt to follow the shape of an old Spanish dagger, but retaining the snake-like blade popular with Malays. The guard and four sections of the handle are made from the horn of the water buffalo; the other four sections are made from ivory. *Blade, seven inches.*

e. Wooden handle, ferrule and guard from one piece of solid brass. *Blade five and one-half inches.*

f. Mounted with brass like bronze. Handle made from the horn of the water buffalo. *Eleven and one-half-inch blade.*

g. Crude wooden handle; iron ferrule. The scabbard is made of two pieces of wood, bound with bamboo. A blow can be struck without first withdrawing the blade, which will cut its way out. This specimen appears to have been so used, as the present bands are not in the same places as the original ones. *Ten and one-half-inch blade.*

h. Brass ferrule and butt cap; handle made from horn of the water buffalo; the scabbard is made from two pieces of wood, bound with bamboo. The blade will cut its way out, so that, in an emergency, it is unnecessary to draw the blade from the scabbard. *Twelve and one-half-inch blade.*

The knife is essentially a weapon for close personal contest: so it illustrates the fighting instinct of human nature in the raw. An Italian whom I once called upon, thinking that I had come upon an unfriendly errand, seized a butcher knife, which had been lying upon the table. Fortunately a tactful word reassured him; but instead of quietly laying the knife aside, his temperamental excitement caused him to drive it almost through the top of the table, with a blow that fairly shook his little house. I thought that the blade would never stop quivering. Here was a cheerful illustration of the racial characteristic which developed the Roman sword and the stiletto.

Just as the American schoolboy takes off his coat to fight, so the Italian rolls up his sleeves, each giving freedom to the muscles about to be employed. This temperamental use of the arm is seen in other things than daggers. What with us are two useless ornamental buttons on our coatsleeves, are useful fastenings in Italy, where the sleeves are sometimes buttoned to the elbows, so as to be the more readily loosened.

In northern Europe the dirk or dagger was usually intended as a guard to ward off a blow from a sword, or for use in the secondary stage of combat, as when Roderick Dhu had been disarmed by Fitz James. In southern Europe the poignard, or stiletto, was rather for a sudden and unexpected assault, to direct a quick sharp blow at some vital spot. I own a specimen of Spanish dagger, with ivory handle and gold-plated scab-

Fig. 5 — NORWEGIAN SHEATH KNIFE
Made by hand during the evenings of a long winter.

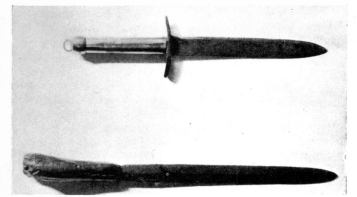

Fig. 6 — HOME-MADE KNIVES
  a. Handle wrapped with sheet brass. Carried by a junk collector who claimed he had found it. *Five and one-half-inch blade.*
  b. Handle made from section of a deer horn. Apparently used for throwing. *Eight-inch blade.*

Fig. 7
  a. Knife with *seven-inch blade* and hard rubber handle. Manufactured. Purchased from an Italian, who was carrying it in a home-made sheath.
  b. Copy of an old Spanish dagger, made in the Philippines, from the iron of a wagon wheel. Crude wooden handle. *Blade nine inches.*
  c. Knife from the trenches in the Great War. Turned wooden handle; undoubtedly originally intended for a pruning knife. *Blade seven inches.*
  d. Crude knife, made from a file; handle is a section of axe helve. *Blade seven and one-half inches.*

bard. It was used by a farmer in southern Maryland to cut holes in hams, in order that they might be hung up for smoking. The man could not give the history of this piece, beyond its having been in his family for a century. The interesting consideration was that the weapon had been designed for the purpose of penetrating flesh, and he had adapted it to his peaceful but similar needs.

Another Spanish dagger in my collection has over seventy pieces of carved ivory and semi-precious stones inlaid on the hilt. The tendency to decorate such fiendish instruments, so that they become part of the personal adornment, presents a combination of the æsthetic and the cruel which suggests temperamental characteristics.

A Matabele dagger from Africa indicates much the same combination of viciousness and vanity on the part of the owner. The hilt and the scabbard are wound with wire, both brass and copper. The blade is double edged, grooved

on one side like a hollow ground razor. It must have taken an immense amount of time to fabricate such an instrument; and yet, since the blade is only three and one-half inches long, I find difficulty in understanding how it could be used as a weapon. I have waded through about twenty books on Africa in the hope of finding some characteristic of the Matabeles which might explain the temperament which would produce such a dagger. Possibly such an instrument might be used effectively to sever the jugular vein, provided an unsuspecting enemy could be approached from behind. Certainly no American would ever think of spending so much time and putting so much ornament upon a dagger possessed of such a short and fragile blade.

In Norway the short winter days cause the members of a household to spend long evenings grouped around the fire. It is customary for the hired man to employ this time in

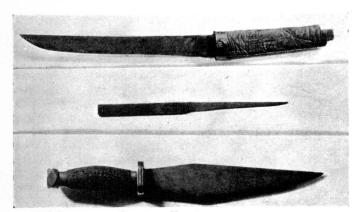

Fig. 8 — CHINESE AND JAPANESE KNIVES
  a. Japanese dagger, brass mounting, handle of carved bone; butt cap missing. *Eight-inch blade.*
  b. Japanese knife carried in a socket of sword scabbard; portion ground as the blade, *four inches.*
    (It is said that it was formerly customary to have a brass effigy soldered upon these daggers, which was similar to a European coat-of-arms. After killing an enemy in battle the Japanese warrior would stick this sword-knife in the body, as a sort of visiting card, so as to show who had killed him, it being considered impolite to fail to do this. But I have not been able to verify the statement.)
  c. Chinese knife. Ferrule and guard are made from one piece of solid brass. Brass butt tip. When the carved wooden handle is slightly moistened, the design changes. It is ground so as to give an upward, backward blow. *Seven and one-half-inch blade.*

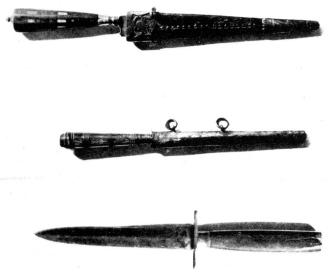

Fig. 9
  a. Dagger obtained from a descendant of the old French nobility. *Six-inch blade;* silver ferrule and hilt cap. Brass mounted scabbard. Handle inlaid with 71 pieces of old ivory and semi-precious stones.
  b. Spanish stiletto, ivory handle, ferrule and scabbard plated with gold; *five and one-quarter-inch blade.* It originally had a fancy guard. Used by a farmer in southern Maryland to make holes in hams, in order that they might be hung up for smoking. It had been in his family for at least a century.
  c. Old French dagger, ebony handle, iron ferrule and guard; butt cap missing. *Six-inch blade.*

making some gift for his employer, for which, in return, he expects a present in the spring. I have a sheath knife so made, laboriously constructed from raw material. While it would be serviceable in a fight, it has the "feel" of a knife intended for ordinary purposes, a fact which reflects the peaceable disposition of the Scandinavian race. These knives are worn on the belt, at the middle of the back, so as to be reached by either hand. The Finlanders carry their knives thrust into their boot tops, after the manner of the original "boot-legger" in America, who carried a bottle in like manner.

I once found an excellent specimen of the primitive knife of the Indian, similar to those discoverable among prehistoric relics in Europe. It consists of a chipped stone, which could be used as a knife, or axe, or hoe, or even as an adze. Although not adapted for use as a dagger, it is the original form from which knives and other cutting instruments have been evolved. On the other hand, the stiletto is probably a development of a sharpened stick, or bone.

Before the coming of the white man, the Indian skinned his game and scalped his enemy with a sharp-edged stone. Every specimen of this kind which I have obtained is chipped on one side only, which seems to be characteristic. It is said that, even today, the Indians sharpen a steel knife on one side only, like a chisel. I have a bowie knive which has been thus sharpened. Hence I surmise that it probably belonged to an Indian. One can tell whether an Indian is left handed or not by the side on which his knife is sharpened.

We naturally think of a murderer as facing the victim whom he stabs. But the Chinese are noted for doing things quite in the opposite way from white folk. In the days of the pig-tail and loose garments, it was practically impossible to identify a Chinaman when only his back was visible. Consequently, when a tong-man wished to eliminate an enemy, he arranged to overtake him in a narrow street. He would brush past him, and then suddenly disembowel him by a sudden upward sweep of his knife. The expiring victim, seeing only the back of the assassin, would usually be unable to offer an ante-mortem identification.

The daggers used for this stealthy method of unfriendliness seem all to be made in the same shape. There is a great deal of character in a hand, and anyone who has ever seen a Chinaman take hold of one of these knives will appreciate why they are made as they are. The fore part of the blade is ground with a view to the upward stroke described.

While scouring my museum specimen I discovered that, when the handle is slightly moistened the pattern of the carving undergoes change, so as to produce a different design. A slight perspiration of the hand holding this dagger would produce a similar alteration. Possibly this was intended to give evidence of luck or nerve. If the tong-man should be suffering from an excess of timidity his moist palm would occasion an alteration in the design on the hilt of his weapon. It would suffice to warn him that there was "bad luck" in butchering on that day.

In the Philippines our soldiers learned that it was not necessary for a native to draw his dagger from the sheath, which was made from two pieces of wood, bound with bamboo. If a blow was struck even while the knife was still in its sheath, the blade would cut its way out.

The Malay makes his kris with a wavy blade shaped like a snake. It is said that, when this is twisted in the flesh the wound will not heal. As an old darkey said "I ain't got no use for no such people, nohow." They must be rather annoying at times.

Formerly, in America, practically every man on the frontier habitually carried a hunting knife. When they became drunk and involved in a fight, they would naturally use their knives, though the primary purpose of these weapons was not for fighting. The Italian stiletto, on the other hand, was intended solely for stabbing. None of my American specimens is decorated in any way. All were intended for use, and not for ornament. Most of them were made from files. The notorious "Arkansaw toothpicks" were made from blacksmith rasps, as was also the original bowie knife, made for Colonel Bowie. This design, which he invented, has now become very popular for hunting knives, and also for the large blade of pocket knives. I have a bowie knife made by a Philippino, but he placed the blade at an angle with the handle.

In some fifteen years' experience in police courts and jails I have seldom found a dagger used by an American criminal. Some, among a certain class of women, sometimes carry a small stiletto for self-defense. But in general, now-a-days, when a crime is committed with a knife, the weapon is usually a common one, siezed in a moment of frenzy, without premeditation. A prosecuting attorney recently explained to me that the American criminal avoids too close personal contact with his victim; he does not like the feel of warm blood on his hands. This reflects an advance in our civilization which must be most gratifying.

Fig. 10 — AFRICAN DAGGERS
  a. From the Matabele region. Handle and sheath made of dark red, closely grained wood, wrapped with brass wire and copper wire. One side of each edge is formed like a hollow-ground razor. *Blade three and one-half inches long.*
  b. Two-handed dagger; iron ferrule. Handle of dark red wood, carved with checks near ferrule; covered with lead beaten into a strip, and wrapped around handle. *Ten-inch blade.*

V Powder Horns and Decorated Military Americana

One of the most fascinating and picturesque facets of military Americana is that of the carved powder horn. Until recently, collectors have concentrated on the powder horn's historical association and have undervalued its artistry. The powder horn is now an accepted form of folk art, and the identification of various schools of horn carvers, as well as an attempt to identify individual artists, has increased the appeal of many horns. The forger, who for many years concentrated his talents (and some were gifted with great ability) on the historical horn, has now turned his attention to the artistic horn as well, and every would-be buyer should exercise extreme caution before making a purchase. Unconditional guarantees ought to be obtained with the purchase whenever possible.

The value that early collectors placed on historical association is reflected in the articles reprinted in this chapter. Having to choose from a limited selection of horns because of his inability to travel widely, the collector of 50 years ago was at a great disadvantage compared with the collector of the post World War II era. Because he was not offered nearly as many examples to look at and to select from, his emphasis, therefore, was placed on that most imposing in appearance. To the collector of the early 20th century, this was the map horn.

Probably the greatest influence to promote the map horn over decorated horns was an English book, *Appendiculae Historicae, or Shreds of History Hung on a Horn* (1891) by Fred W. Lucas. This, the most important published work on powder horns at the time, details the events that were responsible for the carved horn and includes maps of the routes taken during the French and Indian War, with a listing and brief history of each fort. With no major publications to compete with, and a scarcity of fine horns from which to choose, *Appendiculae Historicae* made the map horn famous in the collecting world.

Had the drawings of Rufus Grider (who sketched over 500 different horns during the last decade of the 19th century) been published and circulated freely among the collecting fraternity, the map horn might not have received the renowned recognition that was accorded it. Because the supply of map horns was limited, the faker had an ideal opportunity to make a dishonest profit. Map horns required little imagination, and, supplied with the right dates and names, and with a certain amount of engraving ability, the forger-carver was assured of ready sales. This fraudulent practice continues to this day. Many of these horns are excellent imitations, and those that are good, and are over fifty or seventy-five years old, are difficult to disclaim.

Authentic horns that are artistically engraved with genuine 18th- or 19th-century designs and motifs, however, are gradually becoming recognized. Their amusing rhymes and unique visual qualities have gained the confidence of many new collectors who are pleased to add them to their collections. And even 19th-century hunting horns, long neglected by the collector, are becoming equally important to the folk-art enthusiast.

Another sphere of military-related folk art, one which brings this anthology to a close, encompasses the painted militia accessories of the 19th century. These brightly decorated accoutrements—drums, knapsacks, canteens, helmets, hat plates and flags—add impressive and much-needed color to an otherwise drab wall lined with guns and swords. Most of the decoration was executed by itinerant artists, carriage painters, or just a talented person in a town whose militia desired decorated uniforms.

The Why and How of Engraved Powder Horns*

By CHARLES WINTHROP SAWYER

THERE are wide differences in type among engraved powder horns. In the first place, some horns are American, some are foreign. We may assume, further, that foreign horns are, in the majority of instances, artificially shaped, and are ornamented with formal engraving executed by professionals; whereas American horns retain their natural shape, and, for the most part, were engraved by their maker-owners.

The assumption for American horns covers the case, if we leave a loophole. If we peer through that loophole, we shall see that the best, and, at present, most prized American powder horns, although of natural shape and engraved in America, were *not* engraved by the men whose names they bear; but, on the contrary, even though prepared by their owners, were decorated by hands more skilful with pencil and burin.

All American powder horns qualify as either *military* or *sporting*. High-grade engraved sporting horns made before 1825 are exceedingly scarce. Yet they have not, thus far, become widely esteemed.

Military horns, according to the nature of their engraving, are classed as "map horns" and "culch horns." Culch, in this application, does not mean rubbish, but merely second in quality or interest among American military horns — and this frequently for the sole reason that the fad of the moment has raised the map horn to first place. Indeed, a culch horn may be a work of art, a map horn may be a crudity; and yet, because of fashion's

dictates, the culch horn is less esteemed. In general, however, a culch horn is really a second-grade horn from the standpoint of art. And there is a reason for this: map horns were often ornamented with designs pertinent to military affairs, wrought by men skilled in drawing and engraving. Culch horns, on the other hand, were — not all, but nearly all — engraved by common soldiers who crudely and inaptly traced ill-drawn pictures and poorly lettered inscriptions.

Military horns, both map and culch, were almost always made in camp — important presentation specimens excepted. Even if a soldier or an officer brought from home a satisfactory horn, he was quite likely to make another. Life in certain encampments was so idle and so tedious that horn marking became a welcome method of whiling away the time. It was one of the two — almost the only two — innocent diversions. The other one was keeping diaries and writing home. Diaries and letters written by officers and soldiers of the period 1754 to 1763 still exist in great numbers. They may be examined in state archives, public libraries, and private collections. By piecing together their many accounts of horn marking, we, today, are able to understand not merely why horns were scrimshawed, but also just how the process was accomplished.

Suitable horns in the rough were furnished, free of charge, to officers and soldiers, before

Fig. 1 — MAP HORN (*1757–1760*)
Showing Quebec, Montreal, and Detroit, the route from the Great Lakes to the ocean.
From the Peter Force Collection, Library of Congress

1775, sometimes by the king and sometimes by the provinces. They were all of similar size, and were grown in America, but not in the provinces. As several inches were removed from a horn to prepare it for a base plug at one end and a stopper at the other, the specimen, before the cutting, had to be at least twenty inches long; twenty-four inches was better. Neither British cattle nor those of the thirteen colonies produced horns of such size. It was necessary to secure supplies from American descendants of Spanish bovine stock, such as our grandfathers spoke of as "Texas longhorns."

The king's agents in America, as well as the buyers for the various provinces, secured most of their horn supplies from the Bird family of Dorchester, near Boston, Massachusetts. The men of this family were, primarily, tanners and wholesale dealers in leather. The first of them, Thomas, who arrived in this country about 1635, established a tannery, which eventually developed into a large and many-sided leather business. Hides were gathered in the West Indies, the West Coast, and South America. In those lands, horns — large ones, in countless numbers — were refuse. They went free with the purchased hides. So, in war time, the Birds supplied governments with leather and with thousands of horns. The latter, laid on the wharf in Boston, cost the Birds about a penny apiece, and they brought from king or provincial governor fourpence each in the rough; or sixpence, trimmed and bored.

They were cheap, but, nevertheless, they were very good. Only now and then was there among them one so over-rich in lime as to acquire a white-bone crust and to become brittle. Nearly all were cartilaginous. They were so sound that, even now, nearly two centuries later, a scrubbing with alcohol, soap and water, will make a specimen look almost new. Their age is impossible to determine from their appearance.

Such a horn offered the best possible means of encasing gunpowder. It was waterproof, not only against rain, but even when lost overboard. It was light to carry; and it was also light enough to float. When dropped from boat or canoe it was easily recovered; whereas a leather or a metal box sank like a stone. Horn did not catch fire; and it so thoroughly protected gunpowder as to be safe in a shower of sparks. Furthermore, a powder horn was enduring, tough, elastic; if dropped on a rock, it would bounce instead of break. And it was so soft that its owner could easily mark it with his name — or more — and thus identify it after it had been mixed with all the other horns of the personnel at the powder wagon or other filling station.

Engraved American powder horns usually carried more than simply the name of the owner. Some were spread with a variety of pictures; some bore lines of patriotic doggerel; most of them had both. Such markings, when applied by the soldier-owner, were done a bit at a time during a long period. Hence a date on a horn signifies the moment when the work was finished. It had long before been begun.

From these data emerges a clew to the oft-propounded and always unanswered puzzle: "Why do nearly all the finest engraved American military horns belong to the period of the fourth French and Indian War?" The answer is that this was the only period favorable to the production of such horns by great numbers of soldiers. It supplied the two conditions indispensable to horn engraving: warm weather and the leisure of a long, idle encampment.

The Revolution developed but one long, idle camp; and that one, at Valley Forge, was a winter establishment, where the poorly clad, ill-housed soldiers were too stiff with cold to undertake the delicate task of scrimshawing. During the French Wars preceding the fourth one, soldiering was an active instead of a leisurely occupation.

In the fourth French War, however, great numbers of men were held idle in summer camps during a series of campaigns. The first of these camps, that preceding Braddock's expedition against Fort Duquesne, has left us many culch horns, but few, if any, map horns. There was so little knowledge of the region which the army was to traverse that neither soldiers nor professional engravers could find a map of the region, or a picture or a plan of Fort Duquesne, which they could copy on their horns.

But when the campaigns of the fourth war were transferred to the valleys of Lake Champlain, Lake George, the Hudson, and the Mohawk, the men were operating in regions familiar to many of them and already roughly mapped. Map horns were prepared in advance by professionals — gunsmiths, silversmiths, and block cutters — in all of the centres, and were offered for sale in the stores. Old maps and old engravings of the terrain and of the large settlements were in the hands of civilians and military men alike, and were available for copying.

A single horn, once engraved, was borrowed to serve as a model for others. Hence, nearly all map horns were similar in character. In copying, the maps became distorted, but that was immaterial; they were sure to prove useful to their owners in obtaining information about the point-to-point details of a journey.

For example, an officer in Abercrombie's encampment at the head of Lake George was ordered to start in a week or so for Fort Oswego on Lake Ontario — about ten days' hard travel over a route entirely unknown to him. The officer at once ordered the preparation of a map horn to serve him as an indicator of general direction and of the main settlements which he must seek along his line of travel.

The process of making the new map horn for this officer was, in general, illustrative of the making and engraving of all other such American military horns. The horn had already been cut off at both ends, and the small end bored from tip to chamber. The interior needed to be cleared and smoothed. The exterior was then cut with rasp, drawshave, knife, and file until the piece was satisfactorily shaped and smoothed. The surface was polished with pumice and oil on the palm of the hand. A wooden base plug was now fitted and secured with wooden pins. It was made water-tight by flowing melted tallow and beeswax into the crevice around it. The small end was plugged with a tight-fitting, soft wood stopper.

Pencil-marked with everything that was to go on its surface, the horn was now clamped to its engraver's lap by means of a strap, tensed by foot pressure. The engraver, if a professional, used engraver's tools; if an amateur, a knife point for principal lines and a needle in a stick for fine lines. Whether professional or amateur, as he worked, he gave visibility to the cut lines by rubbing them with his moist and dirty fingers.

When the engraving was completed, he filled it with a weather-proof dark filling of grease and either soot or gunpowder dust. Vegetable oil, made by cooking and squeezing nuts, was better, because it hardened in a short time, whereas the animal fat remained soft.

If color was wanted, either for filling the lines or for staining the surface of the horn, the backwoods were rich in dye materials. There was green in the verdigris of the camp kettle, and black in the soot on the kettle's bottom. Goldthread, growing in swampy places, furnished bright yellow dye, and the pith of sumac furnished another yellow. Brown could be had from alder bark, and other shades of brown from the husks of butternuts and walnuts. Red came from chokecherries and raspberries, and russet-red from sumac berries. There was no lack of stains and colors.

Such a horn, strictly for use and simply marked, could be made, from start to finish, in a few days, by working through all the sunlight hours of long summer days. If done a bit at a time, the task might occupy weeks or months. The elaborately ornamented horns presented by companies, battalions, or regiments to favorite commanders, or wrought by artistically educated young officers or by silversmiths at the behest of worthy military men, represented far more time and labor.

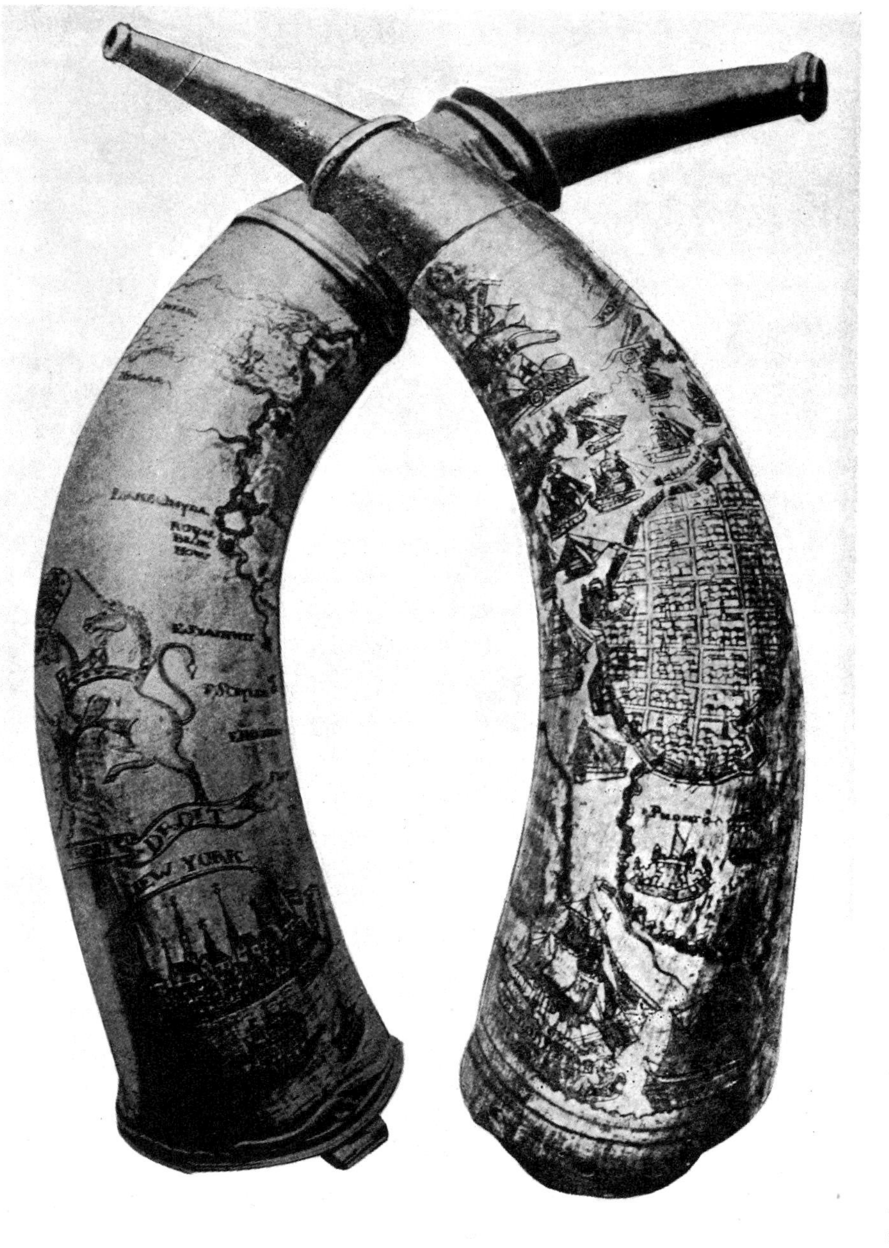

And nearly all the fine old American specimens became family heirlooms. Many are, today, but little faded, and show few signs of wear and age. They afford us as keen pleasure and pride as they gave to their first owners a century and three-quarters ago. They are, as they always have been, articles of merit.

The popular esteem in which map horns are held has been many times erroneously explained on the ground that they are sources from which antiquarians and historians learn the obsolete names of places, the former situations of relocated settlements, the original shape of fortifications. Absurd! Other sources, more abundant, more easily available, are richer in such details and far more accurate. Map horns gained their place among American antiques because they are cultural objects, conveying their own definite proof of when, where, by and for whom they were made. They are made-in-America antiques in a class by themselves.

Fig. 2 — MAP HORNS
That at the left dates from *1757* to *1760*, and shows the route from New York to Lake Ontario. The horn at the right (*1762–1763*) apparently depicts the fortifications about Havana.
From the Peter Force Collection, Library of Congress.

KEEP YOUR POWDER DRY

By F. S. BROCKETT

"A POWDER horn is just a powder horn, nothing more and nothing less." Or so I thought when I began collecting them. But as time passed and both collector interest and the collection itself grew, I found there was a lot more to it than that. It became my aim to assemble examples of all the different kinds of powder horns, and all the associated objects made of horns, used by the pioneers. The Champlain Valley of northeastern New York State and the western border of Vermont, the theater of my exploration, proved a fertile field.

Few relics of the first two hundred turbulent years of English settlement on the American coast played such an intimate and indispensable part in the lives of our forefathers as did horns. During that period there was a continuous series of battles, forays, and skirmishes, of scouting along the Indian war trails leading down from Canada, of long marches into the wilderness, and of scouring the woods and marshes for something to shoot and eat. The possession of a flintlock musket or fowling piece was a prerequisite to obtaining a livelihood, and without the powder horn, bullet horn, and priming horn, the flintlock was useless. Cattle horns were an ideal raw material for many purposes, and they were plentiful and cheap. Horn is light, strong, and tough, and does not sliver, shatter, or break easily. It melts before it burns. Softened in hot water it lends itself readily to the carver's knife and the engraver's burin. Powder horns two hundred years old, in good condition, are proof of great durability, and it is little wonder that horn was a favored container for gunpowder from the time of the invention of firearms.

Beginning about 1825 horn containers were gradually supplanted by copper flasks; they finally reached the end of their usefulness when the muzzle-loading gun, with its accompanying ramrod, was superseded by the breech-loading gun and its ready-made cartridge. Many of the old-timers, however, were loath to shift from horn to metal for containers, as they were to accept the improved gun, and the transition period covered two or more generations. One handsome little priming horn, carved with gray squirrels, is dated as recently as 1848. An ancient hunter on Peru Mountain, Vermont, was using a powder horn in 1923 to serve a small-bore Kentucky-style rifle.

Devon and Durham oxen grew horns twenty or more inches in length. Horns that held from two to three pounds of coarse black gunpowder were the kind usually carried on long marches to the frontiers of white man's civilization. Powder was precious and hard to obtain. It was safest to march with a big horn well filled, in the hope that it might last the round trip.

FIG. 1 — EARLY HORNS. *Top to bottom,* a typical shot horn, length 8 inches. "Six Nations" Indian horn with pewter base and tip; engraved with symbolic motives such as a great horned owl and a large circle enclosing six small circles with a dark spot in center representing the council fire. Dual-purpose horn for bullets and powder. British officer's map horn, inscribed *Jacob Wagner/Año 1760,* engraved by a professional. Powder horn, richly carved with mermaid, two forts, a motto and date *1790.* An unusually large, uncarved powder horn, length, 19 inches. They have acquired a fine patina from many long years of rubbing against buckskin and wool

Most picturesque and rare are the beautifully engraved "map" horns. Prior to and during the Revolutionary War, British officers detailed to regiments stationed in America were provided with finely made powder horns, on whose surface were engraved maps of the region in which they were to serve. After being incised, the lines were traced in ink, in contrasting colors of red and black, and a coat of varnish was applied to clarify and preserve the lines and coloring. The artistry of professional engravers expressed itself in pictorial embellishments covering a wide range of subjects. Their horns show maps of city, country, coast lines, rivers, lakes, battlefields, and forts. Many horns were cut or carved by the owner himself with a knife as his only tool. The American soldiers sometimes carved their own map horns, though the best examples were executed by skilled engravers (see ANTIQUES for May 1925, p. 254, and October 1929, p. 283). If no ink was available, they used grease and soot or home-made dyes to fill in the incised lines. Individuals devised their own patterns, copying familiar objects. Landsmen carved wild animals, oxen, horses, dogs, birds, eagles, guns; seafaring men carved ships, whales, dolphins, sea serpents, mermaids, cannon, pistols, and cutlasses. Horn carvings commonly show mottoes, slogans, verse, names, dates, and personal impressions gained on the march or in camp, sometimes of historical value. Examples of another type bear on their surfaces rings, knobs, collars, flutings, and geometric figures.

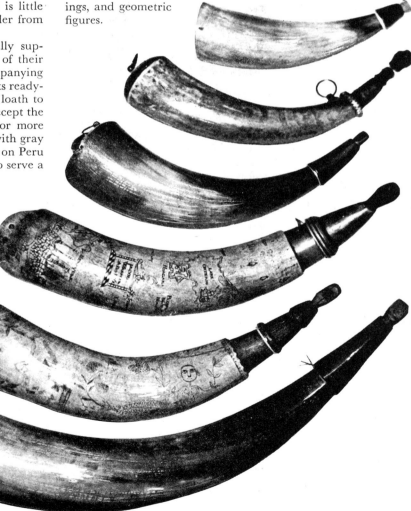

Horns stained with butternut and oak-bark juices give evidence that the old-timers practiced camouflage. Red Devon cattle, the leading breed of oxen in the colonies, had large upright, and beautifully curved white horns. A white powder horn made too conspicuous a target, so colonists toned down the color to minimize the danger.

Traders carried powder horns to barter with the Indians in exchange for furs. Indians were given horns by settlers. Both French and British Indian commissioners were liberal dispensers of war equipment of all sorts, powder horns included, as reward for the taking of enemy scalps. A "Six Nations" horn (*Fig. 1*) belonged to a red warrior-scout under command of Colonel J. G. Van Schaick.

Occasionally horns were made to serve two purposes. A horn in the Fort Ticonderoga Museum has a compartment in its base to hold wadding. Some had false bottoms to conceal a written message. No one will ever know how many messages from one military post to another were concealed in such an innocent-looking, waterproof "envelope." I have read of a horn with a mirror set in its base. Only one dual-purpose horn has come to my hands. It was procured from the previously mentioned Vermont hunter and has a thin board partition set midway of its length, so that the tip end could be used for powder, the butt end for bullets; a cork stoppered the hole bored in the base.

Cannon priming horns were essential equipment for artillerymen, along with rammers, sponges, and vent picks. Priming powder had to be poured into the firing vent of the cannon before the piece could be discharged. The practice continued through the era of

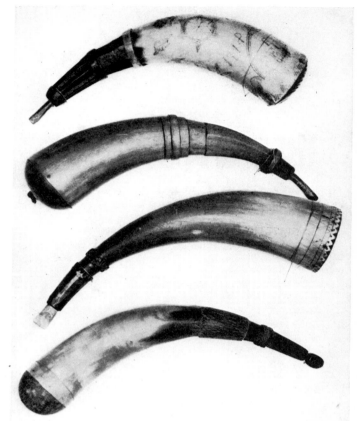

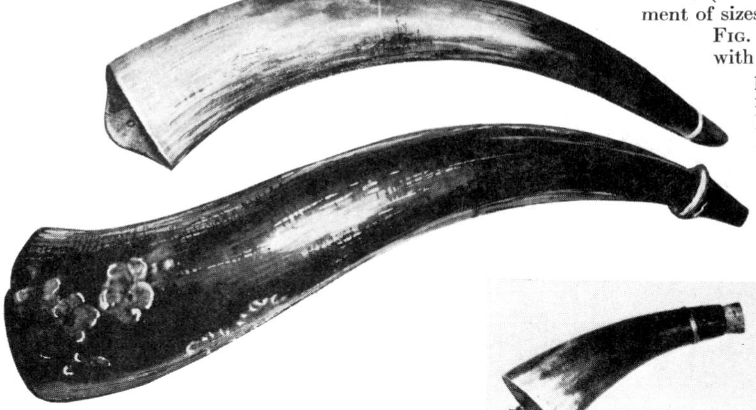

FIG. 2 (*below*) — DRINKING HORNS. Lower horn is a Bennington battle relic, oil painted

Illustrations from the author's collection

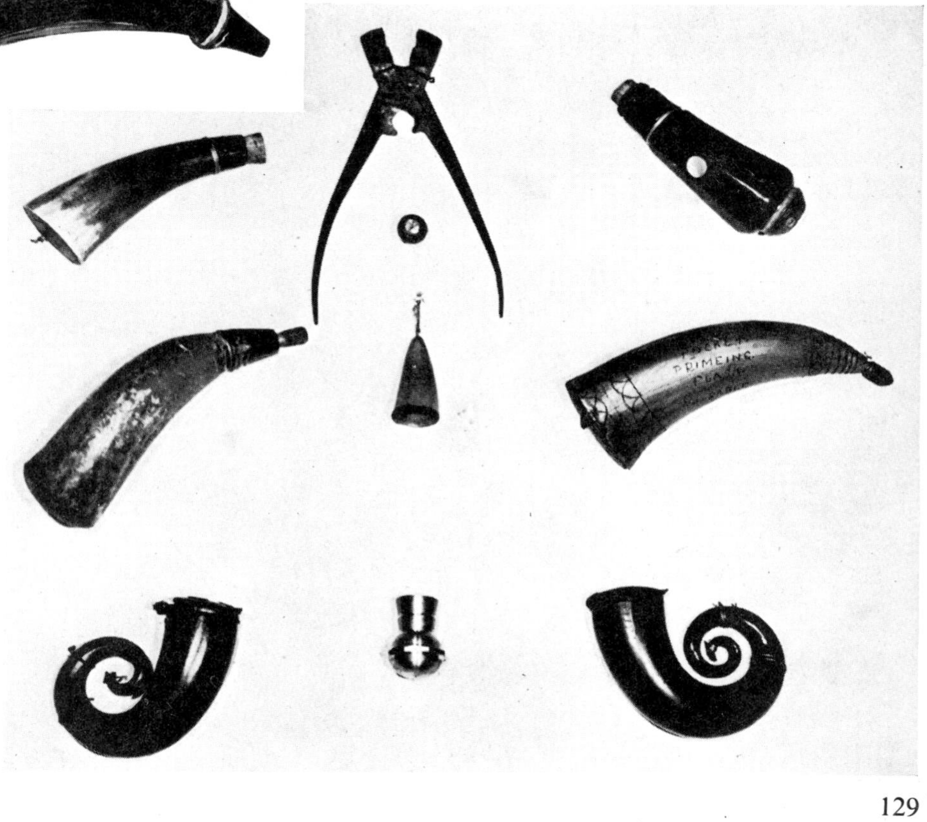

FIG. 3 (*above*) — HUNTER'S AND SPORTSMAN'S POWDER HORNS. A typical assortment of sizes, shapes, and decorative treatments

FIG. 4 (*below*) — HUNTER'S EQUIPMENT. *Top to bottom:* Two bullet horns with corks, length, 4 inches; bullet mold, and musket ball. Richly carved pistol horn; calf-horn powder measure or "charger"; pocket priming flask. Two Scottish Highlands sheep-horn snuffboxes (probably brought into Champlain Valley by members of Caledonian regiments); ox-horn tip made of brass

the cannon-lock and slow-match methods of firing. A cannon primer can be distinguished from a regulation powder horn only when it is engraved as such, or is duly authenticated, or has a large hole with a screw thread cut in the base into which a threaded hardwood stopper is screwed.

Ox horns were used in the production of several other articles that at first glance appear similar to powder horns. All have their place in military affairs. An early bugle horn, for example, looks like a powder horn without a base-board. The tip end of the horn is cut off where the hollow center commences and has a bell mouth. These bugle horns are capable of emitting a quite awful blast, and they have long been used as an instrument of call and alarm. In the early days of this valley, hunters, scouts, lookouts, coach drivers, messengers, and post-boys used them.

The medicine horn was used for ministering to sick horses and oxen. The procedure was to tie a rope around the animal's upper jaw, pass the rope end over a tree limb, raise the animal's head, stick the horn down its throat, and pour. A medicine horn can only be distinguished from a powder horn if the tip end has been chewed, or if the item lacks surface patina.

Drinking horns (*Fig. 2*) and horn cups had their place in the list of regular army equipment. The former are white horns, beautifully polished, from which the tips have never been removed. Cups were made by sawing the horns in two and fitting a base-board in one end of the larger half.

Since a bovine, like a dilemma, has two horns, both were used; but of course the curve of the "left-handed" horn was the reverse of the "right-handed" one. Some men wore the powder horn on the left hip, others on the right. Some used the ramrod with the left hand and others with the right, to wad powder and lead in the barrel of the gun. Deftness of hand governed the choice, and horns could be found to fit either hip. Of the horns I have collected, "rights" and "lefts" are about equal in number.

Cow horns, being small, were used as containers for pistol-horn powder, priming powder, bullets, and shot. Horns of this type were carried in pockets or pouches. In numbers and in importance, the first of the type to be considered is the pocket priming horn (*Fig. 4*). Every owner of a flintlock carried one. They held the fine-grained, high-flash powder used for priming the pan. They are usually about three inches long, and their distinguishing characteristic is the tiny nozzle opening, which is just large enough to emit a thin trickle of powder into the pan. They are usually very handsome little pieces.

Bullet carriers, from four to eight inches long, constitute another important category of small horns (*Fig. 4*). Acquisition of a horn full of round lead balls gave me my first evidence that horns were used in this way. The tips were cut off at a point where the hollow was large enough to accommodate the size of ball used. They were stoppered with corks, instead of wooden plugs, presumably because the roll of heavy lead balls would more easily

knock out a wooden plug. One example of this type is made of buffalo horn, inlaid with pearl shell.

Pistol horns were an accessory of the old-fashioned flintlock, muzzle-loading horse-pistol, with its brass barrel, ramrod, and round hand-grip. Pistol horns are small pocket pieces, three to four inches long, with nozzle opening somewhere in size between those of primer and bullet horn. They cannot be distinguished from primers with certainty, unless by the engraving (*Fig. 4*). Many primers and pistol horns have been flattened slightly, presumably that they might require less room in pockets. Flattening was done by scraping the walls very thin, soaking the horn in hot water to soften it, and then placing a weight on it until dry.

Shot horns were in daily use by members of the average pioneer family. I have found examples that still contain old lead shot much oxidized, often not truly spherical in shape, and always in a mixture of sizes all the way from buckshot down to number six. The olden-time hunter with his "single barrel" went prepared to mow down whatever game he might encounter, from a rabbit to a deer. Shot horns have bell "mouths" (for funnel filling) and a restricted "throat" (to retard the outward flow of shot). This feature distinguishes them from bullet horns.

A small military object is a powder charger, or powder measure, made from a calf's horn, or "button" (*Fig. 4*). It is very light and thin and holds measured gunpowder for one load. Powder horns collected from the original sources still have the straps, of cowhide, deerskin, gut, eelskin, or twine, that suspended them from wooden pegs above the fireplaces of their makers.

In the early days in the Champlain Valley every settler was a hunter, and nearly every hunter was a soldier. Besides the horns already discussed, there is the large group of "hunter's" horns. These were made of cow horns about eight inches long, and held powder for an ordinary hunting expedition. A surprisingly large proportion of them were beautifully made, decorated and polished. Frequently a hunter's horn was worn away to the wars, so that the distinction between hunter's horns and military horns is superficial at best. All played a vital part in the early American settlers' struggle for individual and national existence.

Fig. 5 — The Brockett Collection of Powder Horns

AMERICAN ENGRAVED POWDER HORNS

By STEPHEN V. GRANCSAY

Editor's Note. A monograph entitled American Engraved Powder Horns: A Study Based on The J. H. Grenville Gilbert Collection, by Stephen V. Grancsay is to be published this month by The Metropolitan Museum of Art. It deals with the collection of forty-five powder horns and primers formed by J. H. Grenville Gilbert, of Ware, Massachusetts, and presented to the Museum in 1937 by the late Mrs. Gilbert. One of the features of the monograph is the check list of American engraved powder horns, which records examples that bear the name of the original owner, a date, a map, a rhyme, or other significant inscription or ornamentation. The list is indexed, so that makers or engravers, places, and ships mentioned on the horns as well as the names of the present owners (both institutions and individuals) are readily available. It is a valuable source of information for specialized phases of this study, such as New England, New York, and Pennsylvania map horns, views of cities represented on powder horns, and historical powder horns. A list of rhymes that appear on powder horns is given in an appendix. There is also an annotated bibliography.

The late Alexander J. Wall, former director of the New York Historical Society, courteously granted permission to include in the monograph a record of the Society's large collection of colored drawings of powder horns made by Rufus A. Grider (1817-1900), seven of which represent horns now in the Gilbert collection. A large group of drawings of French and Indian War and Revolutionary horns in the Mohawk Valley was made by the late Robert M. Hartley of Amsterdam, New York, and is now in the Margaret Reaney Memorial Library at St. Johnsville, New York. Still another group of colored drawings of American powder horns, prepared by the Work Projects Administration as part of the material in the Index of American Design, is deposited in the National Gallery of Art in Washington. The Metropolitan Museum has line drawings of all of its engraved horns, which were also prepared by Work Projects Administration artists, and these are illustrated in the monograph. Mr. Grancsay is interested in learning of powder horns that bear the name of the original owner, a date, a map, a rhyme, or other significant inscription or ornamentation. Address him at the Metropolitan Museum of Art, New York 28, New York.

To THE UNINITIATED, engraved powder horns are merely curiosities, like carved cherry stones or flies in amber, but their importance is far greater than that of such trifles. Scratched work is the most ancient form of graphic expression and surface decoration used by man, and powder horns are valuable for their representation of this folk art. When scraped, polished, and engraved, an ordinary steer's horn became a prized possession. On it the soldier demonstrated his skill with the jacknife, just as the sailor on the lee

days carved out scrimshaw work. Many American powder horns belong to a time like the present when every man might be called upon for military service; through their association with men and events such horns now have not only artistic but biographical, geographical, and historical interest.

While most American powder horns were home-made, a certain number were made for sale by professional engravers or gunsmiths as well as by combmakers. George W. Crouse, of Reinholds, Lancaster County, Pennsylvania, informs me that his family have been combmakers since the Revolutionary War. Mr. Crouse, like his ancestors, also makes powder horns. American engraved powder horns were usually made of selected horns from cows, bullocks, or oxen. These natural horns, twenty inches long or more, were beautiful in contour. Professional engraving was executed in fine outline with a sharp, pointed graver and may be distinguished from that crudely engraved with a jacknife by the accuracy and delicacy of the

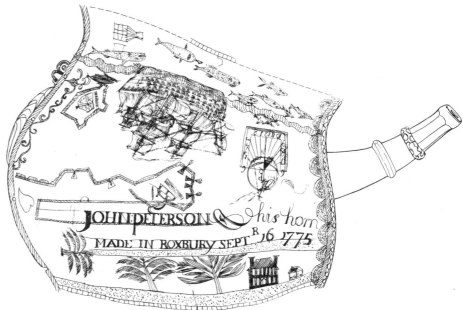

FIGS. 1 AND 2 — POWDER HORN. Inscribed: *John Peterson his horn/made in Roxbury Septr 16 1775.* The engraved decoration includes the plan of a fort. Roxbury Camp, near Boston, is today known as Highland Park. *Comparison of photograph with drawing by Elisabeth Fulda, and Figure 3, drawing of same horn by Rufus A. Grider. Except as noted, illustrations from the Metropolitan Museum of Art.*

ornament. Occasionally the decoration of a powder horn was pricked out with a needle, but a graver was used for the best work. Sometimes the engraving includes a blank cartouche intended for the name of the eventual purchaser.

Color was an important feature in the decoration of horns. Those made by professional "horn smiths" were usually dipped in a yellow dye to give the surface the appearance of amber. A stain made of butternut bark brought out the grain in translucent horn. To accentuate the engraving, sometimes the lines were filled with grease or shoemaker's wax. Soot or gunpowder dust or green verdigris from the camp kettle were also used for this purpose. Sometimes, too, the decorative effect was heightened by picking out details in vermilion red, a technique which is represented on several of the Museum's horns. Some horns were varnished or covered with coatings of shellac, and on these the engravings and coloring are well preserved.

The subjects engraved on powder horns are varied. We may mention maps, sketches of forts and towns, scenes of battle on land and sea, and animals and birds that inhabited the localities represented on maps. In early times every ship that sailed the seas was armed, and powder horns were part of its equipment. That is why so many powder horns

FIG. 4 (above)—JACOB CUYLER POWDER HORN (dated 1761). Shows forts on Mohawk and Hudson Rivers.

are engraved with nautical subjects—mermaids, fishes, ships, and so on. As in scrimshaw work, full-rigged four-masters were favorite designs. At the top and bottom of the horns there is frequently an attempt at decoration in the form of a carved engrailed pattern. On powder horns owned by Americans before the Revolution or by British officers serving in America the British royal arms are often prominently displayed (Fig. 4). Some horns have subjects inspired by contemporary cartoons.

Each horn tells its own story. The horn of Thomas Hastings, in the New Hampshire Historical Society, records the names of men killed or captured by the Indians at Charlestown, New Hampshire, in 1745 and 1746. The State Historical Society of Wisconsin has the horn of a Pennsylvania-German ranger who participated in Colonel Henry Bouquet's expedition against the Ohio Indians in 1764, which date it bears. In the collection of the late Charles Darwin Cook, of Providence, Rhode Island, there is a horn inscribed with the names of the thirteen original states. The New Hampshire Historical Society has a horn that refers to the Declaration of Independence. It is inscribed: *Iohn Abbot H H 1776/Independence ded July 1776.* A Hessian powder horn used during the Revolutionary War, now in the Chicago Historical Society, is inscribed: *Henrich Keller sein horn Georges III Koenig von Gros Bridanien D 2 1776.* The powder horn of Zapnin Smythe, dated April 17, 1774, evidently fell into the hands of a British soldier, for it is inscribed *Ye dam rebel did make ye goode horne G R June ye 29 L. G. 1778 L. Gideon.* This horn is now in the Lexington Historical Society.

On the finest engraved and colored powder horns a map is often shown, usually accompanied by the British heraldic arms. Ever since antiquity maps have been drawn on any object that could be carried conveniently. Among the finds at Salihiyeh, the ancient colony of Doura-Europos on the Euphrates, was part of a Roman archer's shield on which is painted a road map giving names of places and the distances between them. For his exploration of Yucatan, Cortes had native artists paint a map on cloth showing the rivers and mountain chains to be crossed. Apart from his compass, this was his only guide for this dangerous journey. Recently seventeen American aviators, none of

FIG. 3 (below)—POWDER HORN. Drawing by Rufus A. Grider. *From New York Historical Society.*

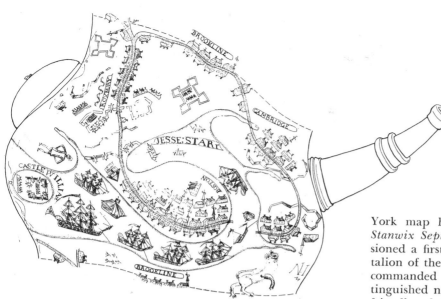

Fig. 5 (*left*) — Revolutionary Powder Horn. This powder horn belonged to Jesse Starr, a Connecticut soldier who took part in the siege of Boston (*1775-1776*), and who while there decorated his horn with a map of Boston in which the fortifications across the Neck are shown, and something of the surrounding country. *Drawing by Elisabeth Fulda.*

whom had ever made the flight before, escaped from the Philippines to the Netherlands East Indies with only a tiny map on a souvenir cigarette case by which to navigate their flying boats.

In colonial and Revolutionary days soldiers and traders frequently had to travel over unfamiliar territory and therefore needed maps. The period of the French and Indian Wars proved to be a mapmaking era, because much of the region that was being fought over had not previously been charted. Few printed maps existed, even for the use of the higher officers. So it was natural that diagrams of the routes followed should come to be engraved on powder horns, for the horn was the indispensable accessory of the frontier rifle, the greatest of all American mapmakers. The maps on the Gilbert horns cover a wide geographical area, including New York and Canada, New England, the Atlantic coast, the Carolinas, Florida, Cuba (*Fig. 6*) and even a view of London. These maps, though picturesque, are inaccurate, but in their day they must have been of inestimable value.

The province of New York was the principal theater of the century-long conflict between the British and French empires, whose aim was the control of the North American continent. Horns with maps of New England and of Pennsylvania are much rarer than those with maps of New York. There are nine New York and Canada map horns in the Gilbert collection. The New York examples have considerable interest apart from the maps. One, elaborately decorated, is inscribed: *Peter Myer hiss horn año 1759* and *Niagara 26 Jullit 1759*, and shows large tracts of forest still scarcely touched by settlers, who usually located their inland towns and farms in the fertile river valleys. Fort Niagara, which is especially noted on this horn, was built by the French in 1726

to prevent the English from controlling this "gateway to the West"; but it was captured on July 25, 1759, by Sir William Johnson, who had succeeded to the command of the British forces when Brigadier General John Prideaux was killed early in the battle. The date *26 Jullit 1759* engraved on our horn evidently refers to this event. Another New York map horn bears the inscription: *Jacob Cuyler Fort Stanwix Septr. 10, 1761 (Fig. 4)*. Jacob Cuyler was commissioned a first lieutenant in 1764 and served in the first Battalion of the Militia of the County of Albany. This body was commanded by Colonel Sir William Johnson, who was distinguished not only for his military exploits but also for his friendly relations with the Indians. Fort Stanwix was important as a defense point during the colonial period because of its strategic location between the upper Mohawk River and Wood Creek.

The soldier prized his horn, the companion piece to his musket and rifle. In times of peace, horn and musket usually hung over the kitchen fireplace, a constant reminder of fighting days and campaigns against the Indians. But the breech-loading rifle (*1866*) and the metallic cartridge (*about 1840*) sounded the death knell of the powder horn for military purposes. It is still used with Kentucky rifles for game.

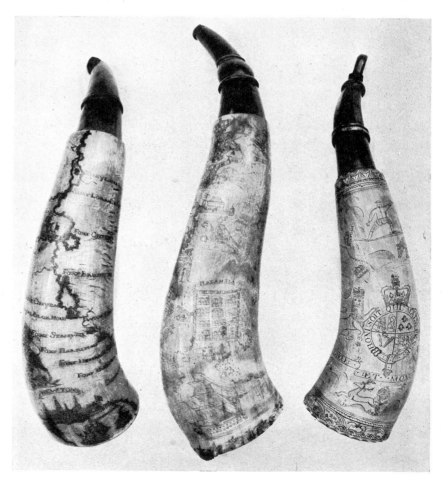

Fig. 6 (*right*)—Engraved Powder Horns (*c. 1760*). *Left*, with a map of New York. *Center*, with a map showing the harbors of "Hauana" and "Matansia." *Right*, with a map of "The Middle Settlement of Cherokees."

Powder horns
of the French and Indian War, 1755-1763

BY WILLIAM H. GUTHMAN

AN EXCITING and unusual mid-eighteenth-century folk-art form has been neglected for more than two hundred years. American carved powder horns have almost always been categorized by historians and collectors not as art objects, but as historical artifacts valued for the persons, places, and events associated with each one. Unscrupulous dealers have fabricated literally hundreds of reproductions over the years which have been sold as originals to careless bargain hunters and naïve descendants of purported original owners of the horns. Fortunately, the fakers have neglected the aesthetic qualities of the horns made at the time of the French and Indian War and have instead emphasized the more dramatic battles, expeditions, slogans, and names that are well known to every collector of Americana.

Even more popular, and more expensive, have been the picturesque horns carved with maps of routes from New York City to Canada via Albany and lakes George and Champlain, or from Albany via the Mohawk River to Lake Ontario and the St. Lawrence River. Once in a great while a map horn showing the route from Fort Pitt (originally the site of Fort Duquesne) to the Great Lakes region appears on the market.

Because a great majority of the historical and map horns are forgeries, many fine collections of Americana today include horns of dubious origin. Some of these are of recent vintage; others have come from collections that were formed in the last century. A number of fakes have been published as originals, and too many spurious examples have figured in major exhibitions for years.

Unlike most collectors, collectors of carved horns appear to act on impulse, buying horns after only the briefest examination of them. Careful scrutiny in strong daylight with a magnifying glass, however, can show whether the carving on a horn is contemporary with it and if a horn has been artificially aged. A revealing comparison can be made between the decorative motifs on a horn and those scribbled in the margins of eighteenth-century account books, on the flyleaves of printed books, and in the pages of diaries. The style of inscriptions on the horns can be profitably compared to the careful calligraphy of eighteenth-century exercise books and tombstones.

Too few horn collectors are familiar with the letters and diaries of soldiers of the same economic and educational backgrounds as those who carved the horns. An awareness of what was important to the average eighteenth-century American soldier would make collectors much more hesitant to buy a horn, for there is a great difference between the amount of emphasis given to events in the eighteenth century and the amount of emphasis given to those same events in the nineteenth or twentieth century.

During the seventeenth and eighteenth centuries England and France played the dominant roles in the wars that were fought in the Colonies for control of the North American continent. Both sides depended heavily upon their Indian allies as well as on provincial militia to reinforce the few regiments of regulars

Fig. 1. Detail of Nathaniel Selkrig's horn, 1758 (see Pl. III, top). *Drums A beating Collers Flieing Trumpeths Sounding Men/A Dieing These are The Bloodde Affects of Wars* is the engraved verse. *Except as noted, the objects illustrated are in the collection of the author. Photograph by Helga Photo Studio.*

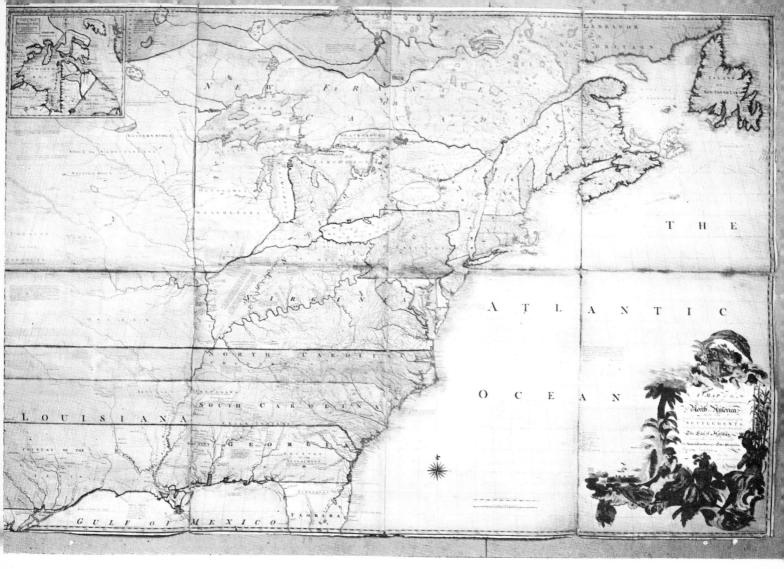

Pl. I. *A Map of the British and French Dominions in North America, with the Roads, Distances, Limits, and Extent of the Settlements,* drawn by John Mitchell, engraved by Thomas Kitchin, and published for Jeffreys and Faden, London, 1755. The eight-sheet folding map is backed with cloth, and measures 53 by 76¼ inches. This may be the most important published map of North America dating from the French and Indian War period (1755–1763). It would have served an officer much more efficiently than a powder horn with a map carved on it. Even the smaller fold-out maps of the areas of conflict that appeared in the *London Magazine* and the *Gentlemen's Magazine* (both published in London) would have been more practical to use than map horns. *Except as noted, color photographs are by Helga Photo Studio.*

stationed in America. As a result of the four major colonial wars (King William's War, 1689–1697; Queen Anne's War, 1702–1713; King George's War, 1744–1748; and the French and Indian War, 1755–1763) service in the militia became obligatory for men between the ages of sixteen and sixty. How-

Fig. 2. This page from the exercise book of a Massachusetts schoolboy, John Barston, is dated January 2, 1777. The second stanza of the patriotic poem incorporates the verse on the Selkrig horn (Fig. 1) with alterations (in italics below) that slanted the poem toward the American cause: "Drums A Beating Colours Flying Cannons Roaring *Tories Dying*/These are The *Noble* Efects of war, *Hozah Brave Boys."* *Helga photograph.*

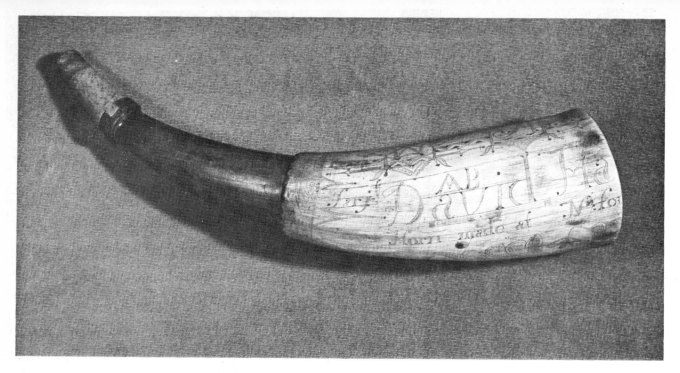

Pl. II. Horn of David Hamilton, a Connecticut ranger who served as a sergeant during the campaign of 1757 in Ephraim Preston's Thirteenth Company of Colonel Phineas Lyman's Regiment of Connecticut Militia. Serving in the same regiment at the time were Nathaniel Selkrig and Aaron Page, whose horns were carved by the same hand (Pls. III, IIIa, Fig. 1). Also members of the regiment at that time were Ichabod French, Isaac Whelpley, David Wheeler, and Josiah Benton, whose horns were carved by other members of the Lake George-Lake Champlain school of carvers (see Pls. IX, IXa, XI, Fig. 14). Hamilton or a subsequent owner cut the horn, probably because it was damaged, but the surviving half continued to be used for many years. The spout has an unusual dovetailed pewter tip.

Pl. IIa. Reverse of the horn shown in Pl. II. Typical of the Lake George-Lake Champlain school of carvers and of the artist who also carved the Selkrig and Page horns is the elaborate calligraphy of the word *Wa*[r]. The letters are neatly spaced with deeply incised fretwork. Other decoration includes sprawling vines with elaborate blossoms and the rhyme, *I Powder with my* [brother ball] / *A Hero Like do Con* [quer all].

ever, such service never extended beyond the duration of a particular campaign, and it was normally confined to the borders of the colony involved. That was not the case during the French and Indian War. The major campaigns occurred in the Lake George, Lake Champlain, and St. Lawrence River regions and the decisive battle took place on Canadian soil. This was the final phase of the colonial wars and resulted in England wresting control of North America from the French.

The majority of the participating militia was raised in New York, Connecticut, and Massachusetts, and the greatest number of surviving powder horns illustrated in this study were owned by New Englanders. A brief review of the militia system will help place these horns in proper perspective.

Most colonies established their militia laws in the seventeenth century [1] and maintained them, with

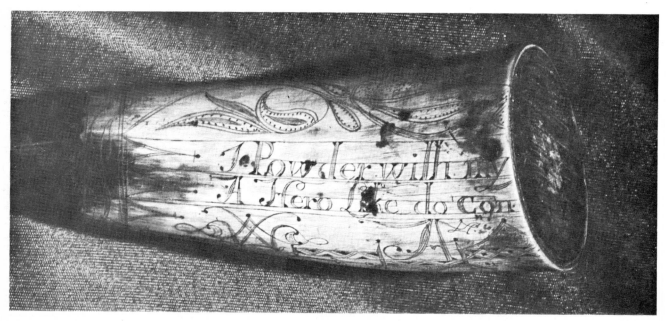

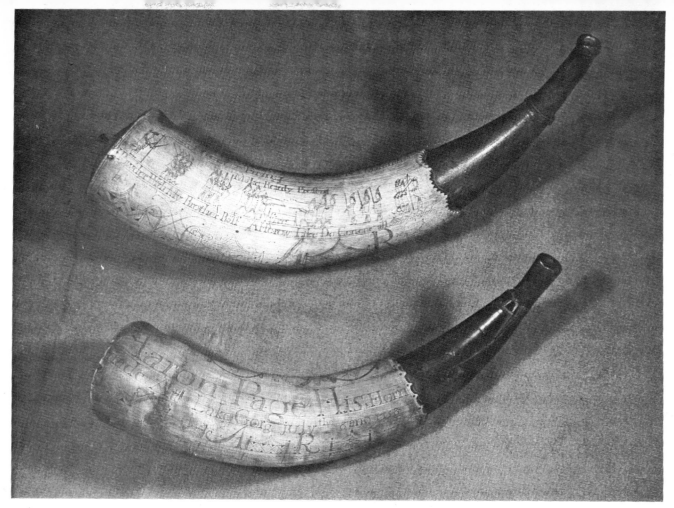

Pl. III. Horns of Nathaniel Selkrig (top) and Aaron Page (bottom). Both men served in Lieutenant Colonel Nathan Whiting's Second Company of Colonel Phineas Lyman's Regiment of Connecticut Militia, which was called into service in February 1757. Their horns were carved by the same hand as Hamilton's (Pls. II, IIa). When enlistments expired in November 1757 Hamilton and Selkrig re-enlisted in a company of rangers at Fort Number 4. Page does not appear on the Connecticut rolls again until April 1758, when he and Selkrig enlisted in the First Company of Colonel Nathan Whiting's Second Connecticut Regiment. Both the Hamilton and Selkrig horns were carved at Fort Number 4, and Selkrig's is dated March 17, 1758. When the troops moved to the Lake George-Lake Champlain region for the summer campaign the carver moved with them, for Page's horn is inscribed *Made At Lake G[e]org[e] july* *the* *8 ano 1758*—the date the French, under Field Marshall Louis

Joseph de Montcalm, defeated the British, under General James Abercrombie, at Fort Ticonderoga. As the horn obviously could not have been made during the battle, it must have been made sometime later, possibly as a commemorative piece. However, since rangers definitely carried powder horns, not cartridge boxes, and since Selkrig enlisted as a ranger in November 1757 and his horn is dated the following March, it is also quite possible that horns already in use were decorated whenever the carver found the time.

Pl. IIIa.   Reverse of the Page horn, depicting opposing soldiers in battle formation, firing at each other. The same scene is shown on the Selkrig horn (see Pl. III, top), and the remainder of the decoration, including the rhyme, is identical to that on the Selkrig and Hamilton horns. The Selkrig horn, however, has one additional scene (see Fig. 1).

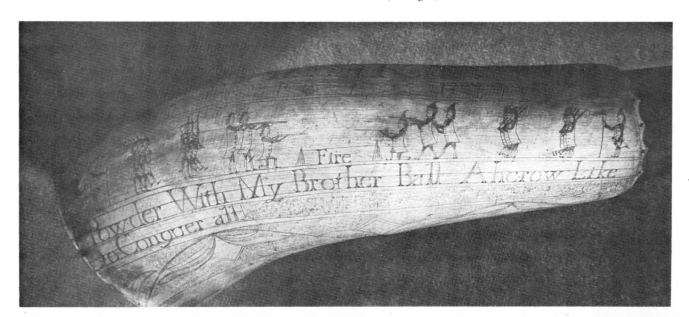

Fig. 3. *Major Robert Rogers* (1731–1795), mezzotint published by Thomas Hart, London, October 1, 1776. Rogers' powder horn is attached to a hunting pouch adorned with Indian bead or quill-work fringes, and both are suspended by an Indian beaded carrying strap. *Collection of John R. Cuneo; Helga photograph.*

then, that the possession of a filled powder horn would have been prohibited in camp.

Since colonial laws specified cartridge boxes, not powder horns, as standard equipment for the militia, it is not unreasonable to ask why so many authentic powder horns survive from the colonial wars. And of these surviving horns, why do the majority date from the French and Indian War? First it must be acknowledged that in both the French and Indian and Revolutionary wars a small number of specialized troops were required to carry powder horns and not cartridge boxes. During the French and Indian War rangers (small volunteer units used to scout and harass the enemy) and many infantry soldiers carried powder horns. Riflemen (but not infantry soldiers) carried them during the Revolution. Artillery soldiers carried priming horns in both wars.

During the French and Indian War, when Connecticut could not fill its quota of troops from volunteer militia, periodic drafts were made from the militia rolls. A temporary resolution of the legislature allowed these recruits to carry either cartridge boxes or powder horns with leather shot bags. During the Revolutionary War the legislature passed no such temporary resolutions and most of the authentic Revolutionary horns that survive today must have been originally intended merely as souvenirs of a soldier's tour of duty. Undoubtedly, many horns from the French and Indian War were also simply souve-

Fig. 4. Drawing of Robert Rogers' horn by Rufus A. Grider (1817–1900), 1889 (see also Pl. IV). At the right Grider has noted that the horn had belonged to William H. Atkinson of Syracuse, New York, since about 1854. To account for the *Wm White* carved above Rogers' name Grider suggests that Private William White "in Cap^{tn} Connie's C^o., Col. Willett's Reg^t., N.Y. troops carried this horn" during the American Revolution. This appears doubtful, for the engraving of the name *Wm White* is typical of the engraving on other horns by or attributed to John Bush, and the precise spacing assigned to the name indicates that it was engraved at the same time as Rogers' name. Note too the similarity of the *W* in *Fort Wm henry* to the *W*'s in *Wm White* as well as the C scrolls adorning the *W*'s, which are typical of Bush's engraving. A William White served in the Connecticut forces that participated in the Crown Point expedition in 1756, and perhaps he had Bush carve the horn as a gift to Rogers to repay a debt. *New-York Historical Society.*

minor changes, throughout the eighteenth century. Although each colony had its own system, the regulations were quite similar. Most colonies required each soldier in the militia to provide his own musket, bayonet (or sword or tomahawk), and cartridge box, unless he could not afford them, in which case the town in which the recruit enlisted was required to supply them.

The cartridge box consisted of a wooden block seven to ten inches long in which ten to thirty holes had been drilled and filled with cartridges that were ready to use, thus eliminating the need for a powder horn and a leather bag to carry musket balls. The box was carried in a leather pouch suspended from the shoulder by a strap or secured to the waist by a belt. Each cartridge was composed of a measure of powder and one or more cast-lead balls wrapped in paper. Cartridges were prepared in a designated structure, called the laboratory, by artillery enlisted men called artificers. Normally soldiers were required to turn in unused cartridges after a battle or a tour of guard duty. Firearms could only be discharged under strict supervision. It must be assumed,

Fig. 5. This drawing of the carving on the Israel Putnam horn (Pl. V) was the frontispiece in volume 2 of *The American Pioneer*, edited by John S. Williams (Cincinnati, 1843). That issue of the rare periodical of the Logan Historical Society, contains an article about the Putnam horn entitled "Ancient Relic," which states that the horn descended in the Putnam family and then belonged to William Pitt Putnam, of Belpre, Washington County, Ohio. *Helga photograph.*

nirs, but many others were functional accouterments.

Because so many temporary resolutions changing equipment requirements were passed by colonial legislatures during the French and Indian War, it is difficult to say today which of the surviving horns were actually used and which were carved specifically as souvenirs. To further complicate the puzzle, were the elaborately carved horns ever intended to be used in war?

To supply troops with fresh meat, cattle were driven behind a marching army, to be butchered as needed. When winter approached and grazing lands were diminished by frost, the herd was slaughtered

and the meat was then dried and salted. Those soldiers fortunate enough to retrieve the horns would boil them, remove the pith, clean and polish the surface, then either carve the design themselves or have a more talented friend do so.

Plain horns, cleaned and ready to use, were available commercially, and no doubt sutlers took a supply to the various army camps to sell as military accouterments or as souvenirs. Possibly they also sold them to soldier-carvers who would decorate the horns and fill in the owner's name once they had made a sale.

Owners of souvenir horns often used them for the first time in hunting or for protection after they had returned home from service and no longer had access to paper cartridges.

Fig. 6. Drawing of Thomas Williams' horn by Grider, 1888. The drawing shows that the horn was inscribed *John Bush: Fecit.* Although Grider inscribed a history of the horn above his drawing, the records of New York provincial troops do not record a Thomas Williams at Lake George on September 8, 1755, the place and date inscribed on the horn. However, the Connecticut rolls show that a Private Thomas Williams served in a militia company called out in 1757 for the relief of Fort William Henry. Since both the David Baldwin (Fig. 7) and Israel Putnam (Pl. V, Fig. 5) horns, which are attributed to Bush, were owned by Connecticut men, it is quite possible that the Thomas Williams who owned this horn was a member of the Connecticut militia who might subsequently have settled in New York State where, in Grider's day, the horn was owned by James B. Williams, a descendant. *New-York Historical Society.*

Fig. 7. Drawing of David Baldwin's horn by Grider, 1891. The carving is attributed to Bush for its similarity to that on the signed Bush horn shown in Fig. 6. Captain David Baldwin commanded the Seventh Company of Major General Phineas Lyman's Regiment of Connecticut Militia for the 1756 campaign. A muster roll for this company in the State Library at Hartford is inscribed *Camp at Fort William Henry, Oct. 13, 1756,* five days before the date on the horn. *New-York Historical Society.*

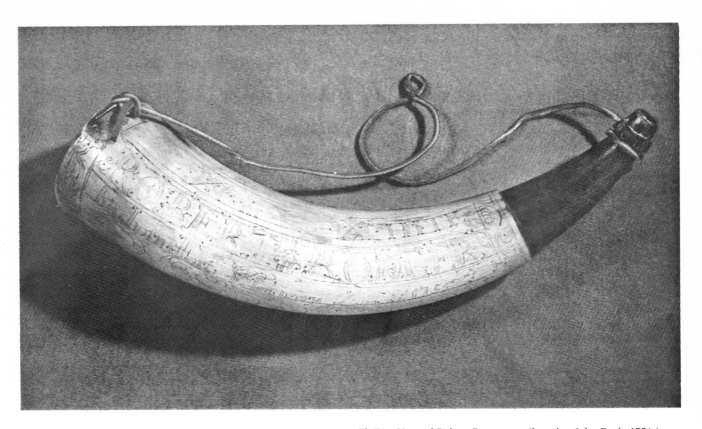

The focal point of this article is a distinctive school of horn carvers who served at the string of British-occupied forts that stretched north from Albany to Lake Champlain and east to the Connecticut River during the French and Indian War. These carvers appear to have been most active in the vicinity of Lake George. Surviving examples of their work exhibit strong similarities in design and style of execution, and it can also be shown that there were certain links among the New Englanders for whom the horns were carved.

The person for whom a horn was being carved was usually interested in having some or all of the following recorded on his horn: his name, his rank, the date, and his location at the time. The type and amount

Pl. IV. Horn of Robert Rogers, attributed to John Bush, 1756 (see also Figs. 3, 4). Rogers was the commander of a detachment of rangers whose exploits were dramatized by Kenneth Roberts in *Northwest Passage*. He was born in Massachusetts but grew up in Concord, New Hampshire, where he spent most of his time in the wilderness, hunting, exploring, and trading with the Indians. At the outbreak of the French and Indian War he enlisted in a New Hampshire regiment, which enabled him to escape prosecution for counterfeiting New Hampshire currency. The effectiveness of his rangers led to his promotion to captain and later to major in command of all nine companies of rangers. In the opinion of many, Rogers was the most romantic figure of the French and Indian War, and probably the most controversial. He made as many enemies as friends, and, after a succession of accomplishments and failures, he died in poverty in 1795 in London. His well-used horn is one of the few surviving examples that actually belonged to a legendary figure. Its decoration is in the style of the school that produced the Selkrig, Hamilton, and Page horns. It appears to have been carved by the hand that carved the horns of Israel Putnam (Pl. V, Fig. 5), David Baldwin (Fig. 7), Thomas Williams (Fig. 6), William Williams (Pls. VI, VIa), and possibly Gershom Burbank (Fig. 8). Since the Thomas Williams horn is signed by John Bush, it may be assumed that he also carved the other four or five horns. The characteristics of Bush's work are his stylized *W*, deeply incised fretwork, flourishing C scrolls on his lettering, neatly executed floral designs, and amusing faces interspersed among the lettering and decoration. *Cuneo collection.*

Fig. 8. Drawing of Gershom Burbank's horn by Grider, 1895. Grider was seventy-eight when he made this drawing, and the precise detail of his earlier renderings is absent. It is difficult to assign a category to the carving, but the stylized *W*, the C scroll on the *G*, the face on the *B*, and the floral designs point to John Bush. According to the upper inscription, James Tobias carried the horn during the War of 1812. The engraver of the latter inscription copied the style of Bush, but there is a strong possibility that the purported 1813 engraving might have been executed around the time the horn was sketched for Grider by Fannie E. Griswold in 1895. *New-York Historical Society.*

Fig. 9. Horn of Jotham Bemus, carved by Jacob Gay (see also Pl. VIII), 1759. Bemus was a soldier, probably in the Massachusetts provincial troops. The horn is dated *Septr/the 30 1759* and was carved at Stillwater, which the British captured from the French on August 4, 1759. The soldiers in battle formation are similar to those on the Selkrig and Page horns (Pls. III, IIIa). Some of the sprawling calligraphy resembles the style exhibited on the J.W. horns (see Pl. IX, Fig. 11). However, the lettering of the rhyme *I powder with my brother ball* . . . appears to have been deepened by a less talented hand than the one that carved the rest of the decoration on this side of the horn. *Metropolitan Museum of Art, gift of Mrs. J. H. Grenville Gilbert.*

of decoration depended upon the carver's talent and the owner's taste. Often one, two, and even three of the four categories were omitted.

The details of a campaign in progress were seldom recorded on horns. They may have been unknown to

Pl. V. Horn of Israel Putnam (1718–1790), attributed to Bush, 1756 (see also Fig. 5). Like the Rogers horn (Pl. IV), this is one of the few authentic horns that actually belonged to a famous historical figure. The horn is typical of those attributed to Bush except for the addition of a plan of Fort William Henry and a simple map showing the road from Albany to Lake George (see Fig. 5). Several other Bush horns bear the rhyme that appears here: "When bows and weighty Spears were Us'ᵈ in Fight/Twere nervous Limbs Declr'ᵈ a man of might/But now Gun powder Scorns Such Strength to own/And Heroes not by Limbs but Souls are shown." Born in Massachusetts, Putnam moved to Connecticut, where he was commissioned a second lieutenant in the Connecticut forces at the outbreak of the French and Indian War. By 1757 he was captain of a company of rangers under the command of Captain Robert Rogers. In 1758 Putnam was promoted to major. He was captured by the Indians, tied to a tree, and rescued just before he was to be burned alive. However, his experiences in the Revolution, particularly at the battle of Bunker Hill, are better known. *Campus Martius Museum, Marietta, Ohio; photograph by Robert P. Etter.*

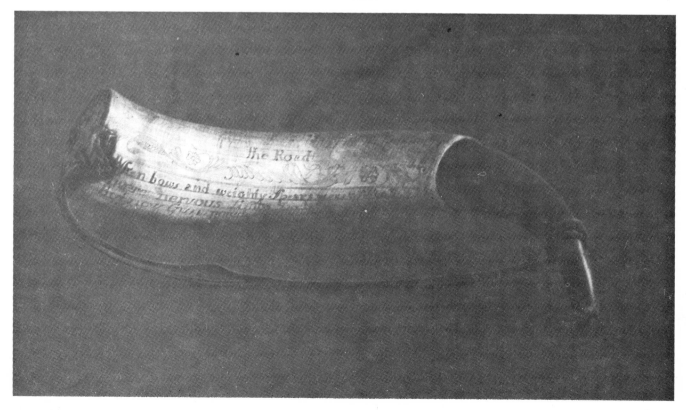

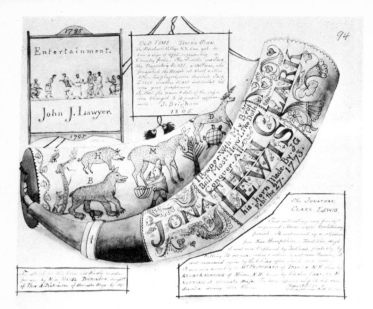

Fig. 10. Drawing of Jonathan Clark Lewis' horn by Grider, 1891. Like the John Mills horn (Pls. VII, VIIa) and the Jotham Bemus horn (Pl. VIII, Fig. 9), this horn, dated 1773, is attributed to Jacob Gay. Stylistically it is almost identical to the Mills horn, which is dated 1760, thirteen years before this one. The notation at the lower right of the Grider drawing is not accurate. During the Revolution Lewis was aide-de-camp to Brigadier General Oliver Prescott of the Massachusetts militia. *New-York Historical Society.*

the carver at the time he was working on the horn, and if known they may have been excluded simply because militiamen were not professional soldiers. They were required to serve during periods of emergency with little if any reward and considerable hardship. Campaigns were almost always planned to take place between the late spring and early fall to take advantage of abundant grazing for the horses and cattle and ice-free rivers and lakes for transportation. Since most militia soldiers were farmers, their tour of duty came at the worst possible season.

The homesick, underfed, frightened, and exhausted soldier was usually worrying more about what might be happening at home because of his absence than he was about the war around him. Although authentic horns carved with detailed accounts of military events occasionally show up, they are the exceptions and should be carefully examined.

The horn carvers whose work is shown here were undoubtedly militia soldiers attempting in a nonacademic way to copy the sophisticated designs of European master engravers. Renaissance, baroque, and rococo engraving styles were combined with imaginative versions of book illustrations of monsters and animals inspired by the East India trade. We can only speculate about how the three styles of engraving were known to the carvers at remote forts such as William Henry, Ticonderoga, and Crown Point. The most accessible models would have been the mountings and lock plates of officers' pistols and fusils and the chasing on their sword hilts. Most of the better-quality officers' weapons were produced in England or on the Continent, and a large percentage of them were embellished by accomplished craftsmen who were influenced by the design books of seventeenth-

and eighteenth-century French gunsmiths. The exquisite designs that had been chiseled into the steel were translated into less complicated versions on horn by the carver.

As most carved horns are unsigned, the majority of the carvers remain anonymous. Rufus A. Grider began a massive compilation of carved horns and a few of their makers late in the nineteenth century [2] and that list was further refined by Stephen V. Grancsay almost fifty years later.[3] To judge by the style of their work, only three of the carvers listed belong to the school under discussion here: John Bush, Jacob Gay (or Gayham), and J. W. (Jonathan Webb?). It is not known whether they knew each other, were student and teacher, had any previous training, were professional horn carvers, or were just talented artists obliging their friends. Gay may have been younger than Bush and J. W., since several existing horns signed by him date early in the American Revolution. It is not known whether Gay, Bush, and J. W. originally copied someone else's style or whether their style was copied by others.

Amusing verses are frequently engraved on the horns of this school, and essentially the same verses often appear on different horns. Examples of these rhymes are:

"I powder with my brother ball
A hero like do conquer all"

"A man of words and not of deeds
Is like a garden full of weeds"

"Drums a beating colors flying
Trumpets sounding men a dying
These are the bloody effects of wars"

Fig. 11. Drawing of Enoch Cooper's horn by Grider, 1890. The horn was carved by J. W. at Lake George in 1758. In addition to the inscription *JW his Pen*, the horn has the stylized birds and free-floating wings of the other J.W. horns (Pl. IX). For the 1758 campaign Cooper served in Colonel Phineas Lyman's First Company of Colonel Lyman's Regiment of Connecticut Militia. *New-York Historical Society.*

Fig. 12. Drawing of Josiah Benton's horn by Grider, 1888. The horn, probably carved by J.W., was made at Fort Number 4 in 1757 when Benton was a member of Captain Andrew Ward Jr.'s Fourteenth Company of Colonel Phineas Lyman's Regiment of Connecticut Militia. During the 1755 campaign Benton served in an independent company, and in the 1759 campaign he was in Ward's Sixth Company of Colonel Nathan Whiting's Second Connecticut Regiment. *New-York Historical Society.*

Stylish calligraphy and embellished letters predominate. Decoration on horns of this school includes floral, geometric, and architectural designs, scrollwork, and amusing animals as well as human figures and faces, birds, fish, and, only occasionally, the British coat of arms. Sometimes ships are incorporated, possibly the ones that brought the soldiers to Albany or vessels observed from the fort. More rarely, formations of soldiers oppose each other in battle order. Ships, soldiers, and battles are hardly ever identified. The drawing is never very detailed and none of the horns could be used for reference.

Sometimes an Indian is represented, but only as a naked barbarian with a feather headdress. The majestic warrior so often portrayed in paintings of the period was seen in a different light by the soldiers who fought against him, undoubtedly feared him, and felt that the Indians and the white men were not members of the same species.

Just as rarely shown as the Indian is the plan of a fort. When one does appear, it is, in contrast to other drawings on horns, fairly accurately depicted and is useful for studying the location of buildings, palisades, bastions, and the placement of artillery. Other appealing decorative devices sometimes used by this school are outline drawings of swords, halberds, cannons, muskets, drums, flags, and tomahawks. Sometimes these devices appear as a border, sometimes to fill an empty space instead of a geometric design.

Deeds are never proclaimed, and the heroes of the day are never referred to on any horns that I have seen. Some of the drawings are mysteries, the meaning of which has vanished with the carvers. Among these are a parrot cage, a large fish swallowing smaller fish, and a whimsical figure—half man half fish—holding a lantern in each hand.

Available records reveal links between some of the original owners of the powder horns illustrated. During the 1757 campaign of the French and Indian War the following all served in Colonel Phineas Lyman's Regiment of Connecticut Militia: David Hamilton, Nathaniel Selkrig, Aaron Page, Isaac Whelpley, David Wheeler, Josiah Benton, and Ichabod French. Page and Selkrig both served in Lieutenant Colonel Nathan Whiting's Second Company. Hamilton was in Captain Ephraim Preston's Thirteenth Company. Benton and French were in Captain Andrew Ward Jr.'s Four-

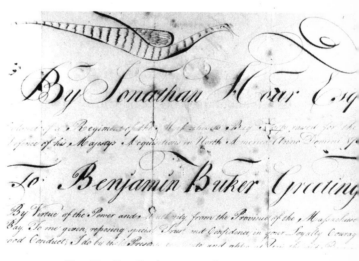

Fig. 13. Detail of a Massachusetts Bay warrant signed by Colonel Jonathan Hoar, appointing Benjamin Buker a sergeant in a company of foot in 1761. The calligraphy strongly resembles that on J.W.'s horns and suggests the kind of source he would have consulted.

Fig. 14. Drawing of Ichabod French's horn by Grider, 1889 (Pl. XI). The rhyme is *A Man of/Vords/And not of/Deeds Is Like/a Garden/Ful of/Weeds.* The date *Jan: 10: 1748* was carved at a much later date, probably in the late nineteenth or early twentieth century. *New-York Historical Society.*

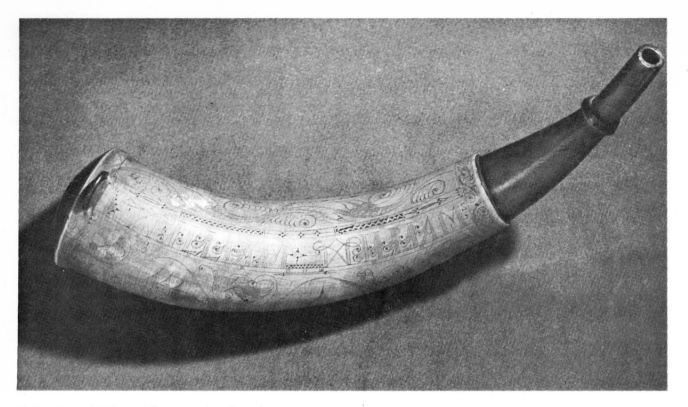

Pl. VI. Horn of William Williams, attributed to John Bush. It incorporates the stylized *W*, flourishing C scrolls adorning the letters, deeply incised fretwork, and handsome floral scrolls typical of Bush's work. Williams' war record is not known, but the horn descended in a Williams family in Massachusetts.

Pl. VIa. The reverse of the horn shown in Pl. VI is decorated with a winged angel's head of the kind often found on New England tombstones, a large fish, and the head of an Indian facing the British flag.

teenth Company. Enlistments expired in November 1757, at which point Whelpley, French, Hamilton, and Selkrig all enlisted for the winter of 1757–1758 in Lieutenant Colonel William Haviland's Twenty-Seventh Regiment, where all were members of Captain Reuben Ferris' company of rangers. The regiment was stationed at Fort Number 4 (today Charlestown, New Hampshire, on the Connecticut River). Israel Putnam was captain of another company of rangers in Haviland's regiment during the winter. In April 1758 Page and Selkrig enlisted in Colonel Nathan Whiting's First Company of Whiting's Second Connecticut Regiment.

For the 1759 campaign Robert Baird and William Patterson were in Captain Thomas Hobby's Fourth Company of Colonel David Wooster's Third Connec-

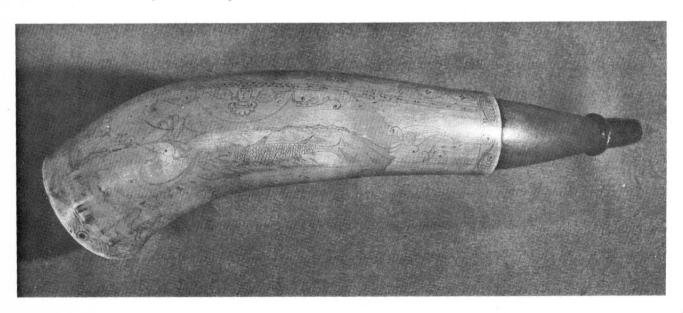

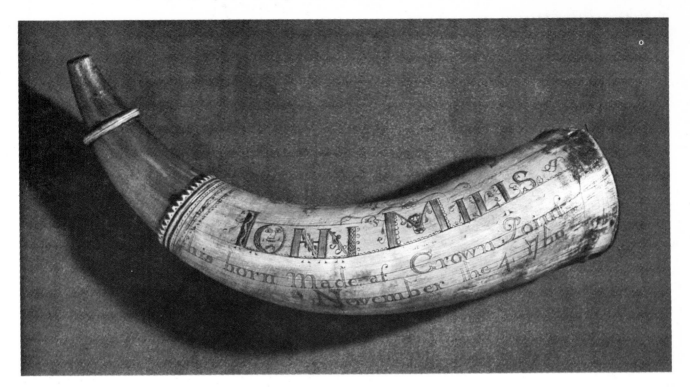

Pl. VII. Horn of John Mills, attributed to Jacob Gay, 1760. Gay's work is remotely similar to Bush's and to that of the unidentified artist who carved the Selkrig, Hamilton, and Page horns. Yet the carving of the owner's name on this horn, the Jotham Bemus horn (Pl. VIII, Fig. 9), which is signed by Gay, and the Jonathan Clark Lewis horn (Fig. 10) is in a unique style that is both amusing and extremely pleasing to view. The comic face in the *o* of *Iohn* and the weird face on the crossbar of the *M* in *Mills*, along with the faces on the uprights of other letters in the owner's name, make this one of the most delightful horns illustrated here. The inscription below the name reads, *his horn Made at Crown Point/November the 4 1760.* Mills probably served with the Massachusetts provincial troops at Crown Point. The horn descended in the Mills family and was acquired from a descendant in Chelsea, Massachusetts.

ticut Regiment. During the 1761 campaign Whelpley, Wheeler, Baird, and Patterson served in Colonel Nathan Whiting's Second Connecticut Regiment. Whelpley and Baird were in Captain Thomas Hobby's Sixth Company, and Wheeler was in Captain Samuel Whiting's Fourth Company.

Hamilton's (Pls. II, IIa), Selkrig's (Pl. III, top, and Fig. 1), and Page's (Pl. III, bottom, and Pl. IIIa) horns all appear to have been decorated by the same artist.

Pl. VIIa. Detail of the reverse of the horn shown in Pl. VII. A hunter shoots deer with his flintlock musket. Below the deer are the distinctively carved initials *J G.* The *G* is embellished with the head of what appears to be an angry Indian.

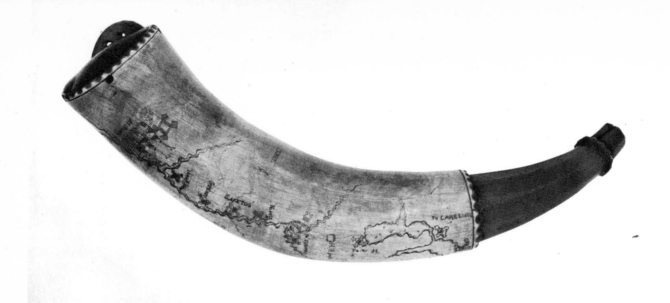

Pl. VIII. The reverse of the Jotham Bemus horn (see Fig. 9) is decorated with a map showing the landmarks from New York City to Crown Point. This map does not appear to have been carved by the same hand that executed the obverse. It seems to have been added later, probably many years later, by a carver who at the same time deepened the letters of the poem on the obverse. *Metropolitan Museum of Art, Gilbert gift.*

Pl. IX. *Top to bottom:* Horns of Isaac Whelpley, 1758, Robert Baird, 1758, and David Wheeler. These, the Enoch Cooper horn shown in Fig. 11, and probably the Josiah Benton horn shown in Fig. 12 were carved by J. W., whose spelling is phonetic and whose decorative style is casual and flowing, with the ends of letters and motifs becoming birds, animals, leaves, and wings. Wheeler's horn bears no year, Benton's is dated 1757, the others 1758; Baird's, Wheeler's and Cooper's were carved at Lake George, and Whelpley's and Benton's at Fort Number 4. Baird and Wheeler do not appear on the rolls in 1758, but Wheeler and Whelpley served in Colonel Phineas Lyman's Regiment of Connecticut Militia during the 1757 campaign, and Baird, Wheeler, and Whelpley all served in the campaign of 1761 in Colonel Nathan Whiting's Second Connecticut Regiment. In that campaign Whelpley and Baird were sergeants in Captain Thomas Hobby's Sixth Company, and Wheeler was a member of Captain Samuel Whiting's Fourth Company.

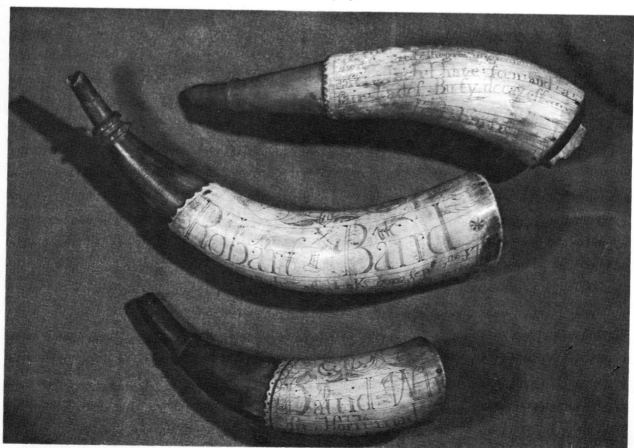

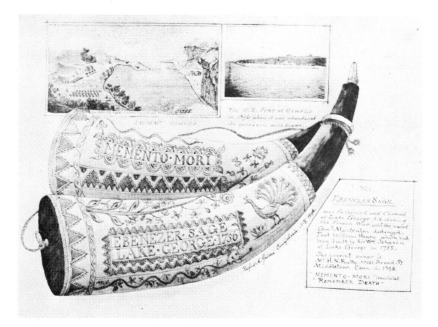

Fig. 15. Drawing of Ebenezer Sage's horn by Grider, 1896. Sage, of Middletown, Connecticut, was appointed commissary in Colonel David Wooster's Second Connecticut Regiment in March 1756. This horn is unlike any of the others pictured in this article, but it is similar to another Connecticut horn in a private collection in Carlisle, Pennsylvania. *New-York Historical Society.*

Another artist whose style is similar carved the horns of David Baldwin (Fig. 7) and Israel Putnam (Pl. V, Fig. 5) of Connecticut, Thomas Williams (Fig. 6) of Connecticut or New York, Robert Rogers (Pl. IV, Fig. 4) of New Hampshire, and William Williams (Pls. VI, VIa) of Massachusetts. Since the Thomas Williams horn is inscribed *John Bush: Fecit,* it may be assumed that the other four horns are also by him. The William Williams horn bears neither place nor date, but the other four are dated 1755 or 1756 and were made at Lake George.

Pl. IXa. Reverse of the horns shown in Pl. IX. The unusual design considered to be a stylized signature of the carver may be interpreted as a *W* encircled by C scrolls and flowering vines. Except on the Wheeler horn the *W* has a crossbar. In addition to the *W,* the Baird horn bears the inscription *JW his Pen* (not visible in the photograph).

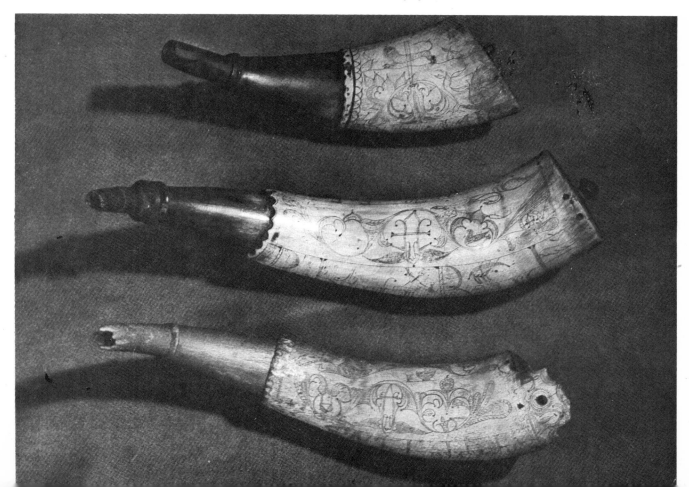

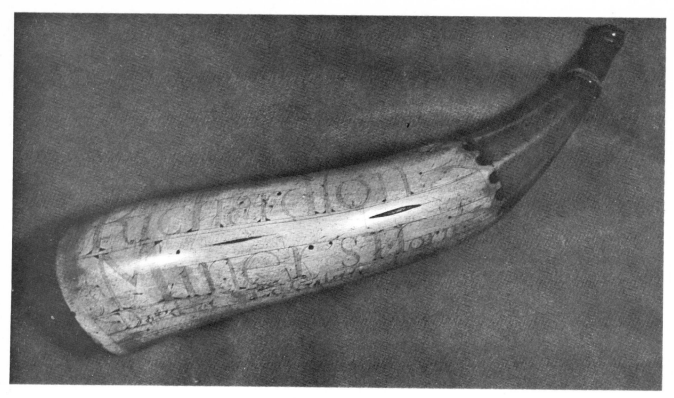

Pl. X. Horn of Richardson Minor (1736–1797), a Stratford, Connecticut, silversmith, possibly carved by himself, and inscribed *Le
Galatte Aug 29 1760*. La Galet is near Montreal on the St. Lawrence
River. Minor served as armorer in Colonel Nathan Whiting's Second Connecticut Regiment from April 5 to November 9, 1760.

The horn of John Mills of Massachusetts (Pls. VII,
VIIa), carved at Crown Point in 1760, that of Jotham
Bemus, probably of Massachusetts (Pl. VIII, Fig. 9),
carved at Stillwater, New York, in 1759, and that of
Jonathan Clark Lewis (Fig. 10), dated 1773, are similar in style. The Bemus horn is inscribed *Iacob Gayham* below the coat of arms, and the Mills and Lewis
horns, *JG*.

Pl. Xa. Reverse of the horn shown in Pl. X. The beautiful floral
design, accented by deep incisions, was carved by a professional,
such as a silversmith.

Another artist appears to have been responsible for
carving Whelpley's (Pl. IX, top), Baird's (Pl. IX, mid-

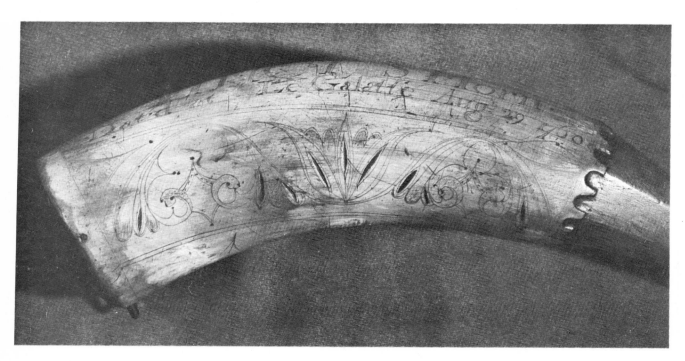

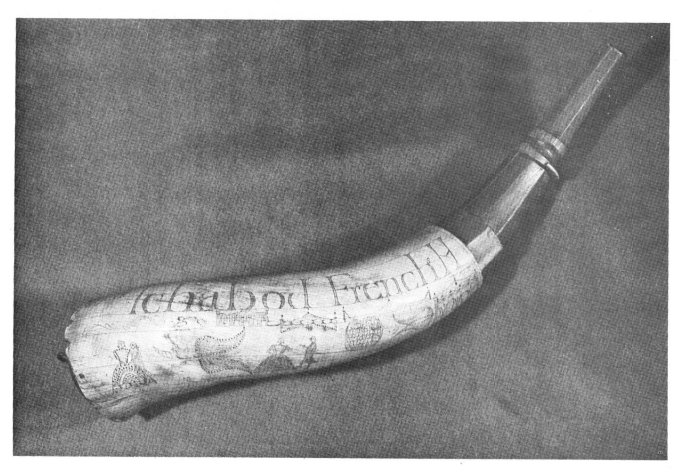

Pl. XI. Horn of Ichabod French (see also Fig. 14), 1755–1758. The large (1¼ inches high), bold lettering of the inscription *Serjant Ichabod French's H*, possibly carved by French himself, characterizes the distinctive style of the Lake George-Lake Champlain school of horn carvers. During the 1755 campaign French served in Lieutenant Colonel John Pitkin's Second Company of Major General Phineas Lyman's Regiment of Connecticut Militia. In the 1757 campaign he served as a sergeant in Captain Andrew Ward Jr.'s Fourteenth Company of Colonel Lyman's regiment. Josiah Benton (see Fig. 12) served in the same company in that campaign. French enlisted as a ranger for the 1757–1758 winter campaign, serving as a sergeant in Captain Reuben Ferris' company of rangers in Lieutenant Colonel William Haviland's regiment at Fort Number 4. Sergeants Isaac Whelpley (see Pl. IX, top, and Pl. IXa, bottom) and David Hamilton (see Pls. II, IIa) and Private Nathaniel Selkrig (see Pl. III, top, and Fig. 1) served in the same company at the same time.

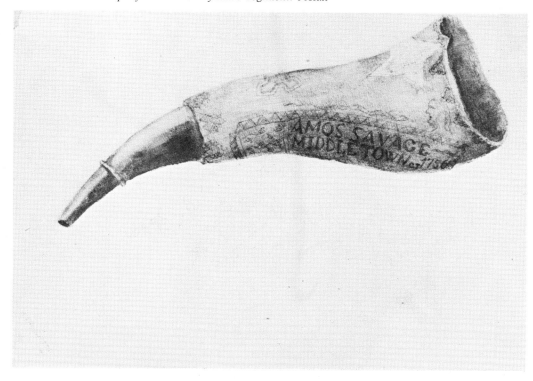

Fig. 16. Watercolor of Amos Savage's horn by N.F. Henderson, probably late nineteenth century. The inscription reads, *Amos Savage/Middletown Ct 1756.* The horn also bears the profile of an Indian and the plan of a fort, probably Fort Edward. The carving is in the style of the Lake George-Lake Champlain school. Savage served with the Connecticut troops during the 1755 and 1756 campaigns. *Helga photograph.*

Pl. XII. Lieutenant Christopher Palmer's horn, made at Fort Edward and dated October 24, 1758. For the 1758 campaign Palmer (of Stonington, Connecticut) enlisted as a second lieutenant in Captain John Denison's Twelfth Company of Colonel Eleazer Fitch's Third Connecticut Regiment. In the 1755 campaign he had served as an ensign in Colonel Eliphalet Dyer's First Company of Colonel Dyer's Third Connecticut Regiment, and in the 1756 campaign as the adjutant of Colonel David Wooster's Second Connecticut Regiment.

Pl. XIIa. Reverse of the horn shown in Pl. XII. A ribbon with tulips attached undulates the length of the horn. Below it a fish resembling a shad chases a school of smaller fish.

dle), Wheeler's (Pl. IX, bottom), and Enoch Cooper's (Fig. 11) horns. Whelpley's was made at Fort Number 4, while the other three were made at Lake George. Cooper's and Baird's are dated September 1758; Whelpley's simply 1758; and Wheeler's only September. (The 1776 on his horn is a later addition.) Both Cooper's and Baird's horns are inscribed *JW his Pen*, while Whelpley's bears a stylized *JW* (Pl. IXa, bottom) and the name Levi Barns (Pl. IX, top). The latter is neither the artist's nor the owner's name but it was carved when the horn was originally made.

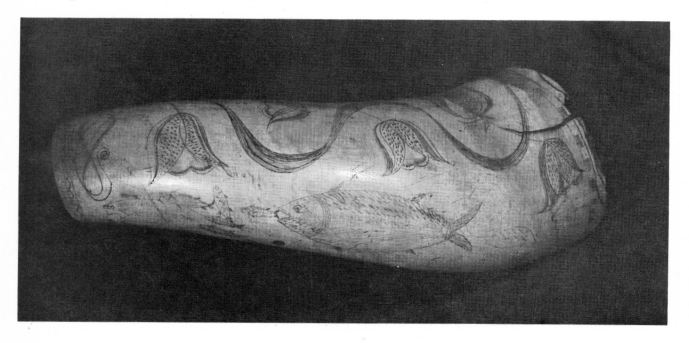

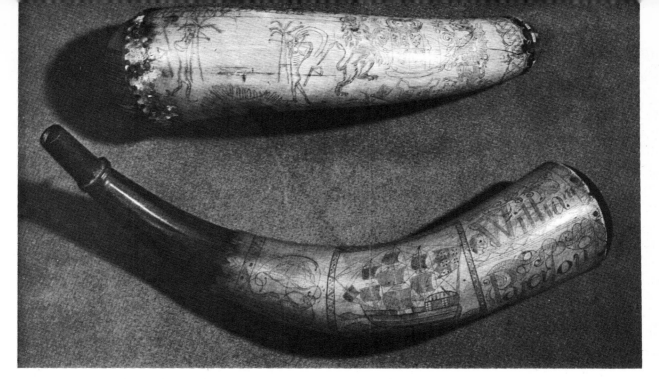

Pl. XIII. Horns of Edward Courtney (top), 1757, and William Patterson (bottom), 1759. The Courtney horn is inscribed *Edward Courtneys/Powder Horn/Fort Edward/1757/Hear I Am Powder/With My* (incomplete). Although the horns are completely different in style of decoration, both can be said to have been executed by carvers of the Lake George-Lake Champlain school. The Courtney horn depicts two Indians, naked except for the feathers on their heads, shooting at each other with flintlock muskets from behind trees. The simple, unsophisticated carving of the Indians contrasts with the elaborate British coat of arms next to them in which a wivernlike monster has been substituted for the unicorn. Except for the ship, which seems to have been executed for the sake of design rather than accuracy, the carving on the Patterson horn is reminiscent of that on the J.W. horns, particularly Robert Baird's

(Pls. IX, IXa, middle). For the 1759 campaign both Baird and Patterson were in Captain Thomas Hobby's Fourth Company of Colonel David Wooster's Third Connecticut Regiment. For the campaign of 1758 Patterson was in Captain Nathaniel Everts' Twelfth Company of Colonel Wooster's Fourth Connecticut Regiment, and for the 1761 campaign he served as a sergeant in Colonel Nathan Whiting's Second Connecticut Regiment.

Pl. XIIIa. Reverse of the horns shown in Pl. XIII. The Courtney horn bears a detailed outline of Fort Edward and, at the left, what appears to be a brick house surrounded by a stockade. Contemporary records indicate that a brickyard was in operation at Fort Edward during this period. Between the house and the fort a deer flees a fox or a wolf.

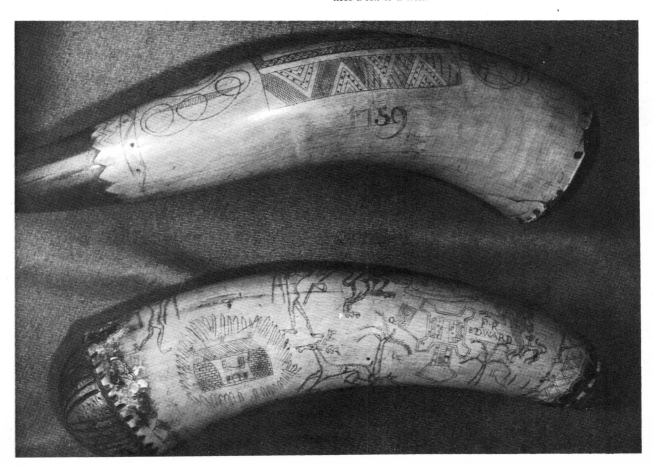

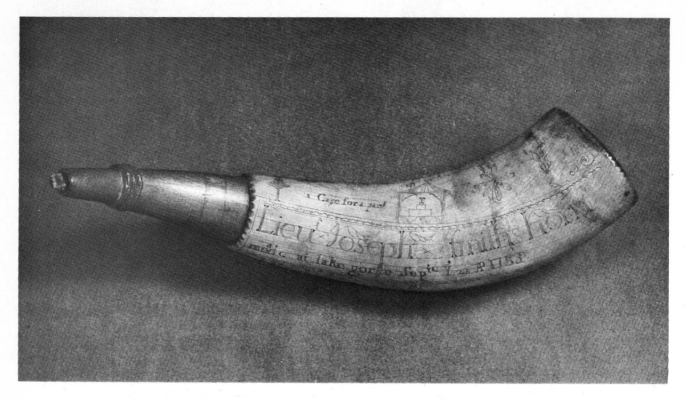

Pl. XIV. Horn of Joseph Smith, 1758. Inscribed *Lieu' * Joseph * Smiths horn/mede* (there is a small *a* above the first *e* in *mede*) *at lake gorge Sep^{te} Y' 25 Ap 1758.* Leaflike projections emerge from some of the letters in the owner's name. Above the inscription are a bird cage and the words *a Cage for a paret.* The calligraphy is excellent and the horn is beautifully carved. Although the rolls contain many listings for Joseph Smiths, none was a lieutenant.

It is hoped that more signed horns will come to light and that eventually a great deal more will be learned about the carvers and their symbolism.

For their help in securing photographs for this article, I would like to thank Richard J. Koke, curator of collections, New-York Historical Society; Thompson R. Harlow, director, Connecticut Historical Society; Stuart Pyhrr, assistant curator of arms and armor, Metropolitan Museum of Art; Donald A. Hutslar, Ohio Historical Society; and John R. Cuneo.

Pl. XIVa. Reverse of the horn shown in Pl. XIV. The letters of the inscription *War* are separated by two accurately depicted, simple American infantry swords of the 1750's.

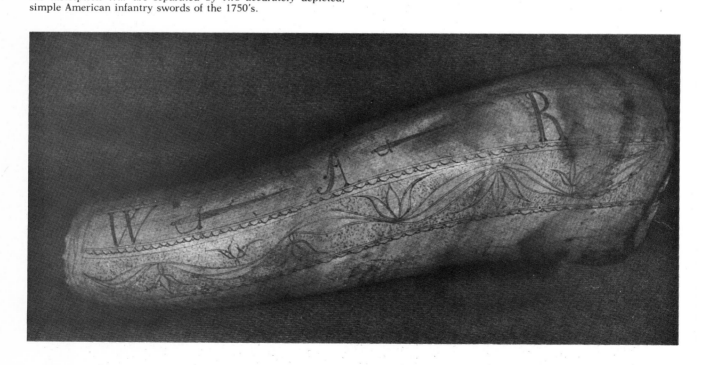

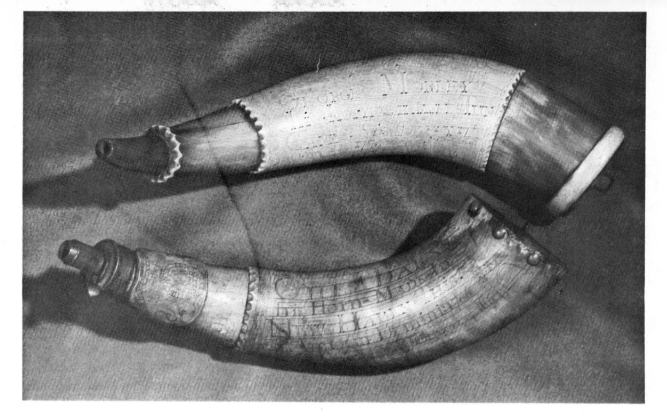

Pl. XV. Horns of George Morley (top), 1775, and Giles Barns (bottom), 1766. The Morley horn is inscribed in superb calligraphy, *George Morley/his horn CharlesTun/Camp N⁰: 3 Decʳ Yᵉ 17ᵗʰ/Ad 1775.* This is one of the most beautiful professionally carved horns in existence, yet it lacks the spirit of true colonial folk art achieved by the Lake George-Lake Champlain school of carvers during the French and Indian War. The Barns horn is inscribed *Giles Barns/his Horn Made In/New Haven * This/27ᵗʰ/Day of/January/Anno ue Domini: 1766/And In The Fifth year of His Majestys Reign/The Brig Lively/Of Sixteen Guns/Commanded by/Capt Alby.* This horn is carved in the manner of the Lake George-Lake Champlain school and might have been made by one of the men who had served with the Connecticut troops during the French and Indian War. The brass charger at the spout and the brass tacks around the plug are nineteenth-century additions.

[1] An exception was Pennsylvania which, because of its large Quaker population, did not establish militia laws until 1755.

[2] Rufus A. Grider made more than five hundred colored drawings of powder horns and annotated them with what he discovered about each one. Much of that collection is now in the New-York Historical Society.

[3] *American Engraved Powder Horns, A Study Based on the J. H. Grenville Gilbert Collection* (New York, 1945).

Pl. XVa. Reverse of the horns shown in Pl. XV. In a tombstone-shape panel on the Morley horn is the inscription *Ty/Liber.* Also on the horn are two finely detailed warships, a church, and delicately carved vines and floral designs. The Barns horn bears a detailed view of the New Haven Green, as well as a British warship—undoubtedly the brig *Lively* named in the inscription.

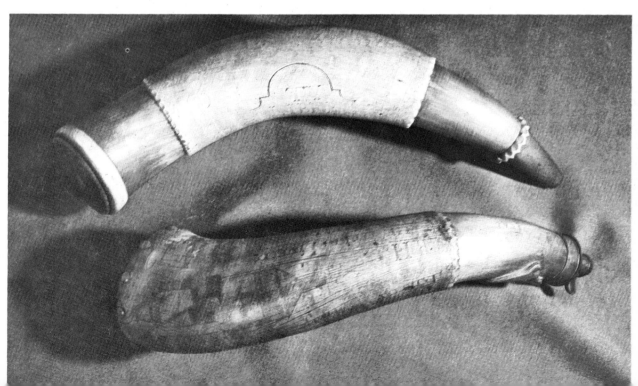

Decorated military Americana

BY WILLIAM H. GUTHMAN

The halberd was used both as a weapon and as an insigne of rank throughout the eighteenth century. This one, with two-piece iron head, has pierced decoration typical of New England.

As a collection develops so does the collector. My first interest was in United States military shoulder arms (rifles, muskets, and carbines) from colonial days to the present, and in forming my collection I took the steps that any serious collector must. The primary step was to acquire the essential, dependable reference books; the next was to find competent sources for the objects I sought; the third was to acquire enough knowledge and experience to tell the original from the reproduction—the untouched from the "humped up"; and the final step was to classify the collection from beginning to end.

In this process, however, I was unexpectedly exposed to many other facets of military collecting and, more important, military learning. I found myself exploring an area in which there are few reference books, if any at all. Attributions gave way to speculations, similar examples were not to be found, and my realization that collecting was no longer "by the numbers" bore with it the true excitement of collecting—the search for the unknown and unattributed, not only in material specimens, but in the form of information in original source manuscripts and uncorrelated papers.

The icing on the cake was the discovery that the collector can engage actively in his collecting, instead of staring at a wall full of guns with an identifying textbook in hand. Probably best of all, my wife can share with me in this newest and most exciting game of learning about what we are collecting.

One of those new facets is what I call decorated military Americana. The colonial soldier decorated his weapons when he could. Late in the eighteenth century the United States required exact specifications for all weapons, and in the early 1800's these regulations became rigid. Then the militia soldier's decorations began to appear upon his uniform and accouterments. The engraved powder horn and belt buckle, the painted knapsack and helmet represent a whole category of American folk art that has been almost overlooked. Collecting in this field is entirely different from collecting regulation military firearms, where each part must conform to specific regulations, and conformity and pristine condition are the ultimate goal. Decorated American militia equipment is full of variety and surprise, and the more individual an item is the better.

The examples illustrated here have all been compared with similar examples at the West Point Museum, United States Military Academy, and the approximate dates given have been arrived at by analogy. Many thanks are due Gerald Stowe and Robert Fish at the museum.

Tomahawks were common soldiers' side arms before, during, and after the American Revolution. This Pennsylvania soldier's weapon carries the exhortation *To your/arms solder* (soldier) *and feight* (fight), the first four words incised on the blade, the last two engraved on a silver half-moon which is inlaid beside them. The initials *J°C* are also incised upon the head.

Examples from Mr. Guthman's collection of decorated military Americana are included in the summer exhibition, *Tools, Woodenware, and Soldiers' Gear,* at the Museum of Early American Folk Arts in New York, which will remain on view through September 11.

If a soldier did not carry a tomahawk he usually carried a sword. Although this example from New England lacks the refinement achieved by the skilled European swordmakers, the crude heart cut out of the sheet-brass guard adds its own simple beauty to the heavy weapon. Little individual features of this kind are largely responsible for the great appeal these American-made weapons of the Revolution have for collectors today.

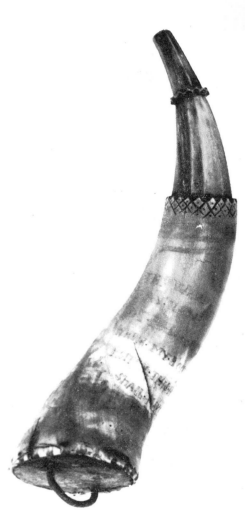

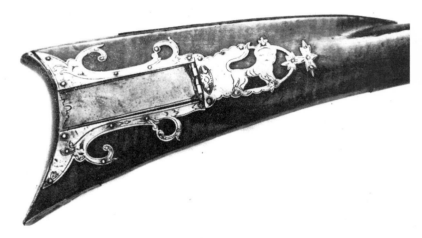

The individual soldier often made his own weapons and accouterments. Thomas Ward crudely decorated his powder horn with incised designs and these lines: "Thos Ward/ is my name/ If I fall bury me/ When my bones/ rotten this horn/ shall make me/ not forgotten." He added the following identification in a scrolled cartouche: *Pvt. Thos. Ward/ 3rd Regt/ New York/ 1779/ A. D.*

Members of Colonel Thomas Crafts' Regiment of Artillery (Massachusetts line) who fought together during the Revolutionary War, organized the Worcester Artillery in 1783. The local engraver probably worked on several brass cross-belt buckles similar to the one shown here, which carries a full complement of military emblems and what appear to be the initials *JJ* (near the bottom hole, which was probably punched later).

When Andrew Jackson defeated the British at New Orleans, January 8, 1815, many of the American militia riflemen carried "Kentucky" rifles made by Pennsylvania gunsmiths. Pictured is the patch box—guarded by a benign lion—of such a rifle.

Early in the nineteenth century the United States began to exact precise uniformity from the national armories and from the private contractors of weapons. Thereafter, aside from a few nonregulation muskets, efforts at decorating the militiaman's equipment were directed toward his accouterments and uniform rather than his weapons. The canteens shown here date between 1812 and 1840.

Militia-day parades must have been extremely colorful events. Among the gaily decorated equipment of the men in the 1825-1840 period were painted knapsacks. The light artillery knapsack shown here has a navy-blue background for the gold eagle, cannon, and initials.

Drums were used to signal commands when large columns of troops were marching into battle or from one fort to another. They also gave the signal of alarm to warn against enemy attack, and soldiers were ordered never to stray beyond hearing of the repeated beat of the drum at the fort. And, of course, drums were an essential part of every parade.

This one, dating from the War of 1812, shows the flag with eighteen stripes and eighteen stars. Not until April 4, 1818, was the act passed establishing that the number of stripes should be thirteen and the number of stars equal to the number of states. The shell of this drum is painted a light maple color, the eagle is light green and yellow, and the lettering and stars are black.

This Civil War artillery drum has a red shell on which are painted white stars and a dark brown and gray eagle with a red, white, and blue shield. The hoops are also red, white, and blue.

This naval powder bucket is similar in style and technique to those of a much earlier period, but the decoration appears to be of the time of the Mexican War. The leather bucket is black and the eagle is gold; the shield is red, white, and blue.

Helmets offered splendid opportunities for imaginative treatment by the decorator. This dragoon helmet in classic form is of leather, almost black with gold stars and red and gold sunburst above a red cloth band. The pierced comb is of tin painted gold and black, and on the front is a tin hat plate painted blue-black with a gold eagle. On the other side the helmet is lettered in gold *5th Regt. Cavalry/New Milford, Conn.;* the 5th Regiment was part of the 5th Brigade, 3rd Division, Connecticut Militia. The style of lettering places the helmet in the 1830-1840 period, but the style of the helmet and the other decoration could be as early as 1810.

This handsome and well-preserved hat is also of leather, almost black with gold decoration. It probably dates about 1815.

Painted tin hat plates were attached to the front of helmets and hats of all kinds. This almost black tin plate, with gold eagle, dates about 1830, though the leather helmet is of about 1810. Militia units often purchased old equipment, which may have been surplus, and then attached contemporary insignia to it.

A tin hat plate of about 1830, painted black with gold decorations.

All illustrations are from the author's collection; photographs by the author.

Index